The Smart Way to Buy Information Technology

The Smart Way to Buy Information Technology

How to Maximize Value and Avoid Costly Pitfalls

Brad L. Peterson
Diane M. Carco

AMACOM

American Management Association

New York • Atlanta • Boston • Chicago • Kansas City • San Francisco • Washington, D.C.
Brussels • Mexico City • Tokyo • Toronto

This book is available at a special discount when ordered in bulk quantities. For information, contact Special Sales Department, AMACOM, a division of American Management Association, 1601 Broadway, New York, NY 10019.

Library of Congress Cataloging-in-Publication Data

Peterson, Brad L.
   The smart way to buy information technology : how to maximize value and avoid costly pitfalls / Brad L. Peterson, Diane M. Carco.
      p.   cm.
   Includes index.
   ISBN 0-8144-0387-5
      1. Information technology—Management.   2. Information technology—Equipment and supplies—Purchasing.   I. Carco, Diane M. II. Title.
   HD30.2.P477   1998
   658.4'038—dc21   *97–40153*
                                                                        CIP

Printing Number

10   9   8   7   6   5   4   3   2   1

To Alexa, my brave little girl
—Brad L. Peterson

To my mother, who gave me life, and to my brother,
who helped me shape it
—Diane M. Carco

Contents

Preface   *xi*

Acknowledgments   *xiii*

Introduction   **1**

Why Information Technology Buying Mistakes Happen • What This
Book Will Do for You

Part One: Why Information Technology Buying
Mistakes Happen

Chapter 1. Technophilia   **7**

What Technophiles Care About • Vendor-Induced Technophilia •
The Hidden Costs of Technophilia

Chapter 2. Vendor Selling Ploys   **17**

Smoke and Mirrors • Fear, Uncertainty, and Doubt • Divide and
Conquer • Sense of Urgency • Bait and Switch • Partnering •
Variations on a Theme

Part Two: The Smart Way to Buy
Information Technology

**Chapter 3. The Deal Wheel: Putting a Business Spin on IT
Acquisitions**   **31**

IT Acquisition Quiz • A Business Spin on Technology Acquisitions
• Who's Who? Acquiring Minds Want to Know • The Question
Chair • The Deal Wheel

Chapter 4. The User   **43**

Defining Success • Defining Needs • User Risk Assessment • Market
Research • Internal Communications • Signing the Contract •
Monitoring Vendor Performance • Reforming the Deal

Chapter 5. Technical   51

Why IT Knows Best • The Technical Assessment Process • Making
It Work

Chapter 6. Financial   61

What Alternatives Should We Consider? • Are We Buying
Something We Don't Need Just Because the Price Looks Right? •
Are We Spending $2 to Solve a $1 Problem? • Finance Can Find
Answers • Crunch, Crunch, Crunch, Crunch: Steps in Finance's
Cost-Benefit Analysis of IT Projects • Are We Applying a Two-Year
Solution to a One-Year Problem? • Are We Assuming Junk Bond
Risk for a Puny Muni Return? • Zooming In From Project Costs to
Transaction Costs • The Report Card

Chapter 7. Negotiating   79

Seven Deadly Negotiating Sins • Control the Process • Know What
the Company Wants • Know Your Vendor • Build an Effective Team
• Beat the Vendor Ploys • Know How to Use Customer Ploys • The
Keys to Negotiation

Chapter 8. Administrative   99

Standards for Goodness' Sake • Rules for the Buying Game •
Unclean Hands in Empty Pockets • Stopping Vendor Performance
Problems • Self-Test: Monitoring Company Compliance

Chapter 9. Putting the Five Roles Together   111

More Than Teamwork • Performance Standards: Stage Directions
That Guide the Actors in Their Roles • Management Support:
Enforcing Organizational Discipline • Casting Call: Management's
Responsibility for Assembling the Right Team • Bringing It All Back
Home • How to Implement the New Paradigm Today

Part Three: Contracting

Chapter 10. Contracting Themes   123

The Vendor's Form • Shackles • Providing Product or Meeting
Needs? • Vague Obligations • Snake-Oil Remedies • Intellectual
Property Indemnities • Boilerplate Ploys • Knowing the Deals

Chapter 11. Request for Proposal   139

RFP Construction • Identifying Vendors • Reviewing Responses

Chapter 12. Software Licenses 147

The Value Pricing Trend • License Pitfalls • The Structure of
Software License Agreements • Setting Context • Granting the
License • Setting Rules and Protocols • Sharing Risk • Warranties •
Providing Maintenance and Service • Conclusion

Chapter 13. Consulting 177

The Benefits to the Company • Locking In the Benefits of Consulting
• Who Owns the Work? • Confidentiality • Keeping Consultants
Independent • Projects by the Hour: The Consulting Paradox

Chapter 14. Equipment 193

Buying Equipment • Maintaining Equipment • Leasing Equipment
• Disposal

Chapter 15. Outsourcing 209

Analyzing Outsourcing • The Vendor's Position • Services • Pricing
• The Company's People • The Vendor's People • Information
Technology Assets • Intellectual Property • Communication
Mechanisms • Liability • Termination • Summary

Chapter 16. Strategic Alliances 233

Key Issues • Contributions • Control • Sharing of Risks and Rewards
• Exit Strategies • Negotiating Technique • Summary

Index *255*

Preface

In our careers, we have seen a real need—which presents a tremendous opportunity—for clarification of a complex and mission-critical process: the way companies buy information technology.

Our informal discussions about this process led us to look for a single, authoritative guide. To our surprise, we didn't find one.

We handle these issues for major corporations every day. We see the pitfalls. We understand how good intentions can be thwarted by a difficult-to-manage process. Out of our experience, we have developed a set of principles for making smart information technology investments. When we discussed these principles with others in the field, they reacted with surprise and delight.

Our desire is to simplify and clarify. A simpler, more manageable process will give companies better value for what they spend on information technology. It will also lower the frustration level of the people involved and allow them to look on technology acquisitions as money well spent.

For all these reasons, we decided to put these ideas in book form. We hope you find that this book helps you.

Chicago, Illinois
August 1997

Acknowledgments

The authors gratefully acknowledge the contributions of Vincent (V. J.) Carco, without whom this book would not have had its life and wit. The authors also acknowledge the time and effort contributed by Christopher Herman, who provided many valuable insights.

Brad also thanks his one true love, Christine, for her patience and support, without which this book could not have been written.

Finally, both authors thank their families, friends, and colleagues for their encouragement and enthusiasm.

Introduction

How long can your company survive without information technology (IT)? One week? One day? One hour?

How much control do you have over vital technology? Network availability? Software usage? Consulting resources? Electronically provided information?

Where you don't have control, your vendors do. Are they looking out for your best interests? Do they want to maximize your long-term success, or do they want to meet their quarterly sales quotas?

Are you confident that you are receiving value for every dollar you spend on technology? Do you understand all the components of your information technology budget? Does your company buy different solutions to solve the same business problem? Does your company buy hardware that will be obsolete in six months? Are the high-priced consultants whom you hired just telling you things you already know? Have you done things just because a vendor told you to?

Do the products and services that you receive match the expectations that were raised by the sales rep? If not, what can you do about it? Can you restructure the deal? Modify the working relationship in time to save it? Change vendors? Spend more money to solve the same problem? Do you have a mechanism in place to learn from your mistakes, or do you keep making them?

No business manager today can read these questions without feeling uneasy.

Companies are making buying mistakes every day. Vendors manipulate the sales process and entice decision makers with features and solutions that may or may not mesh with fundamental business practices. Vendors seduce internal technology enthusiasts with technotoys and costly interim solutions that keep them wanting more. As a result, companies squander precious capital to get the wrong business solution on the wrong terms.

As competition becomes increasingly fierce, maintaining control over technology acquisitions and vendor relationships has become a survival issue. Even if you get the right technology at the right price, an onerous contract can create a harmful dependency relationship in which you are not free to run your business.

Too often, the cost of information technology vastly exceeds both its projected cost and its potential benefits. CEOs, CFOs, and CIOs are not getting the value they expect from their information technology investments.

The Smart Way to Buy Information Technology is the "how to" book that business managers need in order to protect themselves and their companies against bad technology investments and harmful vendor relationships. Business managers today are aware of the symptoms, but until now, no one has pinpointed the various problems and offered a comprehensive, implementable solution.

The Smart Way to Buy Information Technology shows business managers the roles and corporate processes that are needed in order to match technology with business problems, form the right deals, negotiate wisely, monitor relationships, and reform the deals to react to tomorrow's business problems. This book provides the details that people in each role—user, technician, financial analyst, negotiator, contract administrator—should focus on, and at the same time gives them a general appreciation of the responsibilities of the other roles.

Why Information Technology Buying Mistakes Happen

Buying the right information technology products at the right prices and on the right terms is difficult. Why?

Irrationality: "Technophilia" and Vendor Ploys

Some people just love technology. To an engineer, a powerful computer is a delightful toy. To a user, technology looks like a simple solution to a complex problem. As a result, too many companies buy technology because it's "hot" or "sexy" or "new" instead of because it makes business sense. We call that "technophilia."

The irrationality of technophilia is often compounded by vendor ploys. Vendor sales reps can use emotion and obfuscation to distract the company from the real issue: whether buying this product at this vendor's price and on these terms is the best way to meet the company's needs.

Buying Is Harder Than Selling

Even with a top-quality vendor and a sales team too enlightened to use a vendor ploy, sellers generally sell better than buyers buy. Why?

First, vendors know exactly what they want: They want to sell their products at the highest possible prices and minimize their risks. Buyers aren't sure what products they want, or even whether they want to buy a product at all.

For a buyer, the wrong deal can be far worse than no deal at all. The wrong deal can be like a big bag of rocks. It can weigh you down. You won't be able to drag the bag of rocks fast enough to get to the most cost-effective business solution.

What does a bag of rocks look like? A dead-end technology. A contract that prevents you from doing what you want to do with your business. A long-term financial commitment to the wrong service provider. You've got to think four moves ahead to avoid this kind of problem.

Second, vendor sales reps have a single focus: selling their products. They become experts in their products. Companies look at products from hundreds of vendors and only occasionally see the same product twice.

The people who buy products from vendors don't have the luxury of a single focus. Buying products is only one of the many ways in which they serve their companies. They may be in the market for information technology products only a few times a year.

As a result, vendor sales reps generally know their products and the process better than you do. Some sales reps share their knowledge with you in a way that helps you make the best decisions. Others see knowledge as power and tell you only what they want you to know.

Finally, buying information technology is an inherently complex endeavor. It has implications throughout a company. It raises user issues, technical issues, financial issues, negotiating issues, and administrative issues. It involves a complex and continuing process. Doing it well is a valuable skill.

What This Book Will Do for You

Part One describes two key challenges that fill information technology buying with pitfalls: technophilia and vendor ploys. Part One will show you where the pitfalls are so that you can learn to step around them.

Part Two describes the smart way to buy information technology. That continuing process includes forming a deal, negotiating a contract, signing a contract, monitoring the deal, and reforming the deal. Understanding the process allows you to take the right steps at the right times.

As a part of this process, the company's people play certain roles to get the company the right information technology at the right price and at the right terms. Those roles include:

1. *User.* Identifying business challenges and opportunities and confirming that if the vendor's product works, it will produce business value.

2. *Technical.* Understanding technical alternatives, verifying that products can work in the company's computing environment, and making them work.

3. *Financial.* Determining whether a deal is cost-effective and consistent with the company's strategy.

4. *Negotiating.* Getting past the vendor ploys to the best possible price and terms.

5. *Administrative.* Developing rules and monitoring compliance.

Part Two also tells you how the roles work together and provides some quick fixes for your company and your next deal.

Part Three details the contracting process. After discussing contracting themes, Part Three describes key issues in licensing software, buying equipment, hiring consultants, outsourcing internal functions, and forming strategic alliances. Knowing the substance of these types of deals will make you effective at identifying and negotiating key terms.

Technology acquisitions can turn otherwise rational managers into seeming idiots. Read on if you want to know how this happens—and what can be done about it for the sake of the success of your business.

Part One

Why Information Technology Buying Mistakes Happen

1
Technophilia

There is a strange love affair going on in your organization. It isn't likely to enliven office gossip with passionate glances or broom-closet trysts. But this affair has repercussions that far outweigh those of most romantic entanglements. Why? Because this is a case in which Cupid's arrow is aimed directly at the heart of your enterprise. Let the shaft hit home, and your company might never recover.

This dangerous passion is technophilia, or the love of technology. Its victims are usually the technical experts in your organization, from the chief information officer to systems engineers. But anyone in your organization can succumb.

Technophiles love the machines they work with. They love the way software works—even when it doesn't. They pore over computer magazines the way an art collector studies a painting. In their spare time, they play computer games or fiddle with their home computer systems. Their love is practically all-consuming. And their indiscretions ultimately victimize everyone.

What Technophiles Care About

To paraphrase Aristotle, all technical people, by nature, desire to know things. Their innate curiosity drives them. Either physically or metaphorically, they like to take things apart, see what makes them tick, find ways to make them work better.

Technophiles' love of technology can start early or late in life. It might be traced back to a Build Your Own Computer kit received as a tenth birthday present, or it might blossom from a midlife introduction to computers. But there is a common thread: Technophiles love complexity. They revel in complex systems; they love to solve problems. Every physical system is a challenge to be met.

It's no wonder, therefore, that systems people (whether they are engineers, programmers, or related professionals) are always looking for new solutions. Why not? Isn't it their role within the organization to make sure things work? Aren't they supposed to find the elegant solution, the incremental improvement? Doesn't the organization demand the best that technology has to offer?

Actually, no, it doesn't. The organization makes no such demand. An enterprise is indifferent to whether its vital information is stored on papyrus rolls or accessible using a 64-bit processor. It cares only about the way the information helps it fulfill its mission.

But technophiles care. They care passionately. It's what they love. They need to solve problems. While they are professionals in their chosen field (technology), most of them are strictly amateurs in the business world. The solutions they seek are not business solutions.

In a sense, they're like golfers who understand the mechanics of the golf swing but don't know how to keep score. They are capable of playing well. They like to launch a long drive and watch it fly. But they're not sure what the implications of a given shot are for their score, since they aren't keeping one. The occasional snap-hook out of bounds doesn't faze them; why should it?

Technophilia is more than a game to them. We're talking about people whose passion is technology. Like all lovers, they are single-minded in their pursuit of the object of their affection. Obstacles, however insurmountable they seem, mean nothing to them. They love the challenge.

Glitches and Other Flirtations

Technology, like art, is a jealous mistress. It knows how to pique the technophile's interest, to keep the spell unbroken. It can hold a programmer in the palm of its hand for days or weeks in search of an elusive line of code. It can tantalize with seductive promises of seamless integration, only to disintegrate into parts that seem hopelessly incompatible. It can offer a system that works perfectly for months, only to behave erratically all of a sudden for no apparent reason.

To the technophile, this is only technology playing hard-to-get. Glitches, problems, and setbacks are simply opportunities to find more interesting, more satisfying solutions. Every love affair has its ups and downs, and this grand passion is fueled by every contretemps. If the path were smooth, how could it be true love?

With the Blindness of Lovers

Have you ever tried to warn a lover about the faults or behavior of the object of desire? If you have, you were probably rebuffed. And you learned about the remarkable capacity for self-deception that is the one unvarying characteristic of the smitten. When the object of desire is a multimillion-dollar information system that's supposed to help run your business, the results of blind devotion can be catastrophic.

Quite naturally, technophiles lust after "sexy" systems. They want the newest, the most powerful, the fastest, the most complex. They don't want to hear about possible implementation problems. They want a system they can brag about to their friends. Above all, they don't want to be caught with old technology, even if "old" is a matter of milliseconds.

If corporations existed only to be technology proving grounds, this pursuit of the sexy wouldn't be a problem. But there are, of course, other reasons for running a business. Technophiles may acknowledge the importance of corporate marketing, production, and finance priorities (even though there is nothing remotely sexy about them). But they have priorities of their own.

When their technolust starts interfering with the corporation's pursuit of profit, instead of abetting it, it's time for management to tie their hands back. Unfortunately, most managers are curiously reluctant to break out the rope.

Thus begins a dangerous cycle. Technophiles, their eyes on an inappropriate prize, look on the enterprise's basic mission as important, but secondary to the task of keeping up-to-date on the latest technology. The vendors they talk to are naturally happy to play along.

Once needs are expressed in technological terms ("We need bandwidth") instead of business terms ("We need a way to communicate better between departments"), vendors think they know all they need to know about what your company is looking for. The impression thus created in the vendor's mind is a false one. It's better communication between departments that the company needs, not bandwidth. But even if the vendor realizes the mistake, why point it out?

The result is the blind leading the blind, both in a misguided pursuit of the new. Even if the company had the foresight to assign a sharp-eyed chaperone to watch over the acquisition process and raise a skeptical voice when the praise of technology became too effusive, it probably wouldn't improve things much. Too many heads have already been turned.

How to Squander Your Legacy (System)

In the late 1980s, when client/server computing was new and sexy, technophiles could scarcely contain their eagerness to join the revolution. Big iron was out. There was a new paradigm: distributed computing. Its advantages were self-evident. What could go wrong?

A big financial services company we'll call BZB Inc. found out exactly what could go wrong when its payroll processing was taken off the mainframe and moved to a client/server environment. There was no compelling business reason to switch. With the old system, payroll was being processed efficiently, at a reasonable cost. But it was precisely this innocent attribute of the system—that it was "old" and unsexy—that sent the technophiles at BZB Inc. out into the world in search of a solution they could brag about to their friends.

What they (and their friends) never considered was the special nature of the payroll function. A nontechnical businessperson, given a moment to think about it, could come up with a dozen reasons why payroll processing is the last function you'd want to put in an unproven open systems environment.

Payroll needs significant controls. Put it out in the open, in an environment where controls haven't been developed, and you invite some extremely unpleasant consequences. At the time when BZB committed to a client/server payroll system, not only were controls inadequate, but there was virtually no client/server expertise to be bought. Practically no one knew how to implement and maintain such a system.

The internal advocates of BZB's new payroll system envisioned a blissful future of cost savings and improved efficiency. These visions faded fast when the implementation problems started. Trying to solve the problem of inadequate controls in a field not many people knew anything about ended up costing a lot of money. A conversion budgeted at $3.5 million came in at over $12 million. The difference—$8.5 million—would have bought a pretty large number of mainframe-generated and -printed checks.

Speaking of printing checks, the client/server payroll system had one major drawback: It couldn't. The smaller printers in the distributed environment couldn't handle the volume. As often happens in the technophilic rush to the new, someone forgot to check the road map.

Here's an irony. Computer programmers and system developers try to anticipate all future states of the systems they create. If you've ever written a computer program, you know why. And you know what happens if you don't make sure that every line of code leads somewhere the computer can follow—there's a crash.

Isn't it ironic that these system builders failed to ask basic questions about the way their new system was intended to fit into the real world of business? Shouldn't they have been able to step away from their keyboards and apply the same systematic logic they used to build their system to the problem of how to install it?

Maybe the answer is that they don't love the real world. It lacks the internal consistency of a technological system. In the real world, old systems clash with new ones. People do unpredictable things to their computers. There are software conflicts. It's not at all like the world of technology that they love—to a fault.

Vendor-Induced Technophilia

While some are born technophiles, some have technophilia thrust upon them—usually by vendors who understand that every manager of a downsized department is really just an enthusiastic technology buyer waiting to be sold.

Lean, Mean, Technology-Buying Machines

Downsizing, stretch goals, and the unprecedented push to do more with less have department heads and other business managers scrambling these days. People running line operations listen to a constant drumbeat: Improve efficiency. No accommodation is made for "running lean." No matter how understaffed a department is, output is expected to increase.

Put yourself in the position of the manager of such a department. Wouldn't you be tempted to sit down and listen to a technology vendor who promised you a way to meet your goals, however short-staffed you are? With all the demands on your time, how thoroughly would you test that vendor's claim that she can solve your problems? If your department doesn't have much experience in acquiring technology, how would you go about investigating the vendor's claim, even if you had time to do so? If you bought the sales pitch and believed that technology held the answer to your problems, wouldn't you embrace it enthusiastically?

Welcome to the world of vendor-induced technophilia. Line managers and other users with little or no experience end up buying too much technology too uncritically. But not only do they buy; they become internal advocates, even boosters, of the vendors they buy from.

Today's climate of corporate decentralizing has put these managers in a tough spot. People who have never had to assess competing claims from technology vendors are being asked to make fine distinctions that would elude a research scientist. It's little wonder that the results aren't always healthy for the enterprise.

Henhouse, Inc., A. Fox, Prop.

Decentralization of the IT acquisition function has forced too many line managers into a situation in which their only ostensibly credible source of information about technology purchases is the technology vendor. As the sole source of information, the vendor has little trouble framing the manager's problem in such a way that it admits of one and only one solution: the vendor's.

To add misplaced enthusiasm to injury, the manager's acquired technophilia often takes the form of praise for the single-vendor solution she's had thrust into her empty hands. However sincere this enthusiasm, it almost certainly is untempered by the experience and perspective more seasoned technology buyers have acquired.

Managers suffering from vendor-induced technophilia have probably never learned the one immutable truth about IT acquisition and implementation. It is simply this: The solutions that haven't failed yet are the ones that haven't been tested yet. If you've never been involved in a system conversion, you can't imagine all the things that can—and will—go wrong. If you've never seen how the promises in a vendor proposal look six months after the handshake, you're likely to be too credulous for your own, and your company's, good.

You wouldn't let a fox design henhouse controls. Why allow a technology vendor to both make up the rules and score the game?

The Winds of Change

So where are the company's leaders while managers are being mesmerized by technology vendors? Well, they might be off learning how to "think outside of the box" or to "do what you do best, and outsource the rest." In short, they're off attending seminars about the management breakthrough *du jour*. They are learning the formula: Change good, stability bad.

However innocuous the unending procession of catchphrase management fads seems, it has one serious effect: It tells an organization that change is good and the status quo suspect. Change *can* be good, of course, but it is never inherently good, especially the burdensome and risky business of changing information technology.

Whenever a leader catches a new phrase to encapsulate management's commitment to improvement, he or she becomes a change agent. This bias in favor of change is sure to trickle down to an organization's technical people, among others. If presented with a close call between going with new technology or sticking with the old, how would you choose if your CEO was committed to creating an organization that was constantly "reinventing" itself? How can you demonstrate belief in "new paradigms" if you're reluctant to "modernize" your information technology systems?

You can't. And if you're a technophile anyway, you wouldn't even consider hesitating before buying the latest hot item, would you?

The Hidden Costs of Technophilia

Technophilia costs organizations uncountable millions of dollars in unnecessary purchases, but the damage doesn't end there. The most costly effects of misguided, fragmented, technophilia-induced purchases aren't on the vendor's price list. They involve things like inadequate communication within your organization, inability to collaborate, compromised systems, wasted time, corrupted systems, unprofitable activities. Bad business.

Information Systems: A Feudal Vision

Imagine a company in which everybody who needs information gets it—one in which decision makers have what they need when they need it, at the click of a mouse button. Envision full-enterprise executive information systems that make meaningful short- and long-range planning practical and reliable.

Why do these modest goals seem far-fetched to those with experience in the real world of corporate information systems? After all, wide-area networks are up and running in most multi-site companies. Groupware allows a level of collaboration that was beyond imagining just a few years ago. The World Wide Web has taken global information sharing to a place it has never been. Why aren't these tools building us the perfect future?

Part of the reason may be that too many technophiles have been allowed to follow their own partial, idiosyncratic visions of the IT future. Instead of sticking to a stable, consistent, enterprisewide system with reasonable standards and predictable results, too many corporations have come to resemble a medieval kingdom with warring dukes declaring half-hearted allegiance to a weak monarch.

A strong "central government" should be able to set and enforce reasonable, predictable standards for the good of all. Practically all companies pledge allegiance to such a standard. But technophiles, like minor nobility, are too busy building their own fiefdoms to be fully loyal to their liege lord.

His Department, His Castle

In days of old, a single department couldn't afford to buy information technology. It took the full resources of the enterprise to come up with the cash for a roomful of mainframe (complete with white-coated acolytes, glass viewing wall, and special air-conditioning). Decentralization of information technology was impossible.

Today every programmer has more computing power in the notebook computer he carries around than the whole company used to have. Decentralization is easy to achieve. A weak or ineffective central IT department can easily be ignored by a technophile who knows what she loves.

The result? Islands of automation. Castles of antagonistic computing solutions. Warring states of disconnected information technology, each marching into battle under a different vendor's standard.

A Plague Upon All Your Houses

In an unconstrained, uncontrolled computing environment, anything can happen. The technophile who can't get through the day without a quick fix of his favorite home computer game brings it to work. He didn't know it had a virus when he downloaded it from the bulletin board. But now he knows that every computer in his department has a virus.

Viruses are corporate America's dirty little computing secret. Practically every Fortune 500 company has been infected with dozens of viruses (that it knows of). Thousands of worker-hours are consumed every business day while people wait patiently for their virus-protection software to scan their hard drives for known problems (blissfully unaware of the unknown ones). Some companies simply learn to live with viruses that have proven virtually ineradicable.

And, in all likelihood, this is happening because people who love technology intermingle their business computing activities with their hobby computing activities.

Unsupportable Costs

Imagine that you've found the perfect IT system for your department. You've avoided all the mistakes technophiles make. You did your homework. You evaluated the technology dispassionately. You applied a healthy skepticism to the salesperson's claims. You looked at all the costs. Everything looks right. You decide to buy.

Oops. There's one cost you forgot to look at—the cost to your enterprise of supporting one more incompatible system. Your vendors can give you the information you need to assess the cost of running their system, but can they tell you what costs your company will incur by running their system alongside somebody else's in the next department?

Of course not. No vendor has documented the problems of interacting with other vendors' systems. But your CIO could certainly tell you that maintaining multiple types of systems expertise is expensive. And he or she certainly will tell you that, once the word is out that there's another system mouth to feed in the house.

Large companies running multiple systems are seeing support and integration costs on the order of eleven to twelve times software costs. In other words, the $500,000 departmental system that passed your cost-benefit analysis with flying colors can easily turn into a $6 million millstone around the neck of the company IT budget.

The Luxury of Time

Technophiles love to spend time on their pet projects. Long vendor meetings, discussions of the delicious technical details, lovingly careful implementation—for someone who loves computers, is there a better way to spend a workday?

The company, if it could speak, would probably offer an opposing viewpoint. Even if the pet project has departmental value, its net value to the enterprise is probably negligible. The time the technophile lavishes on questionable acquisitions is a valuable corporate resource—squandered.

Loss of Economies of Scale

Economies of scale are critical to IT because of software's high start-up costs and low marginal costs. There are tremendous efficiencies in buying only one product to meet a need or solve a problem, instead of buying different products to solve the same problem in Unix, Windows, and assorted other environments.

These economies of scale can't be achieved in companies that allow technophiles to follow their hearts wherever they lead.

A License to Steal

Technophiles are often uncomfortable (or at least impatient) with the business issues connected to the technology they love. Most vendors know this. Some exploit it. Some use it as the nearest thing to a license to steal—a software license, that is.

All companies of any size face complex software licensing issues. Even if systems were not disparate and fragmented, keeping track of software licenses would be difficult. In the real world, in companies where technophilia is not reined in, software licensing can be the single most vexing problem the IT department faces.

Software companies routinely sue their best customers over licensing issues. Not for deliberate fraud or theft, but rather for failing in a good-faith effort to keep track of how many copies of a given software package they own, which versions they're running and on which platforms, and how much they owe in license fees. For companies that cannot even guess how many computers they own, tallying software usage and deployment to the degree of precision necessary to satisfy software vendors is practically impossible.

There are even software companies that seek out companies at times of major changes, such as data center consolidations and mergers, for the sole purpose of "reminding" them that licensing agreements might be abrogated by the changes they're making, and offering to negotiate a settlement.

In this rapacious environment, technophiles are easy marks. Because they see business as an excuse to work with the tools of technology, instead of rightly seeing technology as a tool of business, they are overmatched in any adversarial business situation, whether it involves software licensing or anything else.

Taken all in all, the costs of technophilia—this odd romance between person and computer—are enough to break your heart.

2

Vendor Selling Ploys

If you're smart about buying information technology, you'll buy the right product at the right price and on the right terms. That's not good news for a sales rep who has the wrong product, or a sales rep whose commission rides on selling you the right product at the wrong price or terms.

The best sales reps use an honest, straightforward, and honorable sales process. They sell only when they can offer the right product on the right price and terms. When they can't do that, they stay out of your way (at least) or help you find the right vendor (at best). In short, they win your long-term respect and loyalty by helping you make the best decision for your company.

All too often, though, sales reps get greedy. Some of them can't see beyond the next commission check. Some of them don't see a long-term relationship with your company. Some of them are made greedy by a greedy or shortsighted vendor's commission and reward system.

When sales reps get greedy, they use vendor ploys to distract customers from smart buying. If the ploys succeed, the customer makes a costly mistake based on misinformation and emotion.

To avoid costly mistakes, you've got to be able to spot vendor ploys. The more you know about these ploys, the better you'll be able to avoid them. This chapter describes six kinds of vendor ploys, and Part Two gives you the strategy you need to beat all of them.

Smoke and Mirrors

In a magic show, a magician uses smoke and mirrors to prevent the audience from seeing how the tricks are done. Smoke covers up what is really happening. Mirrors send the eye to the wrong place.

In selling, the smoke-and-mirrors ploy is used to confuse the customer and avoid the real question. The real question is whether the company should buy this product from this vendor at this price and on these terms.

Fancy Footwork

The classic smoke-and-mirrors ploy is the demo. As a demo, the sales rep shows you a "working" demonstration system. The sales rep shows you how the screens work and what the reports look like. The demonstration system is fast because it has almost no data in it. The salesperson never chooses the menu options that give error messages. If the product fails, the salesperson claims that the same function worked perfectly that morning.

An equal amount of fancy footwork can be done in financial analysis. For example:

▶ A vendor can compare only the hard-dollar costs of implementing the product against the hard- and soft-dollar benefits that might be achieved. What the vendor's analysis ignores are the soft-dollar costs, such as the training time and the lost productivity the company will face while learning the product. That makes the numbers look rosier than they really are.

▶ A vendor can ignore the cost of integrating the product with the company's environment. Analyzing an information technology purchase in isolation may mean ignoring more than half of the costs.

▶ A vendor can assume that nothing ever changes. Vendors often charge for any variation in the use of their products. For example, software vendors often charge for using their software on more powerful computers or in different locations. Ignoring these very real possibilities makes the numbers rosier.

Telling a Story

Humans respond well to stories. It seems to be part of our genetic code. We remember stories better than facts. We quickly attach emotion to stories, loving the hero and hating the villain.

Vendors know that. That's why little companies tend to describe themselves as the underdog, a brave and worthy David fighting a mighty but overbearing Goliath. That's also why big companies cast themselves as strong, old, and wise.

These stories are great on an emotional level. They may even say something useful about the vendor. Mostly, though, they just confuse a purchase decision with powerful and irrelevant emotions.

Building a Personal Relationship

Information technology is often sold through personal relationships. The vendor's salesperson forges a relationship with a company executive over golf and drinks. At the start, it's not about the messy business of buying a product.

Now the vendor is the executive's friend. Executives trust their friends. They even accept oral assurances on important technical, financial, and contractual points. Maybe they even sign their friend's form contract without any review.

Why no review? Because for the executive, this is all about trust. Bringing in financial, legal, and technical advisers is not a trusting thing to do. Also, once the deal and the friendship have merged in the executive's mind, the executive may perceive even well-meaning questions as personal attacks. No one wants that.

Taking advantage of an executive's sense of loyalty is just one example of the ways in which a sales rep can use a personal relationship to confuse and avoid the real question. The real question, again, is whether the company should buy this product now, at this price and on these terms. The confusion comes in when the sales rep raises questions like:

"Don't you trust me?"
"I thought we were friends. How can you do this to me?"
"Doesn't our relationship mean anything to you?"

A little body language from the sales rep is enough to raise these questions. When the sales rep seems to wilt and turns her head to the side, the executive gets an emotional blast. The body language says, "If you love me, you'll love my pitch" on a direct emotional level.

Personal relationships can be so distracting that many companies prohibit their employees from buying from sales reps if there is a personal relationship. A far larger number of companies have implemented ethics policies that prohibit personal gifts, lavish entertaining, and other "relationship builders." These policies, while well intentioned, are usually ineffective.

Using a Fact to Distract

Fancy footwork often feels fact-free. That makes buyers edgy. Appeals to relationships, telling stories, and other tugs on heartstrings worry linear thinkers. For fact-oriented, left-brained buyers, vendors can offer a welter, a veritable barrage, of pleasing but useless information. For example:

▶ *Claims that cannot be verified.* "More than 95 percent of our customers have achieved a 30 percent return on their investment in this product." (How would anyone know if that's true?)

▶ *The wrong fact.* "We're giving you a 50 percent discount on the first 100 hours of training." (Which distracts you from the fact that you'll need 1,000 hours of training.)

▶ *Details of future products.* "We have announced a version of this system that will interface with your existing database." (Announcing is easy. Delivering is hard.)

▶ *Buzzword babble.* "This product provides a dynamic platform for reengineering core processes to achieve world-class synergies." (No chance of missing that target.)

Fear, Uncertainty, and Doubt

Once upon a time, IBM was the undisputed king of the information technology vendors. In those days, it was widely proclaimed that "no one ever got fired for buying from IBM."

To be sure, there were products that seemed better, faster, and cheaper than IBM's. IBM was said to lag the market a bit on price and technology. But could you be sure? Would the better, faster, cheaper alternative really work? Would the smaller company be around to support the product?

What if something did go wrong? Would you want to tell management that you're a risk taker who failed? That you bought a bargain parachute? No. Not that. Better to say you took the safest course.

Big companies have won a lot of business by raising these very questions. The industry called the technique "fear, uncertainty, and doubt": fear of failure; uncertainty about the future; doubt about the smaller company.

Sure, these are good questions. It is important for the product to work and for the vendor to be there to support it. Big companies do tend to last longer than small companies. Companies can die when key products fail. But the fear, uncertainty, and doubt ploy is designed to scare companies into making an irrational purchase.

Is this just a big company ploy? No. It's not even limited to vendors that lead their markets.

Even the smallest vendors can use this ploy. For example, a very small consulting vendor was able to use this ploy to charge a large and sophisticated company a vast premium for shoddy services.

It happened like this: BigCo needed to renegotiate a license agreement with a major software vendor, Computer Agglomerators. The small consulting vendor prepared an analysis showing that Computer Agglomerators' full rates for the license would be over $15 million.

This was a great deal more than BigCo's management was expecting. The consultant portrayed Computer Agglomerators as a merciless profiteer. However, the consultant claimed to know secrets about the pricing at Computer Agglomerators—secrets like where the company was willing to give discounts. The consultant claimed that those secrets would allow TNT to obtain pricing closer to $7 million.

The consultant's ploy was fear, uncertainty, and doubt: fear of Computer Agglomerators; uncertainty about how pricing negotiations would go; doubt about whether BigCo's usual team could do the job without the consultant's secrets. TNT won the business merely because its claims to have secrets might be true.

In the end, BigCo found that it had little to fear from Computer Agglomerators, and little to gain from the consultant's "secrets." BigCo had paid a hefty consulting fee for nothing.

With the fear, uncertainty, and doubt ploy, a vendor makes a company act like Dumbo the elephant. Dumbo could fly with his big ears, but he was too scared to try. When a bird gave Dumbo a "magic" feather, Dumbo found out that he could fly. Later, he lost the feather and realized that he could fly without it all along. A company that's been grounded by fear, uncertainty, and doubt may pay dearly for a magic feather. But, as Dumbo learned, it's the fear, not the feather, that makes the difference.

Divide and Conquer

Selling to Vulnerability

In a simple divide-and-conquer ploy, a vendor goes after the company's weakest point: the person with the most authority and the least judgment.

At the same time, the vendor divides that person from the company. The pitch goes like this: "Look, buying this product is a great idea. You know that. You obviously understand this better than anyone else in the company. The only thing that stands between you and success is the company's bureaucrats. You know that bureaucrats kill deals with their questions and delays. This is a time to make a bold move, even if that's not protocol around here."

This ploy relies on inflating the ego of the decision maker. Most decision makers, left to their own devices, will want to think things over and talk to knowledgeable peers. The vendor needs to inflate the ego of the decision maker to the point where no other opinions appear important.

How does this work in practice? Imagine a decision maker who turns to his financial, technical, and negotiating advisers and says: "You people are all obstructionists. You don't need to protect me. I know what I'm doing here." That sort of decision maker can easily be moved to sign even the most unfavorable vendor form.

Selling the Individuals, Not the Company

In a more sophisticated divide-and-conquer ploy, the vendor sells the product to the users, systems integrators, negotiators, financial analysts, and administrators. The key, though, is to sell to each of them individually, in separate meetings. The heart of this ploy is to keep them from interacting.

With the company's forces thus divided, the vendor can sell a solution to each functional area by focusing on its narrowest interests. The sales rep asks people from each area what they need in order to recommend the purchase. The sales rep then summarizes those needs and confirms that those are that group's only needs. Then, the sales rep presents a solution that meets all of those needs. The sales rep gets approval from each area.

The user looks at the operational problem. The financial analyst looks at the budget impact. The negotiator looks for glaring contract problems. The systems integrator checks the solution technically. With all those recommendations in hand, the sale is made.

What's missing is the companywide view. There's no cost justification because the vendor succeeds in keeping the financial analyst from talking to the user. The technical analyst doesn't verify that the solution will work because the technical analyst doesn't talk to the user either. And so forth. None of these people look at the company's issues; they look only at their own parochial issues.

How can a vendor keep the company's people from communicating? One way is by keeping them busy talking to the vendor. Vendors call this "account control." Savvy vendors often keep enough marketing people talking to the company's people that the company's people don't have enough time to think the deal over, much less time to talk it over with colleagues or other vendors.

Sense of Urgency

Vendors want you to buy quickly. There is an absolute saying among vendors: "Time kills deals." The more time that passes, the more chance there is that the deal could unwind. A competitor might drop its price. A technical analyst might discover technical flaws. A financial analyst might discover hidden costs. A user might actually call some of those reference accounts. The company may find a way to solve its problem without the vendor's product, or the problem may simply go away.

Even if the vendor gets the deal in the end, a quick deal is better for the vendor. One reason that vendors prefer quick deals is that the selling expenses are lower.

The other reason that vendors prefer quick deals is that the faster the sale moves, the more money the company usually leaves on the table. A fast sale generally means that the company hasn't had time to prepare. Haste makes waste. The waste in this case is paying too much for the wrong products on the wrong terms.

By contrast, vendors spend years preparing for sales calls and learning closing techniques. They design form contracts far in advance so that they'll get the terms they want. As a result, they can act very quickly without making hasty decisions.

Scripts for the Urgency Ploy

Some vendors let you fall into the urgency ploy all by yourself. They watch you accept unrealistic deadlines for completing the process. They watch the time you have to evaluate their proposal run out. They do relationship selling, but they don't go out of their way to give you something tangible to evaluate. Then, just before you must decide what to do, they present their proposal. Now it's urgent.

Other vendors are more proactive. They create a sense of urgency with scripts like these.

Annual Price Increases

"Our annual price increase is coming next week. We've got to sign a contract this week to get these prices."

Never to Be Repeated Low Prices

"We're offering these prices only because this is the last week of the most important fiscal quarter we will ever have. You'll never see a better deal."

Scarce Resources

"This product is so hot that we've got a real struggle for the implementation guys. I've got our best implementation team on hold for the implementation date that you committed to with your management. My boss says I can't hold those people any longer unless I can get a signed contract in twenty-four hours. There's just no telling when quality people will be available again."

Take It or Leave It

"We've gone as far as we're willing to go. We don't give anyone the terms that you want, and you've got our best price. We're taking this offer off the table and giving up if you don't sign this contract by 9:00 A.M. tomorrow. You've got a great deal on the table. Take it or leave it."

We're Getting Too Good for You

"I hate to say this, but you don't have much more time to buy this product. We're moving up-market. Pretty soon, we won't even be willing to sell this product to companies like yours."

Lost Benefits

"Your company needs to start getting the benefits of this product as soon as possible. Those benefits dwarf any gains that your company could achieve through financial analysis, technical analysis, legal review, negotiation, and so forth."

Appeal to Machismo

"You need a month to evaluate this? The hotshots at Respected Co. finished the contracting cycle in three days. They really know how to move."

Make Up for Lost Time

"I know how much pressure you're under to get this project done. You spent an extra month choosing us as your vendor, so you're a month behind on your project plan. I want to help. You can make up for lost time by compressing the time required to negotiate a contract from the four weeks you allotted in your project plan to, say, the thirty-two seconds it will take you to sign my form contract."

Why the Urgency Ploy Works

This is a very effective ploy. It appeals to the best in a buyer, offering a good deal in a short time. It also appeals to the worst in a buyer, providing a rationale for avoiding the hard work required to buy the right information technology for the right price and on the right terms.

Another reason this is an effective ploy is that the vendor could be telling the truth. The best choice might be to sign up quickly. This may be the best time to buy. However, in our experience, the same deal is generally available for months after the deadline has passed, and proper analysis saves more money than hasty action.

Bait and Switch

With the bait-and-switch ploy, a vendor sells what sells and delivers what's available. The "bait" part is to lure a company into the sales process by offering a good deal. The "switch" part is to replace the good deal with a lousy one.

Of course, the switch is a delicate maneuver for the vendor. If the switch is too big, too soon, you'll walk away. The vendor needs to get you strongly enough committed to the sales process that you'll keep going even though the deal you want is off the table.

How does the vendor get you committed? By building a personal relationship with you. By getting you to invest so much time in the sales process or implementing the product that you hate to walk away and "lose" that investment. By getting you to sign a letter of intent or a contract. By getting you to publicly announce that you've struck a "deal."

How do information technology vendors make the switch? There are three common approaches.

Boiling a Frog

If you toss a frog into a pot of boiling water, the frog will jump right out. You can boil the frog by starting with nice cool water and increasing the heat slowly. The frog will never feel a big enough increase in temperature to decide to jump out. So the frog boils to death.

Technology buyers are not all that different. If a vendor reveals at the first sales call that it doesn't have a product that meets your needs, you're going to end the sales process.

What a vendor can do instead is to start by claiming to be able to meet all of your needs. The vendor really plans to sell you its standard product. That's bad news for you. But the vendor gives you the bad news a spoonful at a time, switching the deal slowly. No one spoonful is bad enough to convince you to back out, so you pay too much to get the wrong product on the wrong terms.

A Jump to Higher Ground

Another way to make the switch is to pitch it as a great thing for you. Let's say you like the GizmoTron Mark V, except that it costs a wee bit too much. The sales rep likes it too, but she knows that it won't be available when you need it.

The sales rep waits until you make an objection, perhaps to the price of the GizmoTron Mark V. Ostensibly to handle that objection, she proposes the GizmoTron Mark IV. The Mark IV's pricing is quite low now, she explains. And, though it's an older model, it has the features you need. You don't really need a Mark V, in her view.

So you buy the Mark IV. However, the only reason you went to this vendor was because of its new Mark V technology. You might not have even looked at the competitors to the Mark IV.

Just Don't Do It

A third way to switch goes like this: Promise to do something great. Get the contract. Don't do anything great. Instead, do the minimum you can without getting sued.

How does this look in the real world? The vendor brings hotshot programmers to the sales presentation, then provides dolts to do your work. The vendor demonstrates how the software could meet your needs, then provides software that doesn't meet your needs.

What about the contract? The contract can protect you from this ploy, if you do a good job on it. Thus, the "just don't do it" ploy works only if the contracting ploys described in Chapter 10 work.

Partnering

As much as a vendor may talk about wanting the company to succeed, the sales process is mostly about trading products for money.

From the vendor's standpoint, vendors create a great deal of value and receive very little of it. Also, for both sides, the adversarial nature of the sales process means that too little information is exchanged.

The partnering ploy succeeds because real partnerships make a lot of sense. Unfortunately, the partnering ploy doesn't get you a real partnership. Instead, it gets you to buy products on bad terms.

Real Partnerships

Some vendors have succeeded by creating real partnerships with their customers. In a real partnership, the vendor and the customer:

- ▶ Sign a partnership agreement.
- ▶ Conduct a joint business.
- ▶ Share control of the business.
- ▶ Share the profits from the business.
- ▶ Share the losses from the business.

Sharing the risks and rewards of a joint business makes them both want the business to prosper. In fact, because both partners want to achieve the same result, there is far less need for contractual protections.

Sharing of Risks and Rewards

Building upon the success of these partnerships, some vendors and customers have formed strategic alliances. In an alliance, the vendor and the customer share some of their assets, share control over the shared assets, and share the risks and rewards of operating the shared assets. In a successful strategic alliance, as in a successful partnership, the parties want the same things and work well together.

In the short time that they have been in widespread use, strategic alliances have proved to be an effective way to structure business relationships. We describe strategic alliances in detail in Chapter 16.

Alliances are often referred to as "partnering" because in alliances, the allies share the risk and reward of operating shared assets. The concept of shared risk and reward can dramatically reduce the need for other, more conventional contract protections.

The Partnering Ploy

At the same time that true partnerships and genuine partnering were succeeding, the "trust me" ploy was failing. The "trust me" ploy sounds something like this: "You don't need a contract—you have my word on it. Trust me." The "trust me" ploy stopped working because the sales reps who used it often *couldn't* be trusted.

Those same sales reps have now latched on to the word *partnering*. As they see it, just like the old "trust me" ploy, "partnering" means never having to give the company contractual protections. They see partnering as a marketing buzzword, not as a different way of doing business.

These sales reps will tell you, "This isn't about buying and selling—it's about being partners in your success. Don't think of us as a vendor. We're your strategic partner. We have a relationship of trust. Let's not quibble over the terms of my standard form contract." The vendor's standard contract, of course, gives the company a hell-or-high-water obligation to pay the vendor and no right to demand performance from the vendor. The talk is about partnership, but the reality is a one-sided vendor-buyer relationship.

Variations on a Theme

Smoke and mirrors; fear, uncertainty, and doubt; divide and conquer; urgency; bait and switch; and partnering are all variations on a theme. The theme is that the vendor tricks the company into an irrational or poorly considered purchase.

There are always vendors out there creating new variations on these and other ploys—new ways to play to your emotions, new ways to get you to ask the wrong question, new ways to confuse your analysis.

You can spot ploys if you watch the vendor closely. Is the vendor tugging at your heartstrings? Is the vendor inflating your ego? Is the vendor steering you away from the question of whether the company should buy this product now at this price on these terms? Is the vendor muddying the water? Is the vendor ignoring your business needs? Is the vendor telling you what a ridiculous book this is? If the answer is yes, you are seeing a selling ploy.

Remember that you are in control. You have the money. You do not need to do what the vendor wants you to do. No ploy can force you to make a bad buying decision.

Part Two

The Smart Way to Buy Information Technology

3

The Deal Wheel: Putting a Business Spin on IT Acquisitions

Does your company have a rational, disciplined process for buying information technology? Do you understand IT acquisition issues yourself? How would you do on this quiz?

IT Acquisition Quiz

1. What happens to signed technology contracts in your company?
   a. They're filed in a central location, along with amendments.
   b. They're held in the decentralized business units that initiate them.
   c. I think there's one in my bottom drawer.

2. When a technology vendor offers 30 percent off if you buy within the next two weeks, you should:
   a. Stick to a prudent acquisition process without trying to meet artificial deadlines.
   b. Wonder why.
   c. Have a check cut right away.

3. When both the vendor and the user agree on a technical solution:
   a. It still has to undergo a rigorous evaluation process.
   b. The approval process is just a formality.
   c. Someone's going to be treated to dinner in a four-star restaurant.

4. Performing a cost-benefit analysis on a technology project:
   a. Is the only way to determine whether it makes business sense.
   b. Never changes anybody's mind.
   c. Is something the vendor said he'd do for me.

5. If the Software Publishing Association checked your department for unlicensed software, it would find:
   a. Everything licensed and accounted for.
   b. Only a few irregularities.
   c. Can you repeat the question? I was busy downloading Deathstar Golf.

6. Technology projects are to the company's strategic plan as nails are to:
   a. A hammer.
   b. Petrified wood.
   c. A tire.

7. Monitoring a deal means:
   a. Making sure the vendor delivers what was promised.
   b. More paperwork.
   c. Making sure every PC has a monitor.

8. The cost of a technology project should not exceed:
   a. The cost of the business problem it's supposed to solve.
   b. The department's budget.
   c. Forty-eight times the annual dues of the country club the sales rep takes you to.

9. A technology deal should be reevaluated:
   a. Whenever there is a change in business need.
   b. Only after bonuses are issued.
   c. If the vendor says it's OK.

10. A new system should be tested in the user's environment:
    a. Before purchase.
    b. To give systems integration one more thing to gripe about.
    c. If it can fit in the trunk of the salesperson's Lexus.

SCORING: Had this been an actual test, you would have taken the trouble to find a pencil, circled all the ''a'' answers, and scored 100 percent. (Some of you might have done that anyway.)

Few people, and few companies, would score that high in the real world. Unfortunately for the state of technology acquisitions, there are a lot of ''b'' and even ''c'' answers being given. Too many companies give too many vendors too much latitude. Problems are everywhere:

▶ A user, under the influence of unsubstantiated vendor claims, tosses a contract over the transom to a contracts administration area. The deal is fully formed, with little flexibility and no leverage.

▶ A contracts administration area performs a cursory financial analysis and negotiates standard points with the vendor. A detailed analysis is never done. Contract administrators are too busy. Resources are limited. The user's involvement in the analysis is limited to sending E-mails that ask why it's taking so long to get the contract signed.

▶ A contract is signed and thrown in a file, never to be seen again. The user is notified that the contracting is done.

▶ The user and technical teams begin to implement, without knowing how to comply with the contract or how to require the vendor to comply with the contract.

▶ No review is ever conducted to determine whether the project was a success; the organization does not learn from anything but a complete disaster.

As a result, *almost every company pays too much and too often for the wrong things.* Value-oriented CEOs, CIOs, and CFOs are asking: How can we get value for the money we put into IT?

A Business Spin on Technology Acquisitions

At a few companies, a new paradigm for IT acquisitions is emerging. It helps those companies look at these acquisitions in a new way. It takes advantage of an organization's business skill. It combines technical, financial, negotiating, and administrative prowess into a single, dynamic process. This process can cut IT acquisition costs by 10 percent to 30 percent while increasing the value of the technology acquired.

Two ideas are at the core of the new paradigm:

1. *Analysis* of the acquisitions process, breaking it down into the various roles to be played within the acquiring company. These roles are User, Technical, Financial, Negotiating, and Administrative.

2. *Synthesis* of these roles (and the effect they have on the acquisition) into a dynamic process called the *Deal Wheel.*

Why approach the acquisitions process in this way? Because unless each role is examined separately, there is a danger that its functions will be suppressed or overlooked. Similarly, unless the five roles are put back together into a well-integrated unit, there is little chance that the process will succeed.

Who's Who? Acquiring Minds Want to Know

In some companies, the five roles will be played by people in five different departments. In other companies, one person or department will play more than one role. But however the hats are passed around, these are the functions each performs.

1. User

The user is the person who will use the new technology to meet a business need. This role is usually filled by the person, department, or business unit that begins the acquisition process by seeking out the new technology. As the new paradigm is discussed in this and subsequent chapters, think of the user as the business sponsor of the acquisition inside the company (just as the vendor sponsors it to the user).

The user is usually the role that makes the first contact with the vendor, brings the vendor in, and usually advocates the vendor's solution. In the case of a new payroll system, the user role might be played by the chief financial officer, the human resources department, or the payroll manager.

Sometimes the user hat will be worn by people in the company's information technology department. More often, though, the user will be a business unit, a department head, or some other manager or group with line responsibility.

2. Technical

In most companies, the technical function is the province of an information technology department headed by a management information systems (MIS) director or chief information officer (CIO).

The technical role can also be played by IT professionals working for decentralized business units. Whoever plays this role is responsible for:

- ▶ Acting as technical adviser
- ▶ Translating business needs into technical terms
- ▶ Acting as a technical solutions clearinghouse for the enterprise
- ▶ Determining what will be needed to implement and support the acquisition
- ▶ Testing the product
- ▶ Maintaining the new system

3. *Financial*

The person or department wearing the financial hat (perhaps that should be eyeshade?) is responsible for ensuring that the technology acquisition is worth the money. In most companies this will be the finance department under the direction of the chief financial officer (CFO). Some companies will assign this responsibility to management or administrative staff.

The financial role includes:

- ▶ Performing a cost-benefit analysis (CBA) of the project that the technology acquisition will support
- ▶ Figuring out the costs of the business problem that the project purports to solve
- ▶ Comparing the financial impacts of alternate solutions
- ▶ Analyzing the cost-and-benefit impact of delaying, modifying, or redirecting technology projects
- ▶ Analyzing vendor proposals

4. *Negotiating*

Negotiators with experience in information technology acquisitions can be found in the legal profession, in management, or elsewhere. In most companies the person wearing this hat will be found in the contracts department. This role includes:

- ▶ Securing the most favorable price and terms possible
- ▶ Helping the vendor conceptualize the deal in terms of customer business value
- ▶ Eliciting vendor commitments to flexibility and risk sharing
- ▶ Capturing the deal in a contract

5. *Administrative*

The person or department that fills the administrative role must make the rules for the acquisition, and enforce them. In most companies, the wearer of this hat will be found in the contracts department. The principal parts of this role are:

- ▶ Monitoring the company's and its vendors' compliance with contracts
- ▶ Enforcing contracts
- ▶ Setting procurement standards

The Question Chair

Each of the five roles is essential in the acquisition process. The success of the deal depends on all of them working together. It also depends on each getting one question answered.

Imagine people responsible for the five roles all in a room with the vendor. Each role has one question that must be answered. Each has the responsibility to ask this one question at every available opportunity.

Each gets to sit in the question chair from time to time. The questions they ask are:

- *User:* "Will the acquisition provide a competitive advantage, reduce costs, or advance a business objective?"
- *Technical:* "Will it perform the intended function in our environment?"
- *Financial:* "Is this the most cost-effective alternative?"
- *Negotiating:* "How can we cut the best deal with the vendor?"
- *Administrative:* "How can we avoid costly breaches of our contract with the vendor and take advantage of the rights we have purchased?"

Like a single-issue political candidate, the person occupying each of the roles must be able to relate every subject that comes up to his or her special interests. But instead of advocating bimetallism or free trade, the five "hats" represent five essential aspects of corporate oversight. While everything they say or do during the deal process should be an embodiment of their signature questions, they should never lose sight of the general good: business success.

The Deal Wheel

The Prime Mover: A Business Problem

The only reason to set the Deal Wheel (Figure 3-1) in motion is to solve a business problem. The better the problem is understood, the likelier it is that the justification for the purchase will be sound. No company will ever admit that a purchase was made because someone was infatuated with technology (technophilia), or because a vendor's patter clouded the distinction between *want* and *need*. Even poorly thought-out purchases are always justified, at least superficially.

Figure 3-1. The environment of the acquisition process in motion.

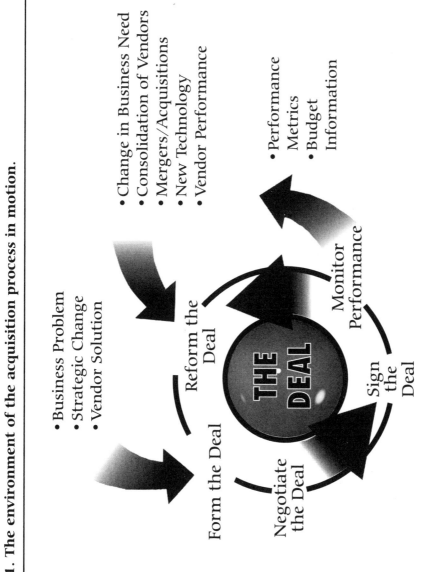

- Business Problem
- Strategic Change
- Vendor Solution

- Change in Business Need
- Consolidation of Vendors
- Mergers/Acquisitions
- New Technology
- Vendor Performance

- Performance Metrics
- Budget Information

THE DEAL

Form the Deal

Reform the Deal

Negotiate the Deal

Monitor Performance

Sign the Deal

The important thing to remember is that something in the business environment has changed. A need may have arisen. There may have been a strategic directional change. The change could have been necessitated by a merger. Whatever the impetus, the immediate reason for the deal must be a business reason.

Remember, though, that a deal, or single vendor transaction, is usually part of a project that flows from a strategic plan. That hierarchy—from strategic plan, to project, to transaction or deal—means that the business problem to be solved by the deal is understandable only in terms of the project the deal supports. The project, in turn, exists only to fulfill a strategic plan.

Forming the Deal

Even at the first stage (forming the deal), it is very important to take advantage of the strength of the five roles. The deal must be examined from a user, technical, financial, administrative, and negotiating perspective while discussions are active with more than one vendor. The advantages of this approach are that:

▶ Deals that don't meet one of the company's key tests are eliminated quickly, before significant user or technical resources are expended on them.

▶ The key terms are established while there are multiple competitors and the company has not made an irreversible investment in a particular solution.

Each role takes its turn in the question chair, even before the vendor field has been narrowed. The user must be sure that vendor solutions being considered meet one of these goals: either providing a competitive advantage, reducing costs, or advancing some other business objective. To answer the question, the user might prepare a needs assessment analysis or similar requirements document. The user might also draft a request for proposal with the help of the other team members.

Technical asks whether the acquisition will work in the company's environment. Incompatible technologies (and solutions with serious design flaws) can be avoided at this early stage. Financial questions whether it is the most cost-effective alternative by helping the user understand the financial scope of the business problem to be solved. It's at this first stage that $2 solutions to $1 problems should be discovered and discarded. The digging done here will also clear the way for the final financial analysis.

Negotiating plans how to cut the best deal with the chosen vendor, helps to identify and prioritize the objectives from all areas that must be included in the deal, and looks at preliminary proposals with an eye to possible talking points. Administrative considers the range of contracting options that each vendor might present and begins to formulate a strategy to maximize the company's rights while minimizing its exposure and to structure a deal that can be easily administered.

Everyone involved should look at the deal in broad terms while remaining vigilant about his or her own role and the question that defines it. Evaluations of hardware and software should be done. User and technical might both do an analysis, or they might work together. Evaluation discussions should be conducted with as few preconditions as possible so that design flaws are not "baked in" at this early stage.

In short, the process of *analysis* (breaking apart the enterprise's skills into specialized roles) and *synthesis* (reblending those roles to execute a dynamic process) has begun.

Negotiating the Deal

As the process continues and deepens, a more detailed understanding is reached with the vendor (or group of vendors) that makes the first cut. The goal of the company should be to build its definition of success into the contract provisions. To do this, it:

► Establishes objectives and priorities for the deal.

► Negotiates specific contractual provisions using expert negotiators. The provisions reflect the understanding that the user and technical people have reached with the vendor. They also include protections for the company so that it gets the benefits it expects and the flexibility it needs.

► Analyzes the financial deal from both the company's side and the vendor's side to determine whether the deal makes sense and whether there is bargaining room left in the vendor's offer.

In addition, the company must design a dashboard for the deal. A car's dashboard shows key indicators for driving, such as distance traveled, fuel remaining, speed, whether you are in drive or reverse, and so forth. It includes "red zones" to indicate when the car is going dangerously fast or is dangerously low on fuel. A dashboard for a contract has the same purpose. It contains key indicators, such as user satisfaction, achievement of milestones, achievement of anticipated savings, and other business value metrics tied to a benefit commitment made by the user. It is easy for an administrative person to watch. It includes the equivalent of red zones that indicate when the administrator must escalate a problem.

Designing the dashboard when the deal is negotiated has the advantages that:

▶ The company knows how to measure success, because it designed the dashboard when the definition of success was understood.

▶ The company is prepared to do low-cost monitoring of the contract, escalating only key problems for user and legal involvement.

Signing the Deal

All five company "hats" must approve the deal. As the contracting authority and rule maker, administrative must ensure that everyone has the chance to do so. To make sure that the company has made a "go" decision on all levels, formal approval by all five roles is important. Before the deal is signed, the user signs on to an ongoing cost-benefit analysis to ensure the continued desirability of the deal and help the company learn from the acquisition. The technical team makes a written commitment as to the cost and time frame for implementation and ongoing operation.

Monitoring Performance

If an efficient dashboard has been designed, low-cost administrative staff can read the gauges and monitor the deal. When they see internal or vendor problems, they can report them to the appropriate person.

Any effective control system has to have three things:

1. Defined criteria for success
2. Observability, so that someone monitoring it can detect whether it is performing according to these criteria
3. Adjustability, so that problems can be fixed

A properly constructed dashboard meets these requirements. It allows both budget information and performance metrics to be reported out in order to keep the deal running smoothly and permit corrective action to be taken

Reforming the Deal

No technology system is an island. As the Deal Wheel graphic shows, the environment affects a deal as much as the deal changes the environment.

The user's business needs may change. A party may not be living up to the terms of the contract. The deal may no longer make sense for other reasons.

The vendor may have undergone an important change. It may have merged or been acquired. There may have been a consolidation of vendors that made a material change in the way service was delivered.

The monitoring process may have revealed structural problems in the design of the deal. The benefits laid out in financial cost-benefit analysis may have failed to materialize. The vendor's performance may be faulty.

New technology may have been developed, so that the deal is no longer the "best solution." Negotiation may believe that market power has shifted and the deal can be improved (from the company's standpoint).

Whether the world has changed or a party is not living up to the terms of the contract, the old deal no longer makes sense. The team's responsibility is clear: Reform the deal.

A new deal is identified at a high level. The Deal Wheel revolves to negotiating the new deal. The negotiation process begins again, this time with the benefit of the experience gained from the original negotiation.

As the Wheel Turns: Life in the Real World

The Deal Wheel paradigm for technology acquisitions is simple, effective, and attainable. Whether it works in your company depends on how well the five roles function, and whether their five fundamental questions are successfully answered:

1. *User:* "Will the acquisition provide a competitive advantage, reduce costs, or advance a business objective?"

2. *Technical:* "Will it perform the intended function in our environment?"

3. *Financial:* "Is this the most cost-effective alternative?"

4. *Negotiating:* "How can we cut the best deal with the vendor?"

5. *Administrative:* "How can we avoid costly breaches of our contract with the vendor and take advantage of the rights we have purchased?"

4

The User

The only reason to buy information technology is to improve the way a company does business, either by allowing it to do what it does faster or at less cost or by allowing it to do things it could not otherwise do. This dictum must always be at the top of a prospective technology user's mind. The user's fundamental question—will the acquisition provide a competitive advantage, reduce costs, or advance a business objective?—should serve as a constant reminder that technology acquisitions must always be linked to business improvement.

In theory, no one disputes the idea that technology acquisitions should be linked to business improvements. But users do not run their businesses, or their companies, in a theoretical business world. The world of business realities that they inhabit is full of confusing signals, tentative projections, and unclear forecasts. That world is filled with companies that adopt new technologies to achieve and exploit competitive advantage. Eschewing the latest technology in such a world is risky. So is adopting it.

The decisions a user reaches—how the need is defined, whether technology is needed to fill it, and what that technology is—should all be seen as results of the crosscurrents of the real business world. Fundamentally, though, the definition of business need remains solely in the hands of the user. While technical, administrative, and financial colleagues may help reframe the user's thinking about the scope and shape of the business need, the user decides both what the problem is and whether a particular technology solves it.

The user has a difficult task. She has to look into the future, try to read the signs to detect new and emerging conditions, and then determine how to continue to create value given those emerging conditions. This strategic planning process often results in goals that can best be met with information technology, such as:

- ▶ Fulfilling new business objectives, e.g., increased market share or expansion into a new product line

► Improving processes, e.g., those things billed as better/faster/cheaper

► Solving existing process problems, e.g., meeting published turnaround times

Defining Success

From a user's goals will flow high-level business requirements. The underpinning of a successful IT deal is to define success in business terms. To define success in technological terms at the start would impair the process of finding the best available solution.

Here's an example. A company's strategic plan requires it to increase sales effectiveness. After some study, the users decide that to increase sales effectiveness, sales reps need to close deals in one sales call. A major impediment to closing deals is that the company's pricing is so complex that a computer is needed to set a price. The sales reps can't close an order in one sales call because they can't put a price on the table. Instead, they return to the main office and use a computer system to generate a purchase contract from six key pieces of information they collect from the customer.

What is the user need here? Many users would express the need as portable computers and printers for sales reps. Meeting that need would allow a sales rep to rapidly print a sales contract. Having a sales contract would allow the sales rep to close the deal.

However obvious it might be to give portable computers to sales reps, the user is better off defining the need as having a sales contract in the sales rep's hand at the first sales call. That need could be met by a variety of technical solutions. For example, giving each sales rep a cellular phone and fax machine, and having a person at the head office run the computer, might meet that need for well under half the cost of providing portable computers for the sales force. Also, defining the business need as sales contracts, not portable computers, opens up nontechnical solutions, such as simplifying pricing. By not prematurely becoming wedded to a specific technical solution, the user is able to keep other alternatives open long enough for the business context to be adequately established and the best solution found.

Defining Needs

In many cases, users consider the deliberate step of setting down business requirements to be a step backward. This is often the case when a bond is formed between users and vendors before the user has developed an adequate formal needs statement. In the end, though, users find that careful definition of business needs acts as an invaluable touchstone to judge at each point whether the deal is delivering the value originally sought.

There are several ways to define a user's need and produce more successful deals. One approach is to create a requirements document. A requirements document is a set of business, timing, and technical requirements. The requirements document should also indicate any service standards that should be achieved in the relationship between the user's company and the solution. It should also include statements about resource availability for implementation and training.

The user must define indicators of success that can be reasonably measured using objective criteria. Commonly, these include contract milestones and specific deliverables or performance specifications that will be set forth in detail in the contract.

Needs should include everything that is required to achieve success, as the user defines it. If a user is relying on the delivery of a significant upgrade to a software product on a certain date to meet a commitment to a customer, that delivery date must be understood to be a priority requirement. If a user knows the volume of transactions that the system must process, that should be a requirement.

Another common way of formally defining need that is often used with larger, more complex acquisitions is a request for proposal, or RFP, process. In an RFP process, the discipline of having to write down requirements that must be clear to a reader outside of the company often helps the user identify the problem to be solved in terms of a specific need. RFPs are described in detail in Chapter 11.

The staff areas support the user in defining needs. In order to choose the right product characteristics as needs, users must understand the trade-offs involved. For example, IT staff should be able to tell the user that a product that meets a particular need, such as increasing the productivity of line employees, would require the company to upgrade all of its mainframe computers. Financial staff should point out any sleight-of-hand factors in vendors' pricing structures that may act as a disincentive to future business growth. Contract administration staff and legal staff should expose any burdensome obligations that may prohibit a future or currently identified business direction.

User Risk Assessment

In addition to defining requirements, users must assess the risks of new information technology. Unless those risks are understood, the company will be unable to decide whether to invest additional money in testing systems, purchasing redundant systems, buying more expensive but more reliable systems, and the like.

Risk assessment should proceed in two stages. The first stage is to identify risks. These risks might include such things as inability to process data, incorrect processing of data, inability to communicate what has been processed, or improper use of the system. They might result from system failures, network failures, equipment break-downs, bad programming, late delivery, incompetence, and other vendor failures. However, a comprehensive risk analysis will also consider risks from acts of God (hurricanes, lightning, floods, and the like), sabotage, malicious acts, and other events that are beyond the vendor's control.

The next step is to assess the possible economic effects of these risks. Only by understanding the probability and magnitude of harm can the user properly orient the company's risk mitigation efforts. The possible harms may include, for example:

- Lost sales, e.g., from erroneous orders or poor customer service
- Lost employees, e.g., from failing to credit sales commissions or from frustration with the system
- Lost revenue, e.g., from failure to properly bill customers
- Lost productivity, e.g., because a production line is down
- Lost management time
- Additional expense, e.g., rework or using outside services to do what the computer system was supposed to do
- Fines or penalties resulting from failure to meet regulatory or contract commitments

Once these risks have been identified and quantified, they should be described to the entire team. Financial needs to understand the potential risks in order to prepare a complete financial analysis. Technical can work to mitigate risks with testing and redundancy. Negotiating can seek to shift many of these risks to the vendor.

However, the user bears primary responsibility for making sure that a computer system produces proper results. If the input is faulty, the output will be faulty. Also, the user is often in the best position to detect faulty output, since the user gets the output first and understands the business best.

Market Research

In addition to obtaining advice and counsel from all internal resources, the user has the responsibility to perform market research from a user, not a technical, standpoint. As Ovid said in *The Art of Love*, it's best not to make fateful decisions based upon an impression formed in candlelight. Ovid advised examining the potential beloved in broad daylight before getting involved. Users will add to their risk-mitigation arsenal by contacting customers who have implemented the proposed solution. Instead of being content to examine product documentation or, worse, relying on a product demo presented at a vendor's site in highly controlled circumstances with hors d'oeuvres and happy talk, the user should seek out other users and learn from their mistakes.

Third-party client visits will potentially provide the broad daylight in which the blemishes of products can be assessed more objectively. If they are allowed to, users should bring their staff support network to identify potential pitfalls.

Good vendors are always willing to supply a list of installed sites and contacts to talk to. Keep in mind that vendors will still attempt to control the impression these sites give. Clients who agree to act as references are usually getting some kind of consideration from the vendor to do so. This may be in the form of a lower up-front price or priority service treatment. There may even have been a term in the contract between the vendor and the client stipulating that the client act as a positive reference for the product.

Obviously, the user should seek out not only other users with the most comparable set of business problems requiring resolution (i.e., users from similar industries) but also other users that may have faced similar implementation problems (such as complex network environments or a huge volume of transactions to process). Users should also ask what solutions the other users have discarded. The answer to that question may identify solutions that the user's company should consider. Users should beware of the vendor who will not quickly and willingly provide them with installed base information and a client reference list.

Users should particularly beware of the vendor who explains that the user is really the first client of its size or in its industry to ever implement the product. In IT, the solutions that haven't failed are the ones that haven't been tried (they don't call it the *bleeding edge* for nothing).

Internal Communications

The user also needs to worry about how a product will need to be implemented in order to realize the assumed or projected benefits. These issues are not trivial. The user needs to communicate all the relevant aspects of the deal to the company in order to help bring about the behavioral change necessary to achieve the benefits originally sought. Sometimes assumed benefits will be entirely unrealized if the rest of the organization doesn't change.

While a program of internal communications may not play a direct part in the negotiation, it may affect the success of the project more than a well-written contract. The user must keep the organization informed of any impending change while not being alarming. The user's challenge is to juggle difficult assignments simultaneously:

- ► Maintaining the old
- ► Preparing for the new
- ► Defining requirements
- ► Communicating requirements to staff
- ► Communicating requirements to other members of the acquisition team

Signing the Contract

Once the user and the staff areas have helped to negotiate a contract that sets forth the business arrangement and embodies the success criteria and remedies for failure, the contract is ready to be signed. The signing of the contract may appear to be a mere and momentary formal event in the long process of meeting a user's business need with an IT acquisition supported by a vendor relationship, but it is more than that.

Signing the deal is the formal process of concurrence among the roles. This action provides a means for all the roles to acknowledge that the negotiations have embodied the concerns they raised as advocates for their own positions, and for the positions jointly determined by the negotiating team.

In particular, the significance of the user's signing the deal is that the user:

- ► Is committed on behalf of the business unit to the acquisition and concurs with the results of the negotiation.

> ► Accepts the business risks associated with the transaction.
> ► Provides budget authority to pay the costs of the transaction.

Monitoring Vendor Performance

If the deal has been correctly designed, with clear, unambiguous criteria for success, monitoring performance against those criteria should be a simple matter. Because the success criteria will be established in different domains (some are business-related, some involve the technical performance of the product, some involve financial measures), the user will have the assistance of various staff areas in the monitoring function. For example, the news that a system is failing to process a defined volume of transactions at a defined speed may come from the IT staff, and the news that the vendor has failed to provide a required insurance certificate may come from administrative staff.

The user will have responsibility for most of the day-to-day relationship with the vendor. As discussed in Chapter 8, "Administrative," it is beneficial to have a separate organization be responsible for the formal communication of performance problems. This separation allows the vendor-user relationship to stay intact in good times and in bad. However, the user needs to stay involved in the appraisal of any disputes and the administration of any remedies. The user's orientation to business needs is an indispensable ingredient in deciding on the amount of company resources to apply to resolve a dispute and the degree to which the company is willing to sour the vendor relationship in order to pursue its remedies.

Reforming the Deal

The user must regularly reassess whether the deal is meeting the current business needs. Business changes. Competition changes. As new needs arise, the user must be ready to seek out new solutions. The monitoring process that is part of the new paradigm for IT acquisitions dictates that all five roles stand ready to reform the deal.

Just as the user is the catalyst for forming the deal, it is the user who must be vigilant in monitoring its success. It is the user's environment that the IT acquisition affects. It is the user who must begin the process, lead it, and reassume leadership whenever the deal must be reformed.

5

Technical

Even if the user has arrived at a new, more businesslike way of looking at the problem to be solved by the acquisition, and even if the
vendor's consciousness has also been raised so that now both user
and vendor are making a good-faith effort to see the acquisition as a
means to an appropriate business end, one very large question remains: Will it work?

Why IT Knows Best

Many years ago, back when the central IT department was called
DP (data processing), the role of the organization's data/information
professionals was a lot different from what it is today. Software
didn't come in a shrink-wrapped box. It appeared character by character in blurry green letters on a cathode-ray tube. Pre-PC information professionals wrote their own code and created their own
systems. They were technology developers, not shopping consultants. No one else in the organization could have done what they did.
There was little need to integrate purchased systems.

Today, with technical talent spread throughout all departments,
the hallways and cubicles are full of people who believe they can do
IT's job of systems integration as well as the MIS director or CIO. True
believers in the idea of open systems have created difficult integration
problems by acquiring systems that are interoperable on paper but
incompatible with the rest of the company in real life. While almost
all kinds of hardware and varieties of operating system software can
communicate with one another, impediments to communication
often occur at the application software level, where the work is done.

The de facto departmental IT expert knows the five or six tasks a
new system needs to accomplish in her department, but she cannot
anticipate the costs and problems of interfacing the new system with
others. Nor is the departmental expert aware of the dozens of technol-

ogy vendors the company has already worked with that might offer more promising solutions, but that have never crossed her path.

Have you ever installed a video card? Debugged a system software problem on your home computer? Hooked up a printer? Used technical terms in conversation? If you have, you might consider yourself the technical equal of the systems integration professionals in your organization. So because what systems integration people do no longer seems mysterious or special, you might not give their opinions about technology acquisitions the weight you should.

That would be a grievous error. Technical knows best, because these days systems integration is practically all that technical does. The "buy, not build" strategy now followed by so many organizations has made acquisitions experts of information technology professionals, while it has burdened them with the problem of finding solutions to complicated integration problems. They hear vendor claims all the time. They're better at evaluating them because they have more practice.

You may be able to spackle a wall, but could you be architect, plumber, and electrician to the ten-story addition to your office?

A History of the World

Rome wasn't built in a day. Nevertheless, the ancient Romans managed to get all their aqueducts to work together. When they needed a new one, it became part of the existing water-supply system. Even the maddest of the mad emperors never thought of demolishing the old system to achieve an incremental benefit.

Integrating old and new into a viable system was no easier 2,000 years ago than it is today, but the alternative—out with the old, in with the new—was just as prohibitively expensive and wasteful.

Which brings us to the point of this history lesson: namely, that when it comes to IT acquisitions, few companies have the luxury of a fresh start. Even in departments where everything is being replaced, the new system will have to be connected to other parts of the organization where things are not so new, not so resilient.

All the upgrades, changes, acquisitions, improvements, realignments, and conversions that have occurred since the dawn of electronic data have left their marks on most organizations. Each change makes incorporating the next change a little more difficult. As in a fragile ecosystem, certain changes—the introduction of a new species of database, for example—can send things spiraling out of control. Not every species can survive in every ecosystem. Some flowers cannot survive a northern winter, except in a hothouse.

Will It Work Here?

No matter how good a proposed system is, installing it in certain environments will cause it to fail or will cause other parts of the environment to fail. Is your environment one of these? What sort of interfaces and bridges and other hothouse technology would you need to avoid failure? Only systems integration can answer these questions with any authority, because only systems integration has the perspective to see what the environment is really like.

Systems Integration as FDA

Here in the United States, the Food and Drug Administration (FDA) is responsible for ensuring that new drugs are both safe and effective before physicians prescribe them for their patients. These two criteria—safety and efficacy—are the same ones that systems integration needs to apply to new technology acquisitions.

And, like the FDA, systems integration sometimes has to endure complaints that the approval process is taking too long, or that it is erring on the side of caution. Just as the FDA is often confronted by interest groups that point out that a given drug was approved in another country long ago, systems integration can be prodded by users and vendors who list all the companies that have already adopted the system under acquisition consideration.

The consequences of the FDA's caving in to pressure and allowing a harmful drug to reach the market without adequate testing can be catastrophic. No such human catastrophes await companies that deny systems integration the proper latitude to fulfill the oversight function outlined in the next section. But the potential for serious harm to the organization ought to be imminent enough for managers to pay close attention to this topic.

Systems integration intervention is necessary to make sure that all new acquisitions meet commonsense standards and achieve specific user goals. While it's true that systems integration professionals won't be able to match the user's knowledge of the business process, they will be able to supply the features-to-benefits analysis far more adeptly than the user or the vendor.

The Technical Assessment Process

Technical assists in the process by translating business needs into technical terms, determining what specific products and tools the company will need, testing them, and defining them in contract terms.

Translating Business Needs Into Technical Terms

Ideally, systems integration should be able to serve as a clearinghouse for available technical solutions, offering a balanced, dispassionate assessment of the strengths and weaknesses of each.

Remember that the vendor has been trained to keep the user focused on a single solution. The vendor's bridge to the promised land of business benefits is intended to be seen as the only bridge.

The primary purpose of this step is to help the user understand that most business benefits can be arrived at in different ways—that other bridges have already been built, and that new bridges can be built. While helping to translate the benefits that the user needs from technology into the features that the technology solution will have, systems integration can introduce technical solutions with which the user may be unfamiliar and remind the user that other vendors or internal technical resources may offer reasonable, or better, alternatives.

Having systems integration examine this critical linkage, and explain that there are many features-benefits links available, is far better than having the user rely on the vendor's help to try to correlate the features of the vendor's preexisting solution with the user's required benefits. Remember that the vendor wants to sell new products with added features, and that the added features can cloud the fundamental business objective.

This step also helps systems integration establish its credentials as the principal source of technology information in the transaction. Clearly it is in the best interest of the company to have its systems integrators, and not the vendor, play this role.

With all kinds of different computing environments spread across multiple sites, today's large companies have difficulty keeping track of the technology they've already acquired. It's a virtually impossible task. Systems integration is in the best position to know whether a technical solution similar enough to the one under consideration is already available within the company. Besides the obvious benefit of not having to write another check, the benefits of finding and using an existing solution include the fact that there are people around who can tell you what it was like to implement an existing system, and how well it works. They can do it faster, too.

Lotzadata Co. had recently decentralized. Being in a regulated environment, it still needed to report corporate information in consolidated form. Its decentralized strategic business units (SBUs) were eager to generate additional information in formats that would suit their individual needs, so they created separate, multimillion-dollar data warehouses independent of the central data warehouse and of each other. As project after project was launched and completed, SBU and corporate managers at Lotzadata Co. started to feel a little queasy. They realized that none of the new systems could feed the old consolidated repository. They also realized that the old repository couldn't be eliminated because of their regulatory reporting requirements. In the end, Lotzadata Co., found itself replacing most of the SBU systems to avoid the horrific cost of building interfaces among its various incompatible systems.

There are undeniable advantages to decentralization, but one thing that cannot be claimed is that decentralized systems will be integrable. Nor can it ensure that the technical needs of a single unit will be consonant with the business needs of the enterprise. Had Lotzadata Co. relied on its systems integrators, millions of dollars would have been saved.

Determining Product Needs

Vendors love to talk about "turnkey" solutions, by which they mean systems that are so complete and ready to run that all the user has to do, figuratively speaking, is walk up to the front door, turn the key, and begin living a life of ease in the marble halls of technology bliss.

If you're a fan of prison movies, you know that turnkey has another meaning: jailer. The guy who turns the key that locks your cell. As in, "Hey, turnkey, this bread is moldy."

Few vendors offer solutions good enough to live up to the first definition, or bad enough to live down to the second. But this much is certain: However comprehensive a new system seems, there are always loose ends, unresolved interface issues, and functionality gaps.

The user isn't positioned to know where these gaps will occur, much less how to fill them. It is essential for the good of the acquisition, and the company, that systems integration plug the gaps.

Consider the example of BZB Inc., the company that acquired software and hardware that allowed it to move payroll processing from a mainframe computer to a distributed computing, client/ server system. (The whole story is in Chapter 1.) BZB's new system seemed complete and self-sufficient to just about everybody involved. But there was one critical gap: operational support services.

Even with the intervention of systems integration, the fact that there weren't enough client/server technicians or print capacity around to support the new system was initially overlooked. Of all the factors that can inadvertently be left out of the mix, ongoing support is one of the most often omitted.

Which is not to say that other, more seemingly obvious, omissions don't occur all too often as well. Software that can run only on Unix-based workstations shows up in PC environments. High-maintenance Unix-based workstations show up in environments without Unix experts (a "high-RISC" blunder). Local-area networks are set up without network managers. Systems that seem to be indestructible during the product demo become eggshell fragile their first day on the job.

Systems integration won't have all the answers. But when you are analyzing the solution, answers aren't all you need. You need questions like this one: "Who's going to support this system?" Or these:

- ▶ Will we have enough backup capacity?
- ▶ Does this alter our current backup implementation?
- ▶ What is the expected system availability? Forty hours a week? Twenty-four hours a day, seven days a week? Are operations established?
- ▶ Are there special database requirements? Will database experts need to be involved? Does the application force the use of a specific database vendor?
- ▶ What are the minimum hardware requirements (processor type, memory per user count, disk usage per user, etc.)?
- ▶ What operating systems are used? Is there staff expertise to support these systems, or do we need to train/hire/contract? What will these staffing options cost?
- ▶ Who will use the system? Where are these people physically located? Is the application real time? If not, what delay is acceptable?
- ▶ Are people at other locations expecting system use? Will they need wide-area network access? Is there enough bandwidth? Is dial-in a requirement? Is there dial-in capability?

Systems integrators have the experience. They have seen how things really happen when promises mature into reality. They have learned lessons.

Testing, Testing, One, Two, Three

Stress testing and analysis provide a broad approach to integration. This analysis gives the systems integrator an opportunity to interpolate the environment when many (or few) users are accessing the system. This testing also proves that the current environment has the capacity to handle the application implementation.

Testing forces the integrator to measure network, disk, processing, and recovery capacities. This process also forces the snapshot measurement that defines an initial point and should (with a seasoned integrator) force the question of scaling for the next few years. If the systems integrator allows for the next few years, this should be adequate because the application implementation could change (as a result of technological advances), or the analysis could yield capacity upgrades in memory, disk, processor, network bandwidth, etc.

The integrator is also the only one in a position to know how many projects in the company rely on that final increment remaining on the existing data line. Thus, only the integrator can react appropriately.

Users eager to get the new system up and running, and vendors eager to get paid, will consider this on-site testing step a waste of valuable time.

Perhaps it does seem a bit overcautious to take a system that is known to work in other companies, has published performance benchmarks, seems easy to implement and use, and comes highly recommended from a trusted vendor—a system with all these assurances of reliability—and put it through its paces before the deal is consummated. After all, who ever heard of a new technology acquisition failing to live up to its billing?

OK, everyone has. So now you see why this step is so important.

Prepurchase testing is a significant bother and expense for systems integration departments that are already overextended trying to make sure the company's heterogeneous environments work and play well together. Systems integration doesn't advocate such testing out of pique over not thinking of the vendor solution first, or from some Luddite-like reluctance to bring in yet another technomarvel.

The real motive? Survival. If technology systems fail, no one's coming after the user. If the new system turns out to be a problem child that takes up so much internal support time that maintenance of other systems suffers, the problems can ripple through the whole enterprise. It won't be the CFO who gets the icy boardroom stares, even if the CFO was the proponent of the new system. It will be IT's systems integrators. And they know it.

So they're more than happy to measure out an ounce of prevention in the form of on-site testing under conditions as close as possible to the ones the system will face if it is bought. Any user or vendor objection to this kind of reasonable testing probably can be attributed to shortsightedness or covert knowledge of system shortcomings or personal incentives.

Feeding Technical Ideas Into the Contract

If the first three steps were conducted rigorously (and the process has not been aborted), it's likely that systems integration will have some additions to be negotiated into the contract.

For example, if it is revealed that the company doesn't have the staff or expertise to support the acquisition adequately, systems integration has to see that support from the vendor is built into the deal.

If questions are raised about the product's ability to run in the company environment, detailed and measurable performance standards must be added that prevent or compensate for product problems that are unique to this environment.

Systems integration might recommend changes such as:

▶ Modifying the vendor product, platform, or function
▶ Developing add-on products
▶ Converting company data
▶ Eliciting a vendor commitment to long-term support of multiple versions of the product
▶ Having the vendor provide source code
▶ Modifying the company's current environment as a prerequisite to acquisition
▶ Requiring the vendor to commit to work with specific third-party products and versions or develop specific interfaces

It is also important that systems integration review the tracking provisions of the deal for technical feasibility. If the contract requires the company to track or count usage, for example, it has to be confirmed that the usage tracking process is technically possible.

Making It Work

Once the deal is done and the new acquisition is in place, IT's systems integration becomes responsible for its care and feeding. Systems integration installs fixes and upgrades. It interfaces with the vendor's help desk. It ensures that the new product doesn't damage any existing systems. In short, it becomes custodian for the new product, with responsibility for all the unglamorous but essential tasks that all custodians face.

For example, if the assessment process resulted in the vendor's writing a specification that enabled the product to comply with the performance standards in the contract, it's up to IT, knowing how the product is working, to report whether the product actually complies with its specifications.

Often the most difficult implementation issue for systems integration is its signature task: systems integration. Figuring out how to get the new system to mesh with the rest of the company's systems—making it function as part of existing IT tools, not merely work alongside them—requires hundreds of assessments and reassessments. A new system doesn't simply enter an environment; it changes it. How the environment changes depends on how well systems integration does this most important of jobs.

Largely because of its monitoring functions, IT's systems integration is in a perfect position to identify technical problems that need to be corrected if and when the deal is reformed.

Reforming the deal, from systems integration's perspective, really means revisiting the whole technical assessment process, from the business-needs-to-technical-tools translation, to determining what additional software, hardware, and services will be required to implement and support the acquisition, to testing, to searching the enterprise for similar solutions that are already available, to negotiating and signing off.

Keep in mind that this revisitation will take place at a future time and in a different place. New information will be available. The vendor's product will probably have changed. Competitors' products will be different and probably better than they were. Completely new kinds of solutions may have been brought to market.

It will be up to systems integration to look at the whole environment to determine what changes should be made to the old deal that will significantly improve the offering. Sometimes these changes will involve modifying the old deal to incorporate new technologies. Changes in the company's overall computing environment (such as changes in system architecture) may cause reformation of existing relationships. In its clearinghouse role, systems integration must be the keeper of solutions. As the computing world turns, it must be ready to realign, to jettison, to trade two bad systems for one good system. In short, it must find a way to keep the enterprise's technology portfolio current, productive, and profitable.

It's probably a little misleading to draw a hard line between these functions when they occur as part of a precontract assessment, and the same functions when they're conducted as part of a postcontract reassessment. The kind of probing and questioning that makes systems integration both author and guardian of an enterprise's information systems is continuous. It doesn't stop and start when a deal is done or undone.

Similarly, systems integration evaluates user systems all the time, not just when a given acquisition is under consideration. Every addition or upgrade an enterprise makes affects every other system, however slightly. Systems integration has to orchestrate all these interactions. So when it's asked to consider a change to a section of the orchestra, it should already have a pretty good idea of the kind of music that's likely to be produced.

It also knows that the audience—top management, board members, and stockholders—expects a good performance. This audience will not be inclined to make allowances for the fact that some of the instruments are newer or less reliable than others. Because the systems integration professionals hold the baton, it's up to them to make sure that all new technology deals can perform in tune.

6

Financial

The technology acquisition process can humble the brightest businesspeople. It can take a major corporation and put it in the same uncomfortable market position as a young car buyer fresh out of college facing a car salesperson for the first time.

The neophyte car buyer can do research on the make and model of car that would best meet the car buyer's personal demands for style and utility, just as the corporation can assess a product's technical suitability and ability to perform the required business task.

The car buyer can take a test drive to see if the published specifications translate to acceptable performance in the real world, just as the corporation can test a product on-site as part of its nexus of already-owned IT systems and networks.

But neither buyer is likely to have the information needed to make the buying decision intelligently. They both are in a buying situation that makes it nearly impossible to understand how much they'll have to spend to get what they want.

The novice car buyer is unlikely to grasp the complexities of installment loans, lease terms, and the time value of money as well as the car dealer. But even if they were both equally adept at understanding consumer lending and vehicle valuations, the buyer would still be at a disadvantage because of the impossibility of assessing future costs. Will this model be discontinued? Will industry standards require retrofitting added features? What will repairs cost for the first three years? What will this car be worth at trade-in time?

The corporation faces similar problems. Trying to figure out a number to hang on the bottom-line value of IT products has stumped more MBAs than W. Edwards Deming. Even the initial price tag is practically unknowable. Hidden costs, like training time and short-term productivity losses, raise the complexity of the computation to something on the order of Riemannian geometry.

Still and all, people buy their first new cars and corporations buy new computer products every day. The difficulties are not insuperable, and they have to be faced, because both groups of buyers need to get where these new purchases can take them.

Overcoming the difficulties starts with understanding that while the financial process is critical to smart IT acquisitions, it is a process that yields answers grudgingly. At least the first questions are obvious enough.

What Alternatives Should We Consider?

An IT acquisition must both be better than doing nothing and be better than anything else you can do. As the first step in the financial analysis process, you should consider many alternatives, one of which must be doing nothing.

Most companies focus only on the question: Do nothing or implement the project under consideration. They see the evaluation process as a bipolar "go/no-go" decision. If the proposed project passes the return-on-investment test, they proceed. As discussed in earlier chapters, vendors may pressure the user to see only one solution. Add the fact that managers have short-term goals and changing responsibilities, and it's easy to understand why it is seldom that multiple options are considered.

A good solution is not necessarily the best solution. Problems that IT can solve may have solutions outside the realm of information technology as well. It's easy to become mesmerized by hardware solutions to problems with business processes, when workflow reengineering, training, or other noncapital investments might solve them even better. Business problems don't always need technology solutions, even in the Information Age.

Are We Buying Something We Don't Need Just Because the Price Looks Right?

A discount is a savings only if there is a good reason for making a purchase. Buying that jar of sliced beets just because the Sunday paper had a 75¢-off coupon is a waste of money in a family that hates beets. Other things being equal, of course, a low price is better than a high one. But are you sure you know what those other things are? "Other things" must start with a clear definition of need. Until you're sure about the necessity for opening the checkbook, how can you be sure that a low price is better than no price?

Vendors try to exploit a buyer's inability to distinguish between a discount and a savings. The vendor gives the buyer the impression that the acquisition under consideration has a value higher than the price at which it is currently offered. Like a discount store owner who marks all his merchandise with two prices, a true selling price, and a higher reference price couched in terms like "made to sell for" or "selling elsewhere for," vendors instill the idea that a deal is worth X but is being offered for 70 percent of X, a 30 percent saving and an unbeatable value if you act now!

Discounts don't matter when you're justifying a project. They do matter (and can sweeten the deal considerably) when a specific technology acquisition has been shown to make sense as a result of an analysis that looks at all the costs and benefits that make the purchase price worth paying.

Are We Spending $2 to Solve a $1 Problem?

Analyzing technology projects should be no different from analyzing other business projects. All IT acquisitions, like all capital expenditures, must make sense in the context of the corporate budget, the overall business plan, and the overall strategic plan. It is unlikely that any of these documents endorses unlimited spending on new technology. If a new system costs corporate money, it had better make money.

Here's a simple example. Chris Clerk spends 50 percent of his time performing a function that could be automated. Your competitor has already automated the function. Chris's salary is $20,000/year plus 20 percent for benefits. The costs to automate include a $12,000 software package, a $2,000 hardware upgrade, a $900 training course for Chris, and 30 hours of a systems integrator's time at $100/hour to load and configure the software. This task is needed for only a year, and no one can pick up the other functions that Chris performs, so you can't terminate Chris. There's nothing else you need Chris to do.

Do you automate? No. You have a nominal manual cost versus higher costs of automation and no benefits. In this example you must ignore the competition and the fact that you can automate. You do the right thing for your set of circumstances.

Finance Can Find Answers

The user of the proposed IT acquisition may have a thorough knowledge of the corporation's profit goals for his or her department. The user may also know that the strategic plan calls for changes that require new technology. But the user probably will not be privy to management decisions that guide project funding. Finance will.

Finance also understands the economic meaning of the various numbers that the company uses. For example, in justifying a project, a company should consider only real dollars and cents. Avoid internal chargeback pricing. Systems designed to allocate costs (chargeback systems) should only rarely be used to drive economic project decisions internally. Because finance understands these issues, it can look at the underlying costs to make the right decisions for the company.

You Can't Lay a Silicon Cornerstone

One of the reasons why so many technology projects elude analysis is that, unlike most big purchases, they're invisible. A multimillion-dollar IT acquisition never attracts the same corporate attention as a multimillion-dollar building acquisition, simply because it just doesn't have the same visual impact.

Have you ever seen a new commercial building go up? If so, you've probably observed a procession of business-suited, hard-hatted people visiting the site practically every day. They point. They make sweeping gestures. They study the tape on the floor that marks the boundaries of their new office or department. They ask questions about the blueprints. They talk to the construction workers and ask how things are going. In short, they make sure they know what's going on.

Their interest in the project is likely to have begun well before the construction phase. They probably studied and commented on the building plans. They stroked their chins while thoughtfully circumambulating a scale model of the project. They talked about moving costs, new furniture, floor plans, parking spaces, and dozens of other features of the new construction.

They're also familiar with the process. Buildings have been around longer than computers. We bump into the concept of a wall (figuratively speaking) a lot more often than we bump into the concept of programmable read-only memory or object-oriented database management systems. Large-scale technology projects are still fairly new undertakings, and most people don't know how to break down their complexities into concepts they can understand and manage.

IT acquisitions might get more corporate attention if the CEO were able to drive past them on the way to work. But because they're invisible, it takes a little more conscious effort, and a lot more corporate discipline, to arrive at an adequate analysis of their costs and benefits.

Carpenters Monday, Electricians Tuesday, Drywallers Wednesday

Even if the world of computers were as familiar to us as the physical world, IT acquisitions would still present challenges at least as formidable as those from the world we can touch and feel. Few experienced people underestimate the complexity of a construction project. They know it involves extensive planning. They understand that, because many contractors are involved, there has to be a way to keep track of what everybody is doing and when they are doing it, or else the whole project suffers.

Things have to happen in a planned sequence. The electrician needs wall studs to mount switches and outlets. If the carpenter hasn't put up the studs, the electrical work can't be done. If the drywaller decides to show up before the electrician, the necessary electrical switches and outlets will have to be cut into or fed around the new walls, adding cost and reducing quality.

Big technology projects have the same need for careful, sequential planning. It isn't because they're technology projects. It's because they're big, complicated projects.

Big projects always require planning. They always force someone to deal with their inevitable complexity. They usually have many contractors whose work has to be coordinated. Their schedules are easily disrupted by a delay in, or a failure of, one of a dozen subsystems. They're important to the company, so if they don't get done on time, significant problems arise.

How Much Is a Brick Worth?

The enterprise cost of a project, like a new plant or a new inventory control system, can be estimated and put in the context of an organization's plans and goals. The enterprise cost of a single component of a project, like a brick in a new plant or a piece of software in an inventory control system, can only be put in the context of a project. The cost side of a cost-benefit analysis is always done at the project level, because individual transaction costs have corresponding value only in the context of the benefits attributed to the project.

You can compare the cost of brick A from Huffenpuff House of Bricks with the cost of brick B from First-Degree Mortar and Masonry. But the answer you come up with won't affect whether the building project is a good investment for the business.

You can't completely analyze the business costs of a single technology transaction, either. You must add all the components and look at the entire project. After the project is approved and the cost side of your cost-benefit analysis becomes your project budget, then all options for each component will be analyzed to pick the best solution.

A single piece of software, however indispensable to a technology project, is still only a brick in the building. It is too far removed from the business justification for the project to have assignable business benefits in itself. Its costs relate only to the project, and it's the project that must justify its business existence. In other words, finance has to make sure that the building is a prudent investment before it can get down to the cost of bricks.

Crunch, Crunch, Crunch, Crunch: Steps in Finance's Cost-Benefit Analysis of IT Projects

The first step in crunching the numbers is figuring out the costs of the problem or the potential revenue from the new solution. Is it a $1 problem? How much are you willing to spend to solve it? Any amount up to a dollar? Fifty cents a year for the next two years? How expensive a problem will it be if you do nothing for six months?

How much will the solution contribute to the bottom line? When will the company see the money? Will it be in productivity gains this year, or over the next five years? Will the solution offer any indirect benefits by making other systems or solutions more valuable to the company?

Identifying these costs and benefits isn't as easy as lifting a price tag and taking a peek. But if you can make a prima facie case for the new acquisition, and it doesn't seem to be a $2 solution to a $1 problem, then the process of looking at all the cost and benefit components begins in earnest. Remember, these projects, like all business projects, must make business sense and fit in with the company's strategic plan.

Save It for the Annual Report: Book Basis vs. Cash Flow Analysis

There's a fair amount of debate in finance circles about whether to analyze projects in terms of their effect on the company's income statement and balance sheet or based on the cash flows they generate. In preparing those financial statements, accountants often reflect one-time costs (like the cost of a mainframe) over many years using depreciation and amortization systems instead of as a one-time outflow of cash. Thus, a technology acquisition may have a far different impact on a company's net income statement from that on its cash flow.

Small companies with cash flow problems don't always have the luxury of looking at the costs associated with a new acquisition from the perspective of a multibillion-dollar public corporation. Sometimes they first have to sneak a peek at their wallets to see if they have the cash to pick up the check.

More than that, they have to look at all the costs—not just the price tag of the new system—from a cash flow perspective. After all, if the checkbook balance says you can't buy the new system, pay for all the telecommunications and networking upgrades it's going to need, pay for the software licenses, and still pay the electric bill, does it really matter if the system will improve the book value of your business?

Moreover, economists and business school professors will tell you that the only right way to decide whether the cash flows resulting from an IT acquisition (some out and some in) would increase the value of your business is to see if their net present value, discounted at the appropriate discount or hurdle rate, is positive. From that perspective, what's important is when you get and pay cash, and how much more a dollar is worth to you today than a dollar will be worth to you when you get and pay cash. The way it's all reported under generally accepted accounting principles is irrelevant.

On the other hand, the big boys of the corporate world (for whom anything under six figures is decimal point dust) probably won't focus as much on a cash flow analysis of a technology acquisition. They generally look at the costs in terms of their impact on net income of the company because net income drives the company's stock price and the value of their stock options.

No Ups, No Extras: One-Time Project Costs

A cost-benefit analysis of all your options starts with the base case. The base case is the company's best estimate of what would happen without the project. All the other options should be looked at as increments above or below the base case. Remember, finance's real assignment is not to evaluate the costs and benefits of a project. Its assignment is to decide whether embarking on the project is a better route to productivity and profitability than every other route and any other course of action, including inaction.

Once the analysis does turn to a specific alternative's costs and benefits, it takes considerable perspicacity to count all the one-time, incremental costs of a new acquisition. Incremental costs here mean costs that would not be incurred if the option under study were not taken. Some of these incremental costs are evident enough:

- ▶ Buying new hardware
- ▶ Upgrading old hardware
- ▶ Buying new telecommunications and networking equipment
- ▶ Upgrading old telecommunications and networking equipment
- ▶ Furniture, fixtures, and leasehold improvements (reconfiguring and remodeling to accommodate the new system)
- ▶ Software licenses
- ▶ Loss on the sale of old equipment (this doesn't enter into a cash flow analysis, only book basis)

The one-time personnel costs are a little more difficult to get your arms around—and they're usually underestimated because of the Christmas morning atmosphere that surrounds most IT acquisitions. They include:

- ▶ Project management costs (including the cost of disruption and reduced productivity during the change process)
- ▶ Testing
- ▶ Contract analysis
- ▶ Installation/conversion
- ▶ Severance (if the benefits the project is claiming include reduced staff)
- ▶ Training and development (including lost productivity during training)
- ▶ Previously incurred feasibility costs (consultants, training, travel, etc.) to the extent that they are not sunk costs, and, thus, irrelevant to the analysis
- ▶ Additional costs required to complete the contract if the company makes a "go" decision

The place to start looking for some of these costs is the company archives. Your company has analyzed these costs before. You may find the information spread out over several projects' analyses. Historical information on training and development costs might be in the file on last year's customer service software acquisition. Installation costs might be in the records of the big client/server conversion. That sort of detective work can be very useful in your analysis of the current acquisition.

Where Will It End? Ongoing Costs

Practically all acquisitions have costs that go on, and on, and on. As you analyze these costs, make sure you assign them to all appropriate time periods within the frame of your study. If you're analyzing costs and benefits over the next five years, you first have to determine how long you think the problem will be around. Then you have to identify which of your incremental recurring costs will be around for all five years, and whether these costs will go up or down during that period:

- ▶ Project management
- ▶ System administration
- ▶ Training
- ▶ Depreciation (book basis analysis only)
- ▶ Lease expense
- ▶ Maintenance fees
- ▶ Software license maintenance
- ▶ Consulting
- ▶ Additional space and utilities

You'll be making lots of assumptions when you estimate these costs. Remember that you're analyzing a complex system—the environment in your organization, and the way it reacts to change. It's a system that is as changeable as the weather. Like a meteorologist, you have to look at this dynamic system and predict its future state. Instead of polar air masses and shifting jet streams, your variables are things like next year's cost of office space and whether systems engineers will be available at a similar salary in two years.

Big changes in the weather start with small perturbations in the weather system. In chaos theory they call this the "butterfly effect," because (so the theory goes) the beating of a butterfly's wings in a distant meadow can begin a chain of events that culminates in a thunderstorm that spoils your picnic. Imperceptible variations in the initial conditions of a system make certainty about its future state an unattainable goal.

That's why the TV weather person talks about a 30 percent chance of rain instead of asserting that it will or it won't rain. That's also why your predictions of project costs can never be perfectly accurate. Make your assumptions flexible and realistic. Be aware of the assumptions you make, and make them visible. When doing these analyses, focus on the assumptions and inputs. They drive the conclusion.

Instant and Delayed Gratification: The Benefits

Most of the benefits of the new acquisition aren't going to be realized right away, but some will be. Remember, benefits count only if they wouldn't or couldn't have been realized in your current state. Instant benefits include:

- ► Gain on the sale of old equipment
- ► One-time incremental business benefit (a new client won because of the acquisition of the new system, for example)

The real payback takes time. Here are most of the benefits that need to be quantified:

- ► Reduction in equipment lease expenses
- ► Reduction in hardware maintenance
- ► Reduction in shared equipment costs (mainframe usage, for example)
- ► Software license cost avoidance
- ► Decreases in personnel (both employee and consultant) costs for project management, system administration, and other technical or operational services
- ► Productivity improvements, such as increased profits from re-engineering, better service delivery, or working smarter
- ► Flexibility, mostly from the expected value of options built into the contract and the scalability of the product that will provide benefits for future activities that haven't yet been contemplated

The broad productivity and flexibility benefits must relate to corporate goals that have already been laid out. A benefit is a benefit only if it's something the enterprise needs. If the company already owns a satisfactory data encryption application, for example, an encryption option that tags along as part of a new acquisition is not a real benefit and should not be a factor in the analysis.

Some benefits can be expressed only in probabilistic terms. The flexibility benefit, for example, can be calculated by multiplying the estimated benefit by the likelihood of the benefit's ever being triggered. Suppose the new acquisition includes a data center software license that can be used anywhere, rather than one that limits use of the software to the existing site only. The dollar value of this benefit depends on the likelihood of a move during the period under analysis. If you know that your company is very likely to build a new corporate headquarters within the time period of your cost-benefit analysis, the value of the portability of the license becomes correspondingly high.

It's another case of trying to predict the future state of a complicated system. You don't know for sure what's going to happen. You think you know what factors are likely to be predictive. To put a number to some benefits, you'll have to wear an economist's hat. For others, you'll wear the hat of a systems analyst, a business cycle expert, a statistician, even a psychologist.

Assigning probabilities is only the beginning. The probabilities have to reflect your unique environment. Consider this example: You leave the house in a delicate suit that cost you $450. If it gets wet, it will be ruined. There is a 40 percent chance of rain. How much is your umbrella worth? How much would it be worth if you lived in Antofagasta, Chile, where the annual rainfall is 0.02 inch?

You Call This a Reward?

Before you take the big risk of making a new acquisition, make sure the reward is worth it. As IT systems improve, the value of each improvement diminishes. Using a PC and Microsoft Word 1.0 to type a letter was a big productivity improvement over using an electric typewriter. The productivity gain from using the current release of Microsoft Word rather than using its immediate predecessor is much smaller. Software maintenance agreements that deliver a seemingly endless procession of new releases, each of which carries a smaller productivity benefit, if it carries one at all, should be looked at with skepticism. Everyone likes to have the newest version, but it usually isn't because the previous release wasn't doing the job. There must be a business benefit.

Diminishing marginal utility is the bane of all maturing systems. If the improvement on the table is too small to be worth the risk and expense of adopting it, your financial analysis should reflect that fact.

A response-time improvement from two to one-and-a-half seconds in a computer system, for example, is probably valueless. Human beings are not cyborgs, and slightly speedier computer functions usually have no impact on staffing and little impact on productivity. While they might determine the order in which certain tasks are performed—that is, whether a worker gets up to get his cup of coffee before, during, or after a set of batched commands—they are unlikely to affect how much gets done or allow you to do more with fewer people.

Are We Applying a Two-Year Solution to a One-Year Problem?

If your rapidly changing business environment will sweep away the problem in a year, it doesn't make much sense to analyze the benefits of a new acquisition over a two- or five-year period.

Even products that can function effectively for five years are likely to be replaced in two with a faster, better, cheaper alternative.

If you're reading this book in the year 2005 or after, that last sentence is probably a real knee-slapper. (Note: Knee-slapper was a mid-twentieth-century expression for a humorous remark.) Five years? Two years? If 1990s trends continue, you, reader of the future, are probably looking at technology generations that are more conveniently measured with clocks than with calendars. Even for us who have yet to see the turn of the century, it is difficult to know how far away the next "killer app" lurks, and whether it will relegate all our closely reasoned analyses to the recycling bin.

Consider yourself a passenger on a fast-moving train traveling through an unknown country. The terrain is relatively flat and heavily wooded. When the train rounds a curve and allows you to see ahead, it's all trees to the horizon. To pass the time, your seatmate proposes a wager on this proposition: Neither the sea nor the mountains will be visible for the next twelve hours. Do you take the bet?

If you complain that you have insufficient data to decide whether to accept the wager, you have grasped the problem—not just the problem of guessing scenery twelve hours down the line, but the problem of guessing the prospects for today's technology solutions when tomorrow comes. The longer the period covered by your cost-benefit analysis, the less likely it is to be accurate.

Are We Assuming Junk Bond Risk for a Puny Muni Return?

With all the uncertainties surrounding any technology acquisition, companies have a right to expect rewards commensurate with the risk. Most IT acquisitions carry at least as much risk as low-grade corporate bonds. So, if the cost-benefit analysis reveals that the return on the company's capital will be more on the order of what a tax-free municipal bond returns, it's time to fold up the corporate checkbook and go home.

The calculus here is straightforward. Start with the company's overall cost of capital. Then increase it to reflect the risks inherent in IT purchasing, such as the risk of rapid technical obsolescence, the risk of failure to operate as promised, and the risk that the project will not be completed as scheduled. Fold in the inevitable softness of some of the numbers underlying the cost and benefit estimates.

You should wind up with a risk-adjusted discount rate that sets an appropriate level for deciding whether to invest in the new acquisition. (See Figure 6-1.)

Zooming In From Project Costs to Transaction Costs

Once the project is justified and approved, or your ongoing operational budget is established, each cost component must be looked at to determine the best source. The best source is not always the one with the lowest price.

Suppose you have a million dollars budgeted (in your project or your operating plan) for bricks. Huffenpuff will sell them for $500,000, but you don't think the company will be around to replace them when they start falling off the building (based on your vendor analysis). First-Degree Mortar and Masonry's bricks will cost $800,000, but because First-Degree is a division of megaconglomerate RockStar, Inc., it's far more likely to be around long enough to stand behind the product. Price isn't the only thing to consider when analyzing a specific transaction.

How Nimble Is the Vendor?

Once you've given the vendor the go-ahead, how long will it be before the new system is up and running? If you know that the vendor you've selected is already overextended, the wait for implementation can be a problem. If the new acquisition has features that are going to result in immediate benefits, a delay of a couple of months diminishes both their value and the overall value of the system.

Similarly, the vendor's ability and willingness to move fast in

Figure 6–1. The risk-return calculation: a few examples.

Example 1: Self-Editing Electronic Mail
(To Speed Internal Communications by Automatically Removing Every Third Word From All E-Mails)

Self-Editing E-Mail	99Q1	99Q2	99Q3	99Q4	00Q1	00Q2	00Q3	00Q4	Total
Projected Costs ($000)	25	50	75	100	90	80	70	70	560
Projected Benefits ($000)	0	10	40	90	120	125	120	115	620
Internal Rate of Return				Net Present Value ($000) When Cost of Funds Is:					
				4%	6%	8%	10%	12%	14%
10.50%				30	19	10	2	-5	-10

Example 2: Hydroponic Data Center
(To Improve Efficiency by Enabling Data Center Employees to Grow Their Own Food)

Hydroponic Data Center	99Q1	99Q2	99Q3	99Q4	00Q1	00Q2	00Q3	00Q4	Total
Projected Costs ($000)	3	3	3	200	10	10	10	10	249
Projected Benefits ($000)	0	0	0	0	2	50	100	100	252
Internal Rate of Return				Net Present Value ($000) When Cost of Funds Is:					
				4%	6%	8%	10%	12%	14%
0.42%				-86	-84	-82	-80	-78	-75

Example 3: Intranet Designer Screens
(To Improve Morale by Installing Intranet Screens Designed by a Leading Couturier)

Designer Screens	99Q1	99Q2	99Q3	99Q4	00Q1	00Q2	00Q3	00Q4	Total
Projected Costs ($000)	200	75	75	20	20	20	20	20	450
Projected Benefits ($000)	0	0	0	0	75	75	75	75	300
Internal Rate of Return				Net Present Value ($000) When Cost of Funds Is:					
				4%	6%	8%	10%	12%	14%
-10.37%				-175	-183	-190	-195	-198	-201

The INTERNAL RATE OF RETURN is the interest rate received for an investment with variable payments and income.
The NET PRESENT VALUE of an investment shows net cash flows discounted by a constant interest rate.

response to changing directions from the company can have tremendous value.

Part of a vendor's nimbleness is its ability to avoid falling flat on its face. Its financial stability must be considered. Is it possible that the vendor will go out of business, or be acquired, or run out of the research and development funds necessary to keep your purchase current? If there are other vendors that need to develop complementary products, their financial stability should be looked at, too. It is important to talk to references, look at the volatility of the vendor's stock price, consider whether the vendor is overextended, and factor all those things into the vendor assessment.

Make sure you assess the risks of dealing with a vendor you know either is backed up or lacks nimbleness. Conversely, credit the agile vendor with lowering your risk.

Flexibility: Risk-Aversion Therapy for Your IT Investment

Pretend that you're the Moody's or the Standard & Poor's of corporate technology acquisitions. Your job is to assess the riskiness of the investment the way the bond rating companies rate debentures. How would you go about identifying areas where risk is high? What factors lessen the risk to the buyer? What would move your rating of a given acquisition from BBB to AA-?

A good place to start looking for the answer is in the vendor's proposal. How much risk, if any, is the vendor assuming? How flexible is the proposal? If conditions change, who bears the consequences?

Flexibility is the most important way in which a vendor can make the acquisition less risky. It's often worth more than a good price (and should be reflected in a lower risk-adjusted discount rate in your cost-benefit analysis). By indemnifying the buyer against certain costs, a flexible vendor can reduce the number of assumptions the user has to make, which makes predicting benefits easier and achieving those benefits more reliable.

Any time the vendor is willing to shift risk away from the user with flexible arrangements and terms, an advantage accrues that should be reflected in the cost-benefit analysis. Remember that a vendor's selfish interest is best served by obtaining a reliable, unvarying revenue stream. That keeps investors happy and avoids future sales costs. So it's natural (although possibly short-sighted) for vendors to push for inflexible arrangements and minimum purchase requirements. With some vendors, the best that can be hoped for is the promise of a discount applicable to future purchases.

Companies find it difficult to forecast their IT needs for several reasons. It isn't only the rapidity of change in the technology environment. Business events that are unrelated, or only partially related, to technology can change needs and put stress on existing agreements or systems.

Here's a two-question quiz to illustrate the point:

1. How many of the companies that merged with, acquired, or were acquired by other companies could have predicted the transaction two years before the fact?
2. How many companies that decided to outsource some or all of their IT operations knew that they would do so more than a year in advance?

If you answered "not very many" to both questions, you're probably right. If such companies are locked into inflexible arrangements with IT vendors, realignments or outsourcing decisions are likely to carry penalties that significantly increase the cost of the IT deal and reduce the benefits of the later decisions.

It's better to pay a little more up front and make sure your analysis reflects the value of the flexibility you're paying for.

The Hidden Risk of "Suite"-ening the Deal

Vendors love to bundle software into "suites." They also like to bundle consulting services with software. Or hardware, software, and services. They'll package deals in dozens of different ways that make them appear more attractive, and more cost-effective. That encourages you to buy more products than you would otherwise buy from the vendor. It also makes the vendor's installation and technical support role easier because there are fewer integration problems.

How do you determine whether a bundle really is more cost-effective than its constituent parts viewed separately, or just looks that way? You have to unbundle it, at least mentally, and do a cost-benefit analysis of each part.

This analysis is further complicated by the fact that bundling often results in costs that cross departmental or functional lines within an enterprise. The only solution is careful allocation of costs by finance.

The Report Card

Finance's cost-benefit analysis, or CBA, is not merely a decision document. Even after a decision is made, it should be used to guide and monitor technology projects, and to determine whether or not they succeeded financially.

Reporting on benefits and costs is essential to understanding the financial success of a project, but the key to business success is good project management. The project manager, typically the user, needs to obtain approval; manage the required resources; develop goals, milestones, and time lines; and communicate the progress and issues associated with a project throughout the organization. Finance's support and the financial monitoring tools help accomplish the project goals.

The cost section of the CBA becomes the project budget. The benefits section becomes a commitment on the part of the user. Report against it. Use it to monitor performance. Urge the user to adopt it as a tool to manage the project. When shortcomings or inaccuracies are uncovered, use them to improve on assumptions for the next project. The CBA can not only give management a comprehensive look at a project, but also help everyone understand each transaction that makes up the project, and how transaction costs affect project success.

It's 11:00; do you know where your benefits are? It's up to finance to find out by monitoring costs and benefits on an ongoing basis in relation to the cost and benefit commitment made by the user. It's also incumbent on finance to identify any significant changes in the numbers. This may trigger a necessary midcourse adjustment, or it may help the company avoid making the same mistakes on the next level. That's what report cards are for, after all.

Ultimately, understanding and comparing alternatives is what the financial assessment is all about. While no one can claim to know precisely what contribution a given IT system makes to the corporation's bottom line, a practical, businesslike review of pertinent costs and putative benefits is the best safeguard an enterprise has against throwing its money away on ill-advised technology acquisitions.

7

Negotiating

Once you've decided on a product, you want to get it at the right price and on the right terms. The way you do that is negotiation.

The good news is that most information technology deals are *very* negotiable. After all, once the software has been developed, the vendor's production cost is often little more than the cost of a diskette and a copy of a user manual. A buyer can often achieve savings of 20 percent on acquisition costs and 30 percent on lifetime costs simply by negotiating well. Vendor ploys can be swept away, giving your company a much more valuable deal. Through negotiation, your company can win the freedom it needs and the remedies it deserves.

The bad news is that negotiating information technology contracts is steadily getting more complex. There are more and more types of contracts, and more and more important provisions, than ever before. Why? Because of:

- ▶ Changes in the law
- ▶ The need for flexibility in an increasingly complex and dynamic business environment
- ▶ Increasing attention to value, not price, in contracting
- ▶ Increasing appetite on both sides for risk sharing
- ▶ More and more money at stake as the role of information technology grows

You'll also face formidable challenges in negotiating with vendors. You're likely to face a vendor negotiating team that has negotiated the same issues dozens of times. Vendors have well-prepared selling ploys, contracting ploys, closing techniques, and other gambits.

The purpose of this chapter is to prepare you to win information technology negotiations. The first step is to avoid seven deadly negotiating sins.

Seven Deadly Negotiating Sins

1. Assuming the Worst

Some negotiators assume the worst of the vendor. They assume that everything that the vendor wants is bad for the company. They see negotiation as a zero-sum game, where one side can win only if the other side loses.

This assumption hurts the company because it ignores opportunities for mutual gain, that is, for expanding the pie. The vendor shares the company's desire for a successful project. The vendor would rather have a good reference account than a collection problem.

In one negotiation, for example, the company's primary concern was implementation. The company's people had never implemented a similar system. Failing to make the cutover date would be very costly. The vendor proposed an increase in the training budget of $150,000. The company rejected that proposal, believing that the vendor was trying to play on the company's fears to pick up $150,000 of training revenue. After the project failed, the company determined that the cause of the failure was an inadequately trained implementation team. If the company and the vendor had found a way to split the $150,000, they would both have been better off by much more than $150,000.

In that case, the company failed to use the negotiating process to expand the pie. Information technology transactions are so complex that there is nearly always an opportunity to modify the deal for mutual gain. Excessive distrust of the vendor costs you that opportunity.

2. Assuming the Best

An equally serious sin is to assume that the vendor always acts in your company's best interests. Wrong. The vendor acts in the vendor's best interests. At times, the vendor's best interests are the same as your company's best interests. At other times, they're exactly the opposite.

A good contract helps to align the vendor's interests with yours. The vendor gains and loses based on how the project goes for the company. Assuming the best of the vendor leads you away from demanding contract provisions that align incentives.

Assuming the best also leads to bad negotiating. If you assume that the vendor will take care of you, you won't take care of yourself. Only by looking out for yourself, and defending your company's interests in spirited discussions, will you get the protections you need for your company.

In good negotiating, you focus on both expanding the pie and dividing the pie. When you are expanding the pie, the vendor's interests are similar to the company's interests. When you are dividing the pie, the vendor's interests are close to being the opposite of the company's interests. Assuming the best of the vendor generally means not fighting hard enough for the company's fair share of the pie.

3. Anchoring

When you are dividing up the pie, you need a reference point to decide whether you've gotten enough of the pie. The vendor would like to anchor that reference point at the vendor's proposal on price and terms. That way, when you evaluate whether you have succeeded in negotiations, you will do so by reference to how much you've managed to move the vendor off of its initial position.

That's an error. The vendor may have picked its initial position out of thin air, or chosen it only in the hope that you will accept it as your reference point. The right question is whether you are buying at the right price and at the right terms. It doesn't matter where the vendor started.

Imagine that you're at a used car dealer. You find a car you like with a sticker price of $10,000. You bargain the price down to $8,000, and you buy the car. Think about how you feel. Was that a success? Did you save $2,000?

Now imagine that you then drive past another used car dealer and see the same car. Out of curiosity, you stop and check the sticker price. It's $7,000. Now how do you feel? Did you save $2,000 at the first dealer?

The reality is that the vendor's list price and standard terms have little to do with the right price and terms. You would have been better off buying the car for $7,000 at the second dealer. Whether you've done well in negotiating depends on how the deal you negotiated compares to your best alternative, not how much you got the vendor to concede.

4. Flying Blind

The only way you can know whether to take a deal is to know how it compares to your best alternative. To compare a deal to your best alternative, you need to know what you want and what alternatives are available. If you don't know that, you're flying blind.

Too often, companies fly blind when they're buying information technology. They haven't done the homework required to know what they want and how they could get it. The result of this error is that they end up paying $8,000 for a $7,000 car.

5. *Irrational Escalation of Commitment*

Another way to end up paying $8,000 for a $7,000 car is to get drawn into the sales process. This cycle is an irrational escalation of commitment. The negotiator becomes more and more determined to make a deal, even if the deal itself keeps getting worse.

One reason why negotiators irrationally escalate their commitment to making a deal is what economists call the sunk cost fallacy. After spending long hours with the vendor, the negotiators can feel a sense of ownership in the deal. From their perspective, they have made an investment in this deal. They would view it as a loss if they were to give up on the deal. In fact, the time spent on the deal is a sunk cost. It's never coming back, and it's never going to justify making a bad deal.

Another reason for irrational escalation of commitment is that project plans and management reviews can bind a negotiator to a path of escalating commitment. If the negotiator becomes focused on a signing date, he or she may continue to escalate commitment to the vendor without taking the time to verify that it remains in the company's best interest to do so. In fact, the confusion between motion and progress, and the negotiator's emotional attachment to achieving the goal, may make it more difficult for her or him to notice warning signs.

6. *Overconfidence*

Just as negotiators often irrationally escalate their commitment to a deal, they may also irrationally escalate their commitment to a negotiation strategy. For example, you can easily be fooled into thinking that if Vendor A, Vendor B, and Vendor C all cut their prices by 20 percent when you threatened to walk away, Vendor D will do the same.

That sort of thinking can make you woefully overconfident. Every negotiation is unique. You've got to develop a strategy for each negotiation based on its own facts. You need to understand how reasonable the vendor's offer is, what choices you have, and who needs the deal more.

Thus, Vendor D may be willing to cut its price in half for you, or Vendor D may not need to cut its price at all. Overconfidence could have you asking for 20 percent when you could get 50 percent, or walking away from a deal that makes sense at the vendor's full price.

7. *Ignoring Leverage*

We've left the worst sin for last. The key to negotiation is leverage. Most of your leverage in negotiating a deal comes from your ability to walk away. Most of your leverage in reforming a deal comes from your ability to terminate the deal or enforce the contract in court. Leverage is why vendors make concessions.

In spite of that, many negotiators take their eye off that ball. They sign letters of intent that make the deal a foregone conclusion. They openly tell the vendor that they have no alternative to the vendor's product. They agree to pay the vendor 100 percent of the price before the vendor delivers. They pay no attention to vendor contracting ploys that strip the company of all of its rights and remedies should the vendor fail.

Control the Process

The most important step in avoiding these seven deadly sins is to control the negotiation process. If the company's negotiators don't control the process, the vendor's sales team will. If the vendor's sales team controls the process, the vendor can drive the company to make an irrational acquisition. The process is that important.

Process Determines Results

The path you take determines where you end up. You can use the process to achieve your realistic objectives. You can get a low price by creating an auction among vendors. You can get high quality by using an engineering-oriented quality evaluation. You can get a creative so-lution by choosing a high-quality vendor, accepting the fact that it may take some money, and creating a safe environment for brain-storming.

There is also a standard approach, recommended by vendors everywhere. It goes as follows: Determine needs, identify solutions, pick a solution, pick a vendor, sign a letter of intent, begin implementation, negotiate a contract. The result of this process is that you buy a vendor's product at very nearly the vendor's standard prices and terms. Why? Because by the time the company begins to negotiate, it has no practical alternative to signing the vendor's form. The company has squandered almost all of its leverage. As a result, the company can achieve little in negotiations.

A Process That Works

What process do you want to use? Expert negotiators craft a different process for each negotiation, depending on the company's objectives. However, as a starting point, the process described here will produce solid results in a wide variety of negotiations.

The core of this process is maintaining leverage. As long as there is competition, you have more leverage than the vendor. The vendor wants your money. As long as you don't irretrievably commit to giving the vendor your money, you have leverage.

1. *Determine what benefits you need from the product.* Write them down. Develop objective measures, or metrics, to determine whether a product is providing the benefits that you expect.

2. *Send out a request for proposal (RFP).* Your leverage is at its peak, since each vendor is competing with every other potential vendor and solution. In the RFP process, vendors understand that accepting or rejecting your requests could make the difference between winning and losing your business. From a leverage standpoint, this is your moment in the sun. Use it to its fullest. In the request for proposal, ask the vendors whether they are willing to commit to providing the benefits you expect from the product. The request for commitment should be in terms of substantive performance standards and key contract terms. See Chapter 11 for a fuller description of the RFP process.

3. *Pick a few key vendors.* This is often referred to as "a short list of three" and generally includes no more than five vendors. By limiting the field, you can give selected vendors enough hope of winning that they are willing to devote significant effort to trying. However, you do not want to give a vendor so great a chance of winning that the vendor no longer feels the need to push to win your business.

4. *Demand that the vendors on the short list prepare more detailed proposals, and encourage them to improve in areas where their proposals are weak.* Avoid disclosing the terms of one vendor's proposal to another

vendor. Showing your hand reduces your leverage. Also, conveniently, you are probably bound by law or contract or both not to disclose one vendor's proposal to another vendor.

Your leverage is very high at this point because several vendors are competing and each has invested a substantial amount in sales expenses to get this far. Thus, this is the time to complete negotiation of all key terms. If you have a form contract, present it and demand comments. Demand explanations of any objections a vendor makes to your form contract. It's not out of place to emphasize that your selection process will favor vendors who are willing to work with your preferred terms.

5. *Select the lucky winner.* You now need to focus your efforts. Deciding to proceed only with one vendor helps you do that.

However, there's no reason to give up all of your leverage. When you downselect to a single vendor, tell the chosen vendor that it is the "preferred vendor" and that you are "suspending" negotiations with other vendors to negotiate with the preferred vendor. Make it clear that the other vendors can probably handle the technical job, and that the financial and contractual concerns are now paramount. Never let the vendor (or anyone on your team) forget that you have alternatives and may need to use them. Nothing is done until an acceptable contract is signed by the company and the vendor.

Even when you've selected one vendor, avoid making any commitments until you sign an acceptable contract. You need to be vigilant to avoid subtle forms of commitment. The best sales reps see no need for the customer to know when the moment of commitment occurs. To avoid subtle forms of commitment:

- ▶ Don't sign a letter of intent that binds you, morally or legally, to anything.
- ▶ Don't let anyone on your team make oral promises.
- ▶ Don't go so far in your implementation of the preferred vendor's product that it would be overly costly to move to another alternative.
- ▶ Don't design your project around the preferred vendor's product.
- ▶ Don't hire people whose sole expertise is in using the preferred vendor's product.
- ▶ Don't accept an "interim" deal.
- ▶ Don't agree to an exclusive negotiating period or a breakup fee if the deal fails.

6. *Negotiate and sign a deal*. Make sure that the deal provides you with remedies and termination rights that will give you leverage in a dispute with the vendor.

Key Subprocesses

This process is a framework for the entire negotiation. To make the negotiation succeed, the person wearing the negotiating hat must:

- ▶ Know what the company wants.
- ▶ Know the vendor.
- ▶ Build an effective negotiating team.
- ▶ Beat the vendor ploys.
- ▶ Know how to use customer ploys.

Know What the Company Wants

If you don't know what you want, you probably aren't going to get it. The same goes for the company. The negotiating team needs to understand the company's objectives and priorities.

Most likely, at the start of the process, the company doesn't know its objectives. Various people wearing various hats have various objectives, but there is no consolidated list of objectives. However, each of those people probably believes that his or her list represents nearly all of the company's key objectives.

We've found that one easy way for negotiation professionals to prove their value is to ask each person on the negotiation team to write down the company's top five objectives for negotiation. Not their own objectives, not their functional area's objectives, but the company's objectives. It's a pop quiz, so no talking is permitted. Then, the negotiation professional reads everyone's list of five. The lists are usually completely different. The negotiation professional then wryly notes that the company can't achieve its top five objectives unless the team agrees on them.

Attaining Agreement on Objectives

Getting the entire negotiation team to agree on objectives requires someone to collect objectives from each team member. Generally, the person wearing the negotiation hat leads that process. One way to approach that process is set forth below.

1. Each member of the negotiation team analyzes the issue. The user talks to other users and conducts site visits. The systems integrator gets an evaluation copy of the product and gives it a detailed technical test. Someone reads the vendor's documentation and whatever the trade press has to say about the product. The financial analyst runs out numbers to do a preliminary cost-benefit analysis. The administrator reviews the company's history with the vendor and its experience with similar transactions. The negotiator considers the vendor's standard terms, gauges market realities, and evaluates the company's leverage.

2. The entire negotiation team meets and discusses the key user, financial, legal, technical, administrative, and other considerations. Each team member should present key conclusions and issues.

3. The team determines its priorities for the negotiation. These priorities will become critical later in the negotiation, when the company will need to trade off some of its objectives.

Each company has its own process for determining priorities. Some use a traditional top-down model, where an executive simply makes the relevant trade-offs. Others have a consensus-oriented style, where talk continues until all agree. A middle-of-the-road format could look like this:

- Each team member writes a full list of objectives for the negotiation.
- The team works together to consolidate the objectives into a single list using a single vocabulary.
- Each team member ranks the items on the list. Any ranking system will do, as long as it clearly identifies the "must-have" and "high-priority" items.
- A consolidated chart is made, showing the rankings prepared by each team member.
- Key differences are resolved by discussion or executive decisions.
- The list of priorities is circulated appropriately for confirmation.

Benefits of Agreeing on Objectives

Getting the team to agree on a single set of objectives can be a time-consuming process. It may lead to considerable discussion and debate. The company may even completely reconsider the acquisition. However, if your goal is to acquire the right information technology at the right price and on the right terms, few processes have a greater return on investment.

Agreeing on objectives adds value because it:

▶ Prevents the negotiating team from inadvertently overlooking a key point. Key points are often lost merely because no one thinks to mention them to the lawyer or the lead negotiator.

▶ Prevents the negotiating team from trading away a critical point for a small point.

▶ Allows the negotiating team to cut its losses by walking away when there is an impasse over a "must-have" provision.

▶ Requires the vendor to respond specifically. Vendors prefer to fudge issues, responding to a general sense of anxiety with general reassurances. Specific answers to clear requests are far more likely to create clear contractual protections.

▶ Allows the negotiator to move quickly, without having to circle back to all participants to learn enough to know how to trade off negotiating points.

Know Your Vendor

To maximize your negotiating success, you need to understand your adversary. To do that, you need to understand both the motivations of the vendor organization and the motivations of the individuals across the table.

You've probably learned a great deal about the vendor through the selection process. However, it's time to hone your understanding of the vendor's decision-making process and negotiation style. Talk to other people who have negotiated with the same vendor. Read descriptions of the vendor in the popular press. And, above all, get a complete organization chart so that you understand the relationships between the people at the table and the people who are not at the table.

Next, you need to understand the people at the table. Most important, how much authority do they have? "Negotiating" with a sales rep who has no ability to make concessions is a waste of time. All you can do is concede points, not win them.

Sales reps often are powerless because the vendor wants them that way. They are often paid to sell, regardless of the terms. The vendor then gives a lawyer, or some other gatekeeper, full responsibility for protecting the vendor. You need to know who will decide key points for the vendor, and seek to understand that person's objectives.

You also want to understand the motivations of the individuals negotiating on the vendor's behalf. Do they have a commission riding on this? Is there a special award program on the product you are buying? The sales reps think about that kind of thing all the time; they just may tell you.

Why do you care about the sales rep's commission plan? Because if you know how the sales rep is paid, you can use your purchase choice to affect the sales rep's personal compensation. That's a lot of leverage. Often, for example, a sale on December 31 would give the salesperson dramatically bigger results than the same sale on January 1. It could mean making quota or winning a special incentive award. The sales rep might be willing to do quite a bit for you in order to do a deal by December 31. That's leverage that will evaporate if you wait past December 31.

Finally, you need to assess your leverage. You need to know how much this deal means to the vendor and the sales rep.

You have leverage in proportion to the amount of money you can provide the vendor in the short term and in the long term. How much leverage is that? It all depends on the revenues of the vendor. A million dollars may mean the world to a one-person shop and very little to a vendor whose sales are billions of dollars every year. On the other hand, even with a billion-dollar vendor, a million-dollar order may give you substantial leverage with a sales rep whose annual quota is $2 million. Likewise if the order is for one of the vendor's most strategic new product introductions. Or if the vendor is putting on an all-out push for revenue, perhaps because its CEO's stock options are about to expire.

Build an Effective Team

Have the Right Skills

An effective team has all of the skills required to identify and resolve the key issues. Missing an issue can be a disaster, and having to hunt for the right expertise is scarcely better.

If the team does not have the authority to sign a deal, consider an executive sponsor. If possible, the executive sponsor should be someone with the authority to make all key decisions in the negotiations. However, if power is distributed, the executive sponsor should be responsible for obtaining a consensus decision from the company's ownership or leadership group. To be effective, the executive sponsor should be fully briefed on the negotiation. That allows decisions to be made quickly.

The negotiation team also needs legal advice, preferably from an experienced information technology lawyer. The team needs legal advice because what the company is buying is a bundle of legal rights. Some of those rights are spelled out in contract language that means what you would expect it to mean. However, most of those rights are built into the legal system as a whole or expressed in legalese. An experienced information technology lawyer is in the best position to get you the right package of legal rights and steer you clear of legal tricks and traps.

Prepare the Team for What's to Come

Preparation is the key to an effective team. The negotiation professional should give the less experienced members of the team a sense of the things that are likely to happen in the negotiation. These six points are worth making:

1. *The angels will stop singing.* The sales reps who couldn't say enough nice things to you during the sales process will now seem colder and somewhat distant. Suddenly, they'll seem more interested in the company's money than in your friendship. This is a normal part of the process.

2. *The company might walk away.* Every member of the negotiation team needs to be onboard with the idea that the company might walk away. Otherwise, the company can't credibly threaten to walk away over "deal points." That will dramatically reduce the company's leverage.

3. *The vendor will complain about the very fact that the company is negotiating.* Expect complaints about the number of changes to the vendor's form. Expect appeals to "keep it simple" ("simple," as in simply giving the vendor what the vendor wants).

4. *The negotiators will spend long hours discussing bad things that probably won't happen.* We all know that thinking about the upside and the potential benefits is what makes businesses succeed. The emotionally rewarding part of a deal is talking about how we're all going to make a lot of money. The team will feel like they've taken the negotiator to a lovely field of flowers, and all the negotiator can talk about is the land mines that are buried in their roots. The team must understand that the contracting process is all about using a for-

mal agreement to handle difficulties and avoid failure. It's not simply an opportunity to rhapsodize about the wonderful benefits that the product will produce.

5. *The vendor will use the full range of human emotion and body language to win points.* The vendor wants you to feel guilty about asking for too many things, asking the salesperson to work hard, and other alleged transgressions. The vendor wants you to be excited by the thrill of victory (a quick deal) and fear the agony of defeat (no deal). The vendor wants you to feel the joy of giving, particularly on key deal points.

6. *There is no shame in demanding a fair deal.* There is no shame in advocating the company's best interest. There is no pride in a mistake, no matter how quickly you managed to make it. Your duty to the shareholders is more important than any warm feelings you may have toward the sales rep.

Speak With One Voice

Making these points is a first step in presenting a united front to the vendor. To be effective in negotiations, the company must speak with one voice. If the company speaks with multiple voices, the vendor will divide and conquer. There are three key steps here.

1. The negotiation team itself must decide to speak with one voice. The team makes a decision, then the negotiator communicates the decision to the vendor. No team member concedes anything in side conversations with the vendor.

You may need a way to let frustrated team members communicate when they feel the need. It's worth having a protocol for sidebar conversations or taking breaks. Experienced negotiation teams often develop signaling systems so that they can communicate concerns without alerting the other side.

2. The negotiation team must warn the rest of the company against side conversations. Sending a message to everyone whom the vendor might call is a good step. Only the members of the negotiating team have enough information to accurately represent the company. Side conversations between the vendor and people with limited information are just going to hurt communications.

3. The negotiating team must control its management. Nothing undercuts a negotiating team like an executive opposing its negotiating positions. Relevant executives should be briefed whenever the vendor is likely to try to go top-down on the negotiating team. That

way, the vendor sees the company as having a unified position on issues.

Ideally, the negotiating team's management will simply refer all calls to the negotiating team. As a fallback position, the negotiating team's management should be convinced to "do no harm." Doing no harm entails supporting the negotiating team generally, and not agreeing or disagreeing with the vendor's arguments.

Handling Internal Vendor Friends

Often, someone on the negotiating team seems to be wearing the vendor's badge. That person, the vendor friend, believes everything the vendor says and gives the vendor full moral and emotional support. The vendor friend may have fallen victim to the vendor's ploys. Or, the vendor friend may be right. The vendor may be your hope and salvation.

Regardless, the vendor friend can be your worst enemy. Vendor friends can undercut your positions by retracting them in private. Vendor friends can also undercut the negotiation team with its own management. Vendor friends can, by their mannerisms at the negotiating table, give the vendor false hopes of prevailing over the company's positions.

The question is how best to handle the internal vendor friend. A common mistake is to isolate the vendor friend, or to treat the vendor friend as a pitiful fool, too silly (or desperate for love) to see past a vendor ploy. That's a mistake. That just drives the vendor friend deeper into the vendor's camp.

Instead, you need to make the vendor friend a part of your team—the vendor friend part. That allows the vendor friend to freely express his or her ideas, and avoids internal team conflict. For example, when you are doing strategy sessions, have your vendor friend play devil's advocate. This will help you anticipate the vendor's responses and avoid groupthink.

Also, there can be value in having the vendor friend develop a personal relationship with the vendor. One benefit of this is that the vendor friend becomes something of a spy in the vendor's camp, understanding the vendor's true motivations and tactics.

Another benefit is that the vendor friend acquires personal leverage. A vendor friend can tell the vendor: "We've become good friends, and I look forward to a long and successful relationship. I've gone to the mat for you again and again with my management. I've put my job on the line for you. Now you need to go to the mat for me." No one else on the team can do that.

All that being said, you need to give the vendor friend a big dose of reality. Vendors are interested in sales, not personal relationships. Lasting personal relationships with the negotiating team are more likely. Much of what the vendor friend thinks she heard from the vendor is wrong. If the vendor won't put it in writing, it probably isn't true. The vendor friend's warm personal relationship with the vendor's sales rep is likely to end when the ink dries on the contract.

Decide What You Will Say

Speaking with one voice allows you to decide what you're going to say to the vendor. Vendors will tell you that sales is the limited release of information. The vendor is thinking hard about what information to provide, and in what order to provide it. For example, vendors tend to:

- ▶ Delay the release of their standard contract and other bad news until the company makes a commitment.
- ▶ Dribble out bad news, or provide it with a flood of irrelevant information.
- ▶ End each meeting on a high note.

All this is based on sound psychological principles. Humans unduly emphasize the last thing they heard. Humans become comfortable with a steady pattern, even if it is the steady drip drip drip of bad news from a vendor. Humans process information slowly and can easily become overwhelmed. Humans who are overwhelmed by information make poor choices.

How does all this help the vendor? A burst of good news creates a commitment to an imagined "deal." Just the right amount of bad news, such as unexpected vendor demands, can improve the deal from the vendor's standpoint without killing it.

The company should be just as careful about releasing information to the vendor. For example, vendors may abuse and misuse the information contained in:

▶ *The company's list of priorities.* The vendor may decide that the low- and medium-priority items are as good as conceded.

▶ *The negotiating team's internal sources of information.* Vendors often call on these people, wasting their time and creating internal dissent with vendor ploys.

▶ *Proposals by other vendors and other information on the company's alternatives.*

Beat the Vendor Ploys

Sidestep Contracting Ploys

In information technology negotiations, the company can win points by presenting a draft contract. "Holding the pen" gives the company the ability to be the side that is "ready to sign" instead of the side that's the obstruction. The company can implement its ideas in its own language and its own time frame.

Vendors fight to use their standard forms. Vendors often claim that presenting a nonstandard contract will delay the review process and will be unacceptable in the end because it fails to reflect the way the vendor does business. However, in the end, vendors who want the business sign contracts drafted by their customers. We find that vendors who badly want the business negotiate and sign buyers' contracts pretty quickly.

The advantage of starting from your own well-crafted form contract is that you beat all the vendor contracting ploys. The vendor can no longer slip innocuous-looking provisions into a form, figuring that you won't know what they mean. Instead, the vendor will have to raise and discuss every issue, which exposes the vendor's true interests and motivations.

Slap Down Selling Ploys

The first step in beating the vendor ploys is to convince the vendor that the company is serious about negotiating. The vendor might start with the assumption that the company is just a vendor ploy away from signing the vendor's standard form. You need to forcefully change that assumption. The vendor must know that you expect to follow a rational, disciplined process to arrive at the right result.

Then, develop a formal understanding that there will be no games and no ploys. If the vendor tries a ploy, issue a sharp reprimand.

A sharp reprimand sounds something like this: "Mr. Sales Rep, the relationship between our two companies is very important— much more important than the deal we are talking about now. That relationship has got to be based on mutual good faith. We were shocked at what your sales team did. We have briefed our senior executives. If these games do not stop now, we're going to terminate negotiations immediately."

These words may sound tough. Remember, though, that you want respect, not love, from the vendor. You want the vendor to fear your response to games and ploys. The advantage to you is that the company will control the negotiations, instead of falling victim to vendor ploys.

Know How to Use Customer Ploys

Still, you may not be able to stop a vendor from using ploys. Some sales reps seem to have ploys written right into their DNA. You may be unable to run a ployless negotiation.

If you can't beat 'em, join 'em. Use customer ploys. Of course, that's not the road to sainthood or good long-term business relationships. But in a cold, cruel world, sometimes you have to fight fire with fire.

To show you the road to the unthinkable, here are some sample customer ploys.

Smoke and Mirrors

Dazzle the vendor with stories of how you could, possibly, need huge volumes of the vendor's product. Shower the vendor's sales team with love and goodies. Talk a lot about a win-win relationship. Make it almost impossible for the vendor's people to stay focused on selling you whatever they've got at a high price on unfavorable terms.

Fear, Uncertainty, and Doubt

Talk to the vendor about a competitor with an unnatural "edge." For example, you might know your ultimate boss went to camp with the competitor's sales rep's brother as a child. It's not such a close connection that the vendor ought to pack his bags. On the other hand, it might make the difference and it's enough to let you stoke up some fear. You can say something like: "Well, I can't tell you that you're going to lose this deal if your bid isn't breathtakingly low. All I can tell you is that it's happened before with the big boss and his childhood connections. You just can't be sure."

Divide and Conquer

The vendor may be going after the person in your organization with the most authority and the least judgment. Do the same. Arrange a final handshake between one of your leaders and one of the vendor's leaders. What you want is for the vendor to present a leader who is simply too important to be briefed. Then, your well-prepared leader mentions a couple of outstanding contract issues. The vendor's leader, unprepared, off guard, and focused on relationship issues rather than contract points, may concede those points.

Urgency

Some vendors need time to make the right decisions. For example, a vendor that is bidding on a complex system development project needs time to understand the nuances. The less time the vendor has, the less accurate its bid will be.

And thus is an urgency ploy born. Give a few fully qualified vendors the opportunity to bid on a project, but demand very fast fixed-price bids. Some will err by bidding too high; some will err by bidding too low. Accept the lowest bid. The lowest bidder has almost certainly underbid because it was a high-speed process.

Bait and Switch

The bait-and-switch ploy can also be turned back on a vendor. Send out an RFP describing a very large and expansive job. Because the job is very large, you will get price bids that are very low. Contract for that price for however many units you choose to order. Order just a few.

Another approach to bait and switch is to get the vendor committed, then gradually worsen the deal. Get the vendor to work up specifications at no charge. Ask for more and more information. Hold lots of meetings to extract useful information from the vendor. Make the vendor jump to meet artificial deadlines. As the vendor's investment in the process grows, gradually increase your demands or reduce your offer.

Partnering

Vendors will often set themselves up for a partnering ploy from the company. Vendors will talk about their partnership with the customer, and how it avoids the needs for contracts. Go right along with that. Get the vendor working without a contract.

Then, withhold money to obtain leverage. Without the usual guarantee of payment, the vendor will be unable to do anything other than perform. If the vendor complains, explain that the relationship is about trust, not money, and that payment thus must follow performance. (Practice that until you can say it with a straight face.)

You can also take this ploy further. If you've bought into the vendor's rhetoric about sharing, you can let the vendor share in your pain. When the product fails, deduct half of your losses from the vendor's compensation.

The Keys to Negotiation

Be prepared. Be rational. Know what you want. Know your vendor. Choose the right process. Control your team. Control your vendor. Fight for what's right. Celebrate your victory.

8

Administrative

The administrative process involves identifying rules and enforcing them. *Rules* in this context are things like the standards the company sets for information technology systems, the written procedures the company uses for making decisions about acquiring those systems, the terms of the contract, and the ways in which the company tracks contracts.

Enforcement in this context means determining whether the company is following these rules. It also means determining whether the other party to the contract (the vendor) is living up to the rules.

Companies cannot abide by contracts or standards unless the rules are effectively identified and published throughout the enterprise. It is up to whoever is responsible for these rules at the corporate level to make sure that these functions—identification and publication—are effectively carried out.

Standards for Goodness' Sake

The first rules that everyone needs to know are the companywide standards for IT systems. These standards are conceived for the benefit of the organization. They may sometimes seem counterintuitive, or even counterproductive, to the individual department head pursuing an IT acquisition. After all, this potential user is not focused on the enterprise's goals of compatibility, security, and efficient corporate purchasing. The user's goals relate to the department's own profit-and-loss picture.

So it's up to administrative personnel to make sure that potential users understand the costs to the enterprise of failure to follow company standards. They include:

► Backup costs
► Security costs

▶ Loss of enterprisewide query capability

▶ Failure (among users or systems integrators) to achieve expertise

▶ The cost of building interfaces to and between incompatible systems

▶ The need to maintain "help desk" capacity in a wider range of products

▶ Security risks caused by a failure to use company-approved interfaces with public networks

▶ Redundant development efforts

▶ Overextension of support and development resources owing to the need to maintain multiple products with similar functions

Overextending finite support resources is a problem that practically all organizations face. Theoretically, an enterprise with complete IT standards should require only one technical support person for every 2,000 technology users. At the other end of the spectrum, organizations trying to do business with a patchwork of wildly heterogeneous, haphazardly cobbled systems could require one technical support person for every twenty users. Few organizations ever approach either of these extremes, partly because the enterprise that needs a high number of support people probably isn't profitable enough to afford them, and the well-standardized company can afford to staff its support functions generously. But it is clear that companies that plan poorly or fail to enforce prohibitions against conflicting or overlapping systems, or that have significant decentralization of the IT function, find themselves faced with unplanned support resource problems.

One of the most important rules is the one that lists the software that will be present on every server and personal computer. The advantage of standardizing operating system software is obvious. The importance of keeping application software standard is not as obvious to all users, but it is just as important.

Other IT standards include rules about whether users may install additional software or add dial-in modems or other peripheral devices. These reduce the security of the company's computer networks and increase the risk that viruses will harm the company's data and systems.

All these standards should be concise, nontechnical, current, and prominently published. The easier they are to find, read, and understand, the easier they will be for all users to follow. They must be known and considered when approving new projects or acquiring new technology.

Rules for the Buying Game

As well as rules about what equipment and software are purchased, companies need rules about how to buy that equipment and software. Purchasing standards enforce the process described in this book by directing users to implement the technical, financial, negotiating, and administrative steps they need to follow if they are to purchase the right solution on the right terms. They are the only effective way to ensure that the company's chosen process will be followed consistently.

Purchasing standards should be simple to understand and to follow. All technology buyers should know, for example, that prospective purchases over a certain dollar level trigger a formal request for proposal, a cost-benefit analysis, a technical analysis, formal contracts negotiated by the acquisitions department, and specified approvals.

IT purchasing standards make sense because they save money. Companies that fail to use them are throwing their money away. Suppose, for example, that your company maintains a fleet of Ford Tauruses. Because of its volume of purchases, the price the company pays per car is about 15 percent below the average retail price that consumers pay dealers for the same model. How much sense would it make to buy your department's Tauruses from your friendly neighborhood Ford dealer instead of getting the fleet discount?

Purchasing standards prevent uneconomical, off-the-beaten-path purchases. They ensure that everyone knows about and uses the volume discounts that the company has negotiated and earned. They prevent the purchase of redundant products or licenses, and they prevent harmful terms and conditions.

Well-crafted purchasing standards also make it easier for administrative people to shepherd contracts through the process. They provide a step-by-step guide that explains what happens next in the approval process. They specify whose signatures are needed. They stipulate how, and by whom, cost-benefit analyses and management summaries are done. They take a complicated process and make it as simple as possible.

Contract Rules and Tracking

All companies should know what they own and what they are contractually committed to do. Every detail relevant to the reporting requirements of software license agreements should be available in a database. The records in this database must be reconciled and appropriate action must be taken with the vendor and the users when key dates occur.

Having this information organized can save big money. Most vendor contracts impose penalties for failing to identify the right payment amounts at the right time. Software vendors (among others) are masters at imposing stiff penalties for missed or improperly calculated payments. These late penalties can amount to an uncomfortably large fraction of the real-world cost of the contract.

Then there are the automatic renewals. Vendors like to see contracts renewed, so they believe that it is in their best interest to make it difficult for the company to cut things off. Like unwanted selections in a sort of Software of the Month Club for inattentive companies, these automatically renewing technology contracts can pile up in the corporate closet at an embarrassing rate. To be fair, it should be observed that large companies juggle hundreds, sometimes thousands, of software and other technology contracts. Nevertheless, it is probable that companies will spend tens of millions of dollars this month on contracts that were renewed automatically only because the transaction type was the routine tendering of an invoice, as opposed to negotiation of an agreement (a process that commands greater attention and provides better results).

Avoiding these sorts of traps for the unwary means tracking hundreds, or thousands, of technology contracts. These contracts may be the result of protracted negotiations leading to lengthy signed documents, or they may fall out of boxes of software when the shrink-wrapped seal is broken. To do this complex tracking, companies must build and maintain a database of technology contracts and their constituent terms. For each contract in the database, administration must track:

> ► Identifying information for the contract (e.g., contract name, signing date, and perhaps contract number)
> ► The user department and any relevant company accounting information
> ► Location of a signed copy of the contract
> ► The scope of the license granted under the contract
> ► The number of licensed users
> ► The location of the product
> ► Maintenance caps
> ► Notification requirements
> ► Renewal dates

- Addresses for notices
- Payment schedule
- Payment criteria, including:
  —Certificate of acceptance
  —Limitations on assignment
  —Upgrade fees
  —Rights to terminate
  —Confidentiality obligations

Maintaining a database of technology contracts is the best way to ensure that the company is positioned to meet its contractual obligations. It is also necessary to assess the impact of acquisitions, divestitures, or outsourcing on your technology contracts without a massive bring-business-to-a-grinding-halt contract review project at every turn.

The contracts themselves should be maintained in a central file. This file must be kept up-to-date with amendments and key correspondence.

Unclean Hands in Empty Pockets

Part of the job of supervision is making sure that the company complies with the terms of the contract with the vendor. Failing to hold up its end of the deal opens a company to several unpleasant possibilities.

The costliest enforcement error of all may be the one that strips the company of its ability to hold the vendor accountable for doing what it's being paid to do. Under the doctrine of unclean hands, the company may not be able to enforce a contract unless it is itself in compliance with it. Like a police officer who is drummed out of the force for speeding, the company can be prevented from enforcing one provision of a contract because of its own failure to live up to another.

Any IT acquisition can go bad. The damage to the company can extend beyond the dollar amount of the contract. Whatever remedies for nonfeasance or malfeasance were negotiated were certainly viewed as important protections for the company when the contract was approved and signed. But the doctrine of unclean hands says that they may be thrown out of court unless the company upholds its end of the bargain.

Vendors always try to entangle some obligation of yours with their obligations in order to excuse their performance problems. So a company's failure to send the vendor usage reports on time, for example, might essentially exempt the vendor from financial responsibility for a total system failure. That may be extreme, but you can't predict the actions of technology vendors struggling to survive in a viciously competitive market.

Software License Compliance: Breaking the Seal Without Breaking the Rules

One of the most important chapters in the company's administrative rule book will be the one on software license compliance. It will be one of the easiest to write—and probably the hardest to adhere to.

Software companies must protect their intellectual property. That's how they make money. To do that, they must rely upon the contracts and rights they are granted. Often, the software company reserves the right to audit a customer's usage and charge for the licenses used but not owned, the cost of the audit, and penalties.

Software companies have a great deal of leverage under the federal Copyright Act. Any unlicensed use of copyrighted software is infringement under the Copyright Act. For example, if you have a 100-user license, it would be infringement to be using 101 copies.

If you infringe a software copyright, the Copyright Act gives the software owner the right to sue for both money damages and injunctions. Money damages could equal or exceed the license fees you should have paid for the infringing use. An injunction could require you to stop using the software. If you keep infringing the copyright after a court issues an injunction against you, the court can put company officers in jail. The Copyright Act also has criminal penalties for copyright infringement, including imprisonment.

If a software vendor has good reason to believe that you are infringing its copyright, it can get a court to provide federal marshals to conduct a surprise audit of your use of its software. Of course, software companies usually call first and offer your company the opportunity to cooperate in an audit (or do your own audit) before they call in federal marshals.

You might think that no software vendor would go to all that trouble to catch your company. You'd be wrong. Software vendors have banded together into collectives, such as the Software Publishers Association (SPA), to stop infringement. The SPA has a large staff devoted solely to getting companies to get clean on software licensing. The SPA can and does use the courts to force companies to submit to audits and pay fines.

Knowing Isn't Doing

Setting the rules is only a first step. Publishing the rules, and making sure everybody knows about them, advances the process. But knowing isn't doing. If it were, speed limit signs would be all the traffic enforcement we'd need.

Vendor transactions put a lot of pressure on everybody involved. Money, careers, and egos are all in play. Administrative's most difficult, and most sensitive, task is to make sure that the rules it sets are enforced.

The next section covers contract rules, guidelines for specific relationships, and the expectations between buyers and sellers.

Stopping Vendor Performance Problems

One way to dramatically improve your vendor's performance, without increasing costs, is to monitor, communicate, and follow up. If you don't monitor, the vendor will not make the effort to meet the performance standards. If you don't communicate, the vendor won't know it's falling behind. If you don't follow up, you won't get the problem fixed.

Monitoring, communicating, and following up can be viewed as a confrontational and an unpleasant part of the vendor relationship. A letter of complaint from the user the vendor works with on a daily basis can be frightening. Making these tasks a routine part of the process lessens the chance that a vendor will misconstrue enforcement as a sign of a deal gone wrong.

Involving administrative specialists who are expert at presenting problems in a constructive manner keeps the user-vendor relationship healthy. It is less extraordinary to receive a letter from an administrator than to receive one from a user. A letter from an administrator is therefore less likely to be perceived as unduly threatening. The company benefits by preserving an important working relationship while pursuing its legitimate right to monitor and correct that relationship.

The Dashboard

The dashboard in a car supplies important information to the driver. The speedometer tells her how fast she is traveling. The tachometer tells her how fast the engine is going, so that she can be sure that it is operating at a safe speed. Other gauges show fuel level, coolant temperature, and oil pressure, allowing her to monitor all these systems at a glance while still concentrating on the road. The gauges have a "red zone" to show when the car is going too fast or is running out of fuel.

Every technology deal should have "gauges" that help the company monitor a vendor's performance without losing sight of the purpose of the acquisition. This deal dashboard should be developed during negotiations under the guidance of the administrative staff. Like different vehicles, different deals need different dashboards. But there are usually common elements, such as:

▶ *Milestones.* There should be a gauge to show what the vendor must do by certain predetermined dates.

▶ *Costs.* Like the red line on a tachometer, the cost gauge should contain a red line that sets the upper bound for total deal costs, as well as costs per time period.

▶ *User satisfaction measurements.* The user's goals for doing the deal should be plotted against a scale of satisfactory outcomes, then monitored to make sure that the gauge reading remains within the acceptable range.

A common mistake is to try to build the dashboard, or something like it, after the contract has been signed. Often both user and vendor see the establishment and monitoring of performance metrics as a formality or a nuisance. They believe that the IT system under consideration will perform perfectly satisfactorily without any mechanisms in place to measure its performance.

It could happen! If no objective performance measures exist, and if satisfactory performance is defined by user impressions instead of metrics, then the new system will always meet expectations— provided the expectations belong to the vendor and the user, both of whom have a home-team interest in the deal.

But someone needs to look out for the interests of the company. Someone needs to point out that there is no such thing as a closed-loop IT system; and that IT systems exist to support, and become part of, business functions, and to provide information to businesspeople. The dashboard provides the information these people need, and therefore is essential to the successful operation of the system.

A car's mechanical fuel system performs its function independently of the fuel gauge on the dashboard. The fuel pump, gas line, and injectors send gasoline to the cylinders just as well whether there's a fuel gauge or not. But without a fuel gauge, the system will fail, because the driver will not know when to refill the depleted fuel tank. The driver is both a part of the system and the reason it exists.

Again, it is administration that has the perspective to see the system in these terms. Administration knows what gauges to design into the dashboard, and it knows that these gauges can't be retrofitted into an already-moving vehicle. It also knows that someone has to be watching for readings that move into the red zone and know what to do when things go wrong.

Save Money: Buy the Top-of-the-Line Instrument Package

Administration can and should pay for itself. By designing the dashboard and linking it to key business metrics, administration enables the company to put provisions in the contract that stipulate that the vendor will pay a financial price if key company expectations are violated. These financial penalties will motivate vendors to achieve full performance and will help pay for the administrative process.

Waiver and Estoppel: Not a Vegas Act, but Potentially More Expensive Than a Trip There

If you don't monitor, communicate, and follow up, your rights under the contract can evaporate. To know why, you need to understand waiver and estoppel.

Let's say you have a contract for buying blue GizmoTrons. Month after month, the vendor delivers green GizmoTrons. After many months, you refuse to pay for a shipment of GizmoTrons because they are green. The vendor sues you for nonpayment.

Do you win the case because the GizmoTrons are green, not the promised blue? Maybe not. The fact that you accepted so many green GizmoTrons without comment might make the court believe that you just don't care whether they are green or blue. The court might decide that you're just looking for a way to avoid your obligation to purchase GizmoTrons. The court rules against you because it just doesn't believe you. The legal name for that is waiver.

Now let's change the example a bit. Let's imagine that you've ordered custom-designed blue GizmoTrons. The vendor sends you specifications for months to show progress. The specifications include a swatch of the green that the vendor plans to use. Even though you ordered blue GizmoTrons, you don't complain. The vendor orders hundreds of custom green panels for your GizmoTrons. When the vendor delivers the very first shipment of GizmoTrons, you reject them because they're green. Your customers demand blue Gizmo-

Trons, and green simply will not satisfy them. The vendor sues to enforce the contract.

Do you win this time? You haven't waived your rights. You rejected the first GizmoTron, and the court has good reason to believe that you care about the difference between green and blue. You could still lose, though, because the court thinks that it's just too late for you to complain. After all, the court might think, the vendor purchased green panels in reasonable reliance on your review of the specifications. The court may want to rule against you because you could have avoided the whole problem by reviewing the specifications. The legal name for that ruling is estoppel.

How do you avoid waiver and estoppel? By carefully monitoring the vendor's compliance with the contract, promptly writing a complaint about any problem, and following up to make sure the problem has been corrected. Communicating and following up avoid waiver by showing that you care about the issue. Being prompt avoids estoppel by making sure that the vendor gets your complaint before doing anything expensive in reliance on your silence. Doing it all in writing means that you can prove to a court that you monitored, communicated, and followed up.

There's more to this than winning a court case, though. The sooner and more effectively you complain about a problem, like green GizmoTrons, the easier it is for the vendor to fix. The sooner and more effectively you complain, the smaller your problems will be. Also, a vendor that knows that you're watching will tend to perform better, if only to avoid getting complaint letters.

Another Glance at the Dashboard

However carefully the contract is negotiated and written, it may fall apart if the dashboard is not monitored and problems recorded when they occur. All parties want the deal to succeed. Identifying problems early allows them to be corrected in a way that will maintain healthy relationships and help both parties realize their goals.

If a vendor's failure to perform is picked up on the dashboard, it's up to the company to draft a clear objection in writing and to expressly reserve its rights under the contract. Even when the dashboard doesn't reveal a true breach of contract, it's still essential that performance be documented. All users, and all administrative staff responsible for monitoring the contract, should know what the contract requires and how to follow its terms and procedures.

The reason to document is to provide a paper trail that you can refer back to in case there is a problem. The process is similar to the one a supervisor would follow when documenting employee performance. Documentation usually involves a letter, or series of letters, to the vendor, with provision for additional internal documentation if the problem worsens. For example, the first letter might serve as a simple notification to the vendor that there is a problem. If the problem is not resolved as a result of this letter, then a second letter would document that fact. It would also repeat the request for resolution.

If there is still no resolution, then the problem needs to be referred by the user to company management. If it cannot be resolved at this level, then management refers it to its lawyers.

The better the dashboard, the better the oversight the company can provide, the greater the chance of a successful relationship, and the greater the likelihood that administrative costs can be fully defrayed in the form of service-level credits or other consideration when the vendor falls short of agreed-upon performance metrics.

Self-Test: Monitoring Company Compliance

Just as administration is responsible for auditing vendor compliance with contracts, it also must audit company compliance with individual contracts, and with company rules for IT systems in general and for their acquisition.

It isn't enough to have rules prohibiting functional redundancies between company IT systems. There must be periodic inventories of systems, in conjunction with IT staff, to ensure that no such redundancies exist. It's fruitless to have a sternly worded corporate policy banning the use of unlicensed software if no one ever checks to see if unlicensed software is lurking on anybody's hard drive.

Rules for purchasing IT systems have to be enforced, not just promulgated. Best practices should be implemented by everyone in the organization. Procedures should be reviewed periodically at every level. Everyone in an organization will give lip service to IT acquisition rules. But it's up to administration to make sure that IT purchasers put the company's money where their mouths are.

Everyone in the organization is responsible for responding to problems by making sure that the right people know about them, then changing procedures, if necessary, to prevent their recurrence. The change might involve renegotiating the deal, or it might be an internal procedural modification. In either case, there has to be a response to that flashing light on the dashboard.

Finally, administration must make sure that monitoring, communicating, and following up are a part of corporate practice for every deal. A technology acquisition is usually invisible, so it doesn't command the interest and oversight of top management the way something physically imposing, like a new building addition, does. Those charged with overseeing technology deals operate under the handicap of this invisibility. Moreover, they are often called upon to raise unpopular issues with coworkers and vendors in the course of following up on compliance issues.

Notwithstanding these difficulties, administration's dual role of identifying rules and auditing compliance with those rules is essential to efficient, orderly deployment of information technology. The companies that recognize this fact realize significant savings that are reflected in productivity gains, lower support costs, and smaller outlays for IT tools.

9

Putting the
Five Roles Together

The five roles—user, technical, financial, negotiating, and administrative—all have important functions in an IT deal.

The previous chapters explored each of the roles in the IT acquisition process separately. This chapter looks at all of them together and discusses how their relationships to one another, and to management, affect successful implementation of the new paradigm for IT acquisitions.

More Than Teamwork

While the roles are discrete functions, each is supported by the others. Like the legs of a three-legged stool, they depend on one another for support. The work they do can be done only in an environment in which all are working together.

Without the user, what would be the purpose of the technical function? If finance did not analyze risks and benefits, on what basis could negotiation operate?

Not only is each role defined by the others, but each enhances all the others. At those times when a single role takes the lead, the other four all must support it, or it fails.

The key to success is a balanced support structure. The process cannot go forward without it. No matter how well an individual role is performed, its success will always remain contingent on how well the other roles are played.

Synergy or Cynicism?

Before looking at the way the five roles should work together, consider the reasons why they might not work well together. Like method actors, they might well ask about their motivation. Without a clear understanding of the organizational importance of the process, their personal motivations are just as likely to exert centrifugal force away from the process as to impel them to a meaningful consensus. But no matter how clear the organizational mandate for interfunctional harmony in the IT acquisition process, problems can arise.

The purpose of presenting these issues is to help you think about some of the ways in which cynicism, resistance, or other problems can creep into the process, and how to make sure they don't.

The IT acquisition process described in this book depends on organizational harmony. Each player's strength must be enhanced by the others'. Everyone involved in the process has to learn to look ahead and consider what needs to be done to help the others do their jobs. Without this intentional synergy, inertia, functional parochialism, and indifference will overwhelm the process.

Here's a fanciful look at some of the ways the five roles get subverted in many organizations. As you read, visualize the people in your organization and whether they are ready to accept the interdependence necessary to make IT acquisitions systematic, businesslike, and successful.

The Devil, the Angel, and the User

The user must support the other roles in the process by:

- Providing technical with a clear and complete definition of the needs to be met with technology
- Establishing for finance the potential benefits to be achieved
- Identifying the key issues negotiation is to fight for, supporting the negotiation team in taking positions, and participating in creative efforts to forge better contracts
- Identifying the key success factors that administrative uses to form the dashboard, and providing the day-to-day data on compliance by the vendor and the company

No matter how well a user understands these needs in spirit, the flesh may be weak. Managers of strategic business units like autonomy. No one likes to be told that his or her one-person show is now an ensemble piece. At the very least, some personal ambivalence is inevitable, as illustrated in the following interior monologue:

> **User** [*to herself*]: Let's see, what's on the schedule today? Hmmm, Bill from IT is coming over to talk about that new

software we need. I hope he isn't going to make this an issue.

Tiny Devil [*standing on user's shoulder, waving pitchfork, yelling in ear*]: Get rid of him! He's gonna try to talk you out of it. And you know we can't make the numbers without it.

Tiny Angel [*on opposite shoulder, strumming harp*]: That's just not true. He only wants to make sure the software is the right choice.

Tiny Devil: That's a hot one. You know he's jealous 'cause the vendor likes you. Besides, he's a control freak.

Tiny Angel: Heavens, he only wants to talk about the possibility of using a software solution the company already owns. Is it unreasonable to discuss whether we really need to buy something new?

Tiny Devil: That's all anybody ever does around here: discuss. How are you supposed to get any work out of this department if you have to get three approvals to buy a paper clip? Just sign the contract and tell him to go to the devil.

Tiny Angel: I wouldn't do that if I were you. Why forgo heaven for the hell of vendor failure?

User: I shall repent of my evil ways.

Of Mice and Modems

Technical must support the other roles by:

- ▶ Translating what the user needs into technical specifications, and stopping projects that are based on unrealistic views of the state of the technology
- ▶ Verifying for finance the costs, benefits, and time frames for the vendor's technology, and identifying technical alternatives that will solve the same problem
- ▶ Determining for negotiation the key risks to be placed with the vendor during contract discussions
- ▶ Identifying the company IT policies for administrative and providing the tools required to verify compliance

The technical role is most susceptible to the disease of technophilia, described in Chapter 1. When technophiles talk about the way technology will solve business problems, it is sometimes difficult for them to restrain their enthusiasm. If this enthusiasm is infectious, it can lead to others in the organization expecting something that cannot be delivered, thus spoiling the best-laid plans:

> Lenny looked out over the water. He kicked an exposed sycamore root rhythmically, like a child, but with a huge man's foot. He was fondling a diskette. Then he stopped and turned his head. "Tell me about client/server, George," he said.
>
> "Aw, shucks, Lenny, I done told you about client/server so many times you'd think you'd be sick of it."
>
> "C'mon, George. I'll listen real quiet," wheedled Lenny.
>
> George flipped his cigarette butt high in the air. He sighed. "OK. Nowadays we're workin' real hard for somebody else's data center. But someday, if we can lay some acquisition capital by, we're gonna get a little computin' power of our own. An' we'll have servers . . ."
>
> "Real fast ones, George."
>
> "That's right, Lenny. Real fast ones, with big databases, and . . ."
>
> Lenny interrupted again. "No, George, it's supposed to be big relational databases."
>
> "See, you heard this so often you know it by heart. OK, big relational databases, and we'll have real-time sales figures, and charts . . ."
>
> "I get to make the charts, and use all the colors of the rainbow," Lenny added with a delighted giggle.
>
> "And you get to make the charts, with all the colors of the rainbow." George paused and reached behind him.
>
> "And we won't never have no computer problems again." Lenny looked far off.
>
> "Can you see it, Lenny? Our new system?"
>
> "Where, George? Show me where."
>
> "It's way out in the distance. Don't turn around."

Hamlet, *Prince of Finance*

Finance must support the other roles by:

▶ Providing the user with the framework and analytical support for evaluating whether an IT project is the best use of scarce resources

▶ Helping technical focus on the issues that affect the bottom line

▶ Giving negotiation the cost-benefit analysis needed to combat the vendor's rosy projections of financial benefits and thereby drive down price

▶ Helping administrative determine which rules justify a compliance effort based on risk assessments and other analysis tools

The occupational hazard here is inaction. By considering costs and benefits, pros and cons, in a thorough manner, finance runs the risk of forever contemplating a course of action, but never being able to carry it out. Sort of like the all-time champion of irresolution, the melancholy Dane:

> *To buy, or not to buy, that is the question,*
> *Whether 'tis nobler in the company to test*
> *The costs and benefits of outrageous systems,*
> *Or to stake harms against a sea of dollars,*
> *And by opposing, spend them. To lie, to speak—*
> *No more, and by a silence say we end*
> *The heartache, and the thousand natural shocks*
> *That deals are heir to; 'tis an acquisition*
> *Devoutly to be wished. To lie, to speak—*
> *To speak, perchance to buy, ay there's the rub,*
> *For in that purchase yet what costs may come*
> *When we have shuffled off this contract's coil*
> *Must give us pause—there's the respect*
> *That makes necessity of all these plans.*
> *For who would bear the vendor's tricks and ploys,*
> *The user's wrong, the spreadsheet's slow delay,*
> *But that the dread of something worse than death,*
> *The undiscovered contract, from whose costs*
> *No company recovers, vexes still,*
> *And makes us rather run to costs we have*
> *Than fly to benefits we know not of?*
> *Thus cash flow does make cowards of us all,*
> *And enterprises of great pitch and moment*
> *With this regard their buying turns awry,*
> *And lose the name of bold and best in class.*

The Wild, Wild Deal

Negotiators are sometimes seen as hired guns. The perception is that they're all swagger and no substance. Deals are simply an opportunity to prevail.

Negotiation has a legitimate role to play in the deal, of course. It supports the other roles by:

▶ Spotting and crystallizing the key concerns of the user, taking a hard line with vendors when the user relationship does not allow the users to do so, identifying the vendor ploys, and knowing where to push vendors

► Protecting technical from the distraction of vendor ploys, thus allowing them to focus on their central responsibility

► Helping to identify the key financial issues, negotiating savings, and generating alternatives

► Easing the role of administrative by obtaining unambiguous contractual terms and by avoiding terms that are difficult to administer

But what happens when ego supplants business goals? The other roles, and the business itself, could get caught in the crossfire.

Miss Billie's Short Branch Saloon. The Vendor Kid enters, leers at Miss Billie, and walks menacingly to the bar, spurs jingling, with a bag of ice slung over his shoulder.

Vendor Kid: Barkeep, whiskey. And I get to own the bottle.

Miss Billie: Hold it, Kid. That thar's my bottle. Now you can have the drink right enough, but you ain'ta gonna get to keep the bottle. And by the way, how 'bout sellin' me some a that ice? Could sure use some.

Vendor Kid: Glad to oblige, ma'am. But it's gonna cost ya.

Miss Billie: If ya wanna talk about hard bargains, looks like I'ma gonna haveta go get the Delaware Talker.

Vendor Kid: You just go right ahead, little lady. I ain't afeard a no outside negotiators.

Voice From Outside Swinging Doors: I'ma callin' you out.

Vendor Kid: I'ma ready for you, Delaware.

High noon, outside Miss Billie's. People run for cover. Shutters slam. The Vendor Kid and the Delaware Talker face off at a distance.

Delaware Talker: Kid, you just go ahead and reach for that legal pad.

Vendor Kid: You ain'ta gettin' the jump on me this time, Talker. Not like that Abilene data center conversion. Let's hear your best offer first.

Delaware Talker: I ain't talkin'. I'm waitin'.

Vendor Kid: Me too.

The two stand frozen in the street, Mont Blancs in hand, glaring angrily as the Western sun melts the ice.

Waiting for Vendot

Administrative must support the other roles by:

▶ Setting expectations for the user, making sure that both parties stay in compliance, and taking the burden of detail off the user
▶ Providing technical with a clear and consistent methodology for its analysis
▶ Allowing finance to assume that the organization will be able to comply with agreements, creating a reference database of existing agreements, and requiring financial analysis at the right stage of the acquisitions process
▶ Providing negotiation with clear standards, thus permitting straightforward compliance

People who are inclined to flout rules usually find ways to justify their behavior. Rules are stupid, they say. Rules are unnecessary. Rules inhibit real work.

The administrative staff who enforce rules sometimes react to resistance before it occurs. They can become defensive or officious. In the eyes of others, they may seem to obstruct the freedom that is necessary if an enterprise is to flourish.

In a sense, administrative has the thankless job of keeping the devil out of the details. It has to sound the alarm over things that are too small for other people to notice. Its vigil can be unrewarding. To the other roles, administrative may seem to be anticipating things that never happen:

Adnim: Vendot said he would come.
Minad: I am expecting him as well. Have you prepared the compliance rules?
Adnim: Of course. As you know, our database of software contracts is completely up-to-date. In addition, the database is not only backed up continuously but each backup is in turn backed up hourly at seven remote sites in abandoned missile silos.
Minad: When Vendot comes, I must discuss his tardiness with him. The terms of the meeting were fully set in preliminary discussions.
Adnim: This desert sun is hot.
Minad: It is not something I stipulated.
Adnim: Irksome.
Minad: Most irksome.

Performance Standards: Stage Directions That Guide the Actors in Their Roles

Achieving true synergy among the five roles is not impossible. If all the actors understand how important their support of the other roles is to the success of the play, a successful performance is practically ensured.

The best way to remind the role-players of this point is to make it part of their performance standards. Write standards that measure more than individual accomplishment. Tie the standards to the success of the deal process.

If you really believe that the five roles are, and must be, interdependent, how could you assess an individual's performance without looking at the group outcome?

If the individual really believes that interdependence is the only road to successful IT acquisitions, how could he or she indulge in the luxury of selfish behavior or ungenerous motives?

Performance standards should reinforce a group perspective. They should provide real incentives for helping the other roles do their jobs. Most important, the performance they measure should be weighed pragmatically. The metric should be group success attributable to individual effort, not individual attainment disconnected from the success of the IT acquisition process.

Management Support: Enforcing Organizational Discipline

Organizations that are committed to making IT acquisition a rational, disciplined process imbue the whole process with rigor.

Management must take its governance responsibility seriously and be willing to penalize employees who flout or try to circumvent the process.

Whatever the benefits of organizational flexibility, of continual reinvention, and of outside-the-box thinking, there are certainly serious drawbacks to disorder and inconsistency. Management owes it to the vast majority of employees, who make good-faith efforts to follow agreed-upon processes, to discipline those who do not.

Casting Call: Management's Responsibility for Assembling the Right Team

Because the five roles in the acquisition process are so interdependent, management must ensure that they are filled by individuals or groups that can perform them well. Managers who understand the roles must assess which employees in the organization will complement each other. When the user is known to be a forceful person, an equally dynamic technical person must be chosen to represent the interests of the company. When the technical person is known to be fond of the technology under consideration, the finance person must be able to neutralize this technophilia with unwavering advocacy of economic issues.

When management takes the trouble to assemble the right team, it sends the right message: namely, that the company is dedicated to the process and that it expects all five roles to be competently played.

Sometimes management will have to go outside the company to find the right people to fill the roles for a given acquisition. Not only does such a step help to neutralize intramural issues, but it also serves as another reminder of the corporate commitment to the new paradigm. This powerful team will send the right message to any vendor.

Bringing It All Back Home

If you carry away only one concept from this book, let it be this one: The only reason to buy information technology is to improve the way a company does business.

If you are a manager responsible for overseeing IT purchases, let this single concept be your mantra. Remind everyone in your organization that the tools of technology are only tools. When you are evaluating an IT acquisition, come back to the putative business benefit at every meeting, at every opportunity.

When everyone involved in the acquisition process understands that you're serious about looking at these purchases in terms of business success, they will be, too.

How to Implement the New Paradigm Today

Don't fall into the trap of waiting until everything is in place before you try to apply these concepts. Begin today.

Here are some first steps:

1. Look at all your negotiations in process, whether you're in the proposal stage or exchanging drafts of the contract. Clarify the roles and establish a negotiating strategy based on the principles in this book, and use that strategy going forward.

2. Look at your organization and see if you can easily identify which functional areas wear which hats; if you cannot, consider a reorganization or re-missioning of certain areas.

3. Review your projects in process; reconfirm the approval based on what you know now.

4. Look at your project management methodology; does it include all the steps in the acquisition process talked about in this book?

5. Take the time to analyze past negotiations, recognize the similarities in deals, and learn from prior mistakes.

6. Look at your policies for financial, technical, and administrative approval of technology acquisitions; do they foster a collaborative process, or work against it?

7. Collect all contracts in a central place.

8. Create a database of key terms.

9. Develop guidelines to help your organization follow the process laid out in this book.

10. Make this book required reading for everyone in your organization who is involved in the technology acquisition process.

Part Three
Contracting

10

Contracting Themes

The contract makes a difference. No matter what the sales rep says, the company and the vendor are legally bound by what's in writing. When all the people who negotiated the deal have gone on to other things, the contract will remain to bind the companies.

Vendors can use clever contract language to write themselves better deals. Understanding contract issues and contract language is vital to buying information technology on the right terms.

Why do you care? Because some of this contract language could impose hidden costs on your company. Contract language that seems innocuous when you're signing up could look like an iron shackle a year later. Your company could find itself with a nasty choice between living with that shackle or paying the vendor to release it. Either way, it's a hidden cost.

Other contract language may make the contract useless to you. Contract language that seems to bind the vendor to provide the benefits you expect could turn out to give you little or nothing. With that sort of language, the vendor washes its hands of responsibility.

The language that's missing from the contract can be as important as the language that's in the contract. Most of a well-drafted contract will be designed to protect the company. Thus, short agreements generally favor the vendor.

The Vendor's Form

Vendors typically begin contract negotiations with their "standard form contract." In a vendor's paradise, the company would simply sign the vendor's form without negotiation. That's generally a bad idea for the company because the vendor's form is usually nothing more than the vendor's wish list.

Vendors will put their full efforts into getting you to sign their forms. If a sales rep can get you to sign the vendor's form, the sales rep has won every contract point. A grand slam. Figure 10-1 shows some of the things that sales reps say to defend their form, with translations.

Vendors use all their selling ploys to sell you on the standard form. For example, a common smoke-and-mirrors ploy is to "present" the standard form contract instead of having you read it. Of course, the sales rep's presentation doesn't highlight the pitfalls hidden throughout the form.

The most common selling ploy for the vendor form is the sense of urgency ploy. Your vendor may seem simply unable to generate a contract. Then, once signing a deal has become urgent, the sales rep presents a contract and says that the vendor cannot go forward without a signed contract. The vendor's attorney is on a three-week scuba diving cruise, and thus the vendor will be unable to even consider making changes.

To get the right terms, you'll need to be able to spot the contracting ploys in a vendor form. This chapter gives you the tools to do that.

Shackles

Information technology contracts can shackle your company. They can deprive it of the liberty to pursue competitive advantage. They

Figure 10-1. Some things sales reps say—and what they really mean.

What the Sales Rep Says	What the Sales Rep Means
"You don't need to see my promises in the contract. You have my word on this."	"This is a personal deal. Me and you. My company would never back me up on this."
"I'll have to get that approved by corporate. That'll take weeks. That will blow our time schedule."	"You lost all the contract points when you fell for my sense of urgency ploy."
"That's just the way we do business. We never change that."	"It's OK that you're getting a bad deal because everyone who buys our products gets a bad deal."
"Our form is very reasonable."	"We have our reasons for wanting every provision."
"Well, I'm sure that we can work something out on this, but this is going to be a long, tough road to a contract."	"Resistance is futile. Our form is your destiny. Give in to the dark side."

can prevent smart business. They can keep you from doing what you want to do.

Vendors know that as markets and technologies change, their customers will need the keys to unlock those shackles. When things change, vendors will be able to exact some price to amend the contract. Perhaps the price will be an order for other products. Perhaps it will be some sort of fee to amend the contract.

Not all vendors exact a price to unlock the shackles in their contracts. Some amend their contracts just to maintain relationships, or to create a market perception of dealing fairly with their customers. On the other hand, some vendors hear the sound of cash registers ringing when you come to them to talk about unlocking shackles. Of course, vendors in financial distress are more likely to demand payments than vendors with growing businesses.

A few good places to look for shackles in a vendor form are the confidentiality, assignment, and scope of use provisions.

Confidentiality

The confidentiality section requires you to keep the vendor's secrets. This sounds reasonable, but it can mean unreasonably large hidden costs.

Using information technology products generally requires training, installation, systems integration, operation, maintenance, and so forth. You need those services to make the product work in your environment.

The vendor is often the highest-cost provider of those services. You might want to reduce your costs by hiring other vendors to perform those services. That may be smart business compared to using the vendor or hiring more employees.

Often, the confidentiality clause prevents you from giving a consultant access to the vendor's product. How can you find another source for training, installation, systems integration, operation, maintenance, and so forth if you can't give a consultant access to the vendor's product? You can't, of course. So you find that your only choices are to use the vendor's overpriced service or to ask the vendor to unlock the confidentiality shackles.

Vendors don't see this as just a ploy. Rather, in their view, confidentiality is necessary to protect their trade secrets. That may be true. Some vendors have genuine trade secrets. A smaller number of vendors have trade secrets and could be harmed if you let a consultant in on their trade secrets.

Most vendors, though, have few truly secret ideas. Most of their products are like this book: a good collection of well-known ideas applied to a particular problem. Vendors implicitly acknowledge this when their contracts make everything concerning their enterprises, their prices, and their products confidential. If they had a trade secret, it would be described with reasonable specificity so that you would know to protect it.

Even vendors with real trade secrets to protect often would not be harmed if the trade secrets were disclosed to a consultant who agreed in writing to keep those secrets. You have to ask yourself whether there is a risk that the vendor will lose legitimate revenue opportunities because you have the right to give limited access to the vendor's product to consultants.

Assignment

The assignment clause is often the last clause in the contract. In spite of that, in our fast-changing economy, it can be the most costly clause in the contract.

Assigning a contract transfers your rights and obligations to someone else. Why would you want to do that? Usually it's because you sell a business, merge, or outsource. If the business relies on a particular software product, for example, you may need to assign your license to use that software to a buyer of the business.

What happens if the assignment clause prohibits assignment? You can't assign that contract without the vendor's consent. If you want to sell a business, for example, the vendor will have the opportunity to demand that you buy the contract all over again. If you're getting a good price for that business, it may be worth your while to buy the software again. If the price isn't high enough, you might give up the opportunity to sell that business. Either way, you'll wish you had negotiated the assignment clause when you bought the software.

Scope of Use

When you license technology, you license it for a particular "scope of use." The license permits you to use the technology only within that scope of use. So, for example, if the scope of use is limited to 221B Baker Street, you cannot use the technology anywhere else.

In software licensing, the scope of use is often defined by:

- ▶ Who can use the product (for example, your company and its wholly owned subsidiaries)
- ▶ What computer the product can run on (for example, a Gizmo-Tron Mark IV computer, serial number 890916)

▶ Where the product can be used (for example, a state or a street address)
▶ Whose data can be processed using the product
▶ How many people can use the product
▶ How long the company can use the product

These restrictions often seem innocuous. After all, you may intend to use the product to have three people process your own data at your headquarters on GizmoTron Mark IV serial number 890916. The restrictions don't bother you because you don't intend to do anything else with the software.

Over time, though, those restrictions can feel a lot more like shackles. You may want to have more people use the product. You may want to move your operation. You may want to upgrade from the GizmoTron Mark IV to the GizmoTron Mark V. You may want to outsource the function, or to perform the function for someone else.

Then, just as with the confidentiality and assignment provisions, you could face a nasty choice: Live with the shackles (and without doing what you want to do) or pay the price the vendor wants. Regardless, it's probably a cost you didn't consider when you acquired the technology.

Providing Product or Meeting Needs?

You buy products to meet needs. When you buy a product, you want the vendor to promise that the product meets your needs. If the product doesn't meet your needs, you want to be able to return it to the vendor for a full refund.

A vendor's form usually promises only that the product meets the vendor's specifications for the product. Often, those specifications are so brief, vague, and basic that it's hard to imagine how the product could fail to comply with them. On the other hand, it's often easy to imagine that a product could meet its specifications without meeting your needs. Often, the vendor doesn't even give you a copy of those specifications unless you demand one.

In the rest of the business world, this would be called an internal control issue. The vendor is writing its own performance standards. The performance standards are weak enough that they can't be audited.

This problem is not limited to hardware and software vendors. Service vendors often want to promise only that they will supply people with the right titles. For example, the vendor's form contract for a project might promise to provide four "senior programmers" and one "project manager." Is that a promise that those people will meet your needs? No. It's just a promise that they'll have those titles.

How Vendors Sell Benefits—Then Contract for Product

Vendors are surprisingly successful at closing deals based on oral promises that their products will meet needs, then using the written contract to absolve themselves of responsibility for the products' meeting those needs. How do they do that?

The Path of Least Resistance

People take the path of least resistance. That's a selling fundamental. It's not always true, but it's true often enough.

Although sales reps often sell on the basis of meeting needs, vendors generally make it easy to contract for product and hard to contract for meeting needs. Vendors design their forms for providing product, not for meeting needs. Changing the vendor's form requires new language and a clear definition of the needs that you expect the product to meet. You can't get the vendor to promise that the product will meet your needs unless you've described your needs clearly and completely, in writing.

A clear, unambiguous description of needs is hard to create. You need a precise, unambiguous document that considers all of the angles. Creating such a document takes time. It takes experience. It's an art. The company must understand, in detail, what it needs from the product.

Producing this list description of needs often seems a thankless task. The process is often regarded as a useless delay in a high-priority effort. Also, it may create discord and further delay by exposing the many and varied beliefs that the various parts of the company have about what the product is going to do. It may even expose the lack of a sound rationale for going forward with the purchase.

All this makes the project team ready to fall into the vendor's trap by taking the path of least resistance. It requires negotiating expertise and leadership to avoid this trap. With expertise and leadership, the various participants will understand that it is vital to commit the vendor to meeting the company's needs.

Sharing the Blame

Making contracting for product the easiest thing to do is just one way in which vendors get their customers to contract for providing product instead of for meeting needs. Another way is by sharing the blame.

Sharing the blame looks like this: The company says it wants to contract for the benefits that the vendor promised in the sales pitch. The vendor agrees, but the contract makes it clear that any success or failure is in part, perhaps in large part, the result of the company's efforts. The contract doesn't define what the company must do in order for the product to meet the company's needs, so the company can't prove that it had the right to expect the product to meet those needs.

Certainly, there are benefits that require both the right product from the vendor and the right effort from the buyer. Vendors can't control the way their products are used. Buyers make a lot of mistakes. It doesn't make sense to ask a vendor to be liable for a buyer's mistakes.

That would be a fine argument if the vendor merely sold a product as meeting its specifications. However, if the vendor sold the product by promising that it would meet the company's needs, the vendor should know what the company must do in order for the product to meet the company's needs.

Companies can defeat themselves by trying to overreach on this issue. For example, the company may insist that the vendor be responsible for the company's achieving its goals (such as increasing sales by 20 percent) instead of for meeting appropriate needs (such as being able to print a list of all products purchased by a customer in the prior year). The vendor can win that argument because the vendor has too little control over whether the company increases its sales.

This is a trap for the unwary. It will fail if the company starts out with a clear set of needs that can be met by the product, regardless of the quality of the user's efforts. You need smart people working hard to properly analyze the issues and to translate the expected benefits into objective performance standards that will appear in the contract.

Vague Obligations

A contract is a bundle of legal rights. The legal rights have value only if you can enforce them. You can enforce a legal right by going to court and proving that the vendor had a legal obligation that it did not perform. Your ability to enforce a legal right in court gives you leverage to get your vendor to perform.

Thus, you want the ability to prove to a court that the vendor had a legal obligation. To do that, you need a contract provision that imposes a clear legal obligation on the vendor. If the contract provision is vague, or does not impose a clear legal obligation on the vendor, you will probably lose.

Vendor Victory by Vagueness

Let's take a very common example. You contract for a consultant to develop software. The only warranty you get is that "The services will conform to industry standards." The vendor's performance is horrible. How does your case go when you get to court?

First, you need to demonstrate what this obligation means. The contract doesn't say what industry standards will be applied, so that's an issue in front of the court. The vendor says that the contract requires the court to apply the self-serving standards of the Fly-by-Night Consultants Association. If the vendor wins that, you've probably lost your case.

Second, you need to prove that the vendor's services didn't conform to the standards. Let's say you win on the choice of standards. You choose high standards. The vendor will argue that its services were just fine, and that you're complaining only because the results were horrible. The problem, the vendor will say, was that you asked to have the wrong things done. Also, whatever standards you propose will turn out to be mostly inapplicable. Thus, you will appear to be cherry-picking your standards.

Now the question goes to a jury, because there are issues of fact to resolve. The jury will probably consist of a varied group of people, united only in their confusion about information technology. You'll be hanging your hat on a complex and mostly inapplicable set of standards, not an unambiguous contract provision.

The bottom line is that it will be very costly and difficult to prove anything in court. If you can't prove anything in court, your leverage is limited to preventing the consultant from continuing to bill time on the project. For the vendor, this is victory by vagueness.

Weasel Words

Vendors can make a contract provision uselessly vague with just one or two weasel words. For example, a vendor's form might require the vendor to provide the product "as available." With those two little weasel words, the vendor can escape all obligations. If the vendor isn't making enough money on you, you may find that the vendor's product simply isn't available—at least, not to you.

A common weasel word in software maintenance agreements is *update,* as in "so long as the company pays the annual maintenance fee, the vendor will provide all updates to the software." The word *update* does not include "new products." The vendor decides what's an update and what's a new product. At the extreme, everything will be a new product. Thus, with one slippery weasel word, the vendor has greatly limited the value of the maintenance you're buying.

Another common weasel word is *reasonable,* as in "the vendor will cooperate with the company's reasonable requests for assistance" or "the company may allow other users to access the system, with the consent of the vendor, which consent will not be unreasonably withheld." In each case, the word *reasonable* changes what might be a clear obligation that a judge can interpret without a trial to a fact question for a jury. That makes any potential litigation far more expensive, and possibly prohibitively expensive.

The way to spot weasel words is to read the contract very closely. Small words can make big differences. "Vendor may" is worlds away from "vendor shall." This is no place for speed reading.

Drafting Clear Obligations

Clear obligations say *who* will do *how much* of *what* by *when.* For an example of a clear obligation, look at the payment provision of almost any vendor's form. Almost certainly, it will say something like, "The company will pay the vendor the amounts set forth on Exhibit A within ten (10) days of the date of vendor's invoice." There's no room for argument there.

Clear obligations rarely result in protracted or expensive litigation. Instead, the party that will clearly lose the lawsuit settles it quickly. There is little point in spending time and money litigating a doomed position.

If you want to enforce your agreements, you need clear obligations from your vendors. For a consulting vendor, you can fairly ask that: "Vendor will develop the software to perform in accordance with the specifications set forth in Exhibit B within six months of the contract effective date." Exhibit B can be loaded with clear statements, such as: "The software will display the outstanding balance of the customer's account if the operator presses the F7 button."

Snake-Oil Remedies

So let's say that you manage to prove that the vendor breached an obligation. What happens next? What do you get? What does the vendor have to do for you? The answer to those questions is called your *remedy*.

Some of the remedies that vendors offer are of no more help to you than snake oil. For example, a prominent software vendor's form contract states that if its software doesn't conform to the vast majority of its specifications, the vendor will either cause the software to conform to the vast majority of its specifications or change its specifications.

That's the remedy that a successful licensor offers. Would it help you to have the vendor's specifications describe the problem that brings your network down at the worst possible times? Of course not. Yet that may be the only remedy available to you.

Reasonable Efforts

A common "sole and exclusive" remedy is for the vendor to use "reasonable efforts" to solve the problem. What efforts are reasonable is difficult to determine, but it's probably not reasonable to ask the vendor to spend more money fixing a problem than the vendor will make because the problem is fixed.

Also, these remedies rarely say when the vendor has to use these reasonable efforts. Thus, the vendor can choose to do so sooner or later. You might even find yourself offering the vendor a bit of cash to meet this obligation sooner instead of later.

What kind of efforts do you want when you report a problem? You want the vendor to respond to your call within a set period of time, perhaps an hour, and to have someone working on it within another set period of time, say four hours. You want that person to work continuously on the problem. If the problem is of high priority, you want the engineers who created the problem to pitch in. You may even want them to fly to your location at the vendor's expense to fix the problem.

Refund Rights

If the product doesn't work, you would expect that you would have the right to return it for a full refund. It's rare, though, that the vendor's form gives you that right. Some forms expressly take that right away from you.

Money Damages

If the product fails, and the failure proximately causes you to lose money, contract law gives you the right to sue for the money you lost. That amount of money is called your damages.

Vendors tend to divide damages into two categories. The first category is called direct damages. Direct damages are the out-of-pocket expenses incurred as a result of product failure. For example, you might have to buy another product to solve the problem.

The other category is much bigger. This category includes lost profits, lost savings, consequential damages, indirect damages, punitive damages, and everything else that isn't a direct damage. For example, it includes the sales you lose because your new order entry system fails.

What you want, of course, is to be made whole. You've been damaged by the vendor's failure, and you want to be put in the position that you would have been in if the vendor's promises were true. If the contract was silent on the matter, that's what you could sue for in a court of law.

Instead, the vendor's form usually limits direct damages to the contract price or less—sometimes a lot less. Some vendors' forms limit the vendor's liability to the vendor's profits on the deal. Other vendors' forms limit the vendor's liability to the amount paid for the part of the product that caused the problem. That part might be an hour of a consultant's time or a line of code.

A vendor's form will usually exclude all consequential damages. That means that the vendor does not pay one penny for the sales or savings you lost because the product failed. Think about that, particularly where the benefits you hope to receive are increases in profits or savings.

Together, the limitation on direct damages and the exclusion of consequential damages give almost all of the risk that the product will fail to you, the buyer. Caveat emptor.

Intellectual Property Indemnities

This provision is often so shrouded in legalese that buyers just skip over it. That's a mistake.

What's an intellectual property indemnity? Let's start from ground zero. Intellectual property laws give owners of intellectual property certain exclusive rights with respect to the intellectual property. These are relevant:

- ► Patent laws give the patent owner the right to prevent others from making, using, or selling the patented invention.
- ► Copyright laws give the copyright owner the right to prevent

others from copying, displaying, performing, or distributing a copyrighted work.

▶ Trademark laws give the trademark owner the right to prevent others from using confusingly similar trademarks.

▶ Trade secret laws give the trade secret owner the right to prevent others from improperly using or disclosing the trade secrets.

If the vendor uses someone else's patented invention, copyrighted work, trademark, or trade secret without a license, that's called infringement. Infringing intellectual property is similar to stealing a car.

If the product you buy infringes someone's intellectual property, the owner of that intellectual property can go to court to:

▶ Sue you for money damages.

▶ Stop you from using the product.

That's a bad result for you. The intellectual property indemnity clause tells you what the vendor will do for you in this situation.

Vendors generally offer to pay some portion of the damages. Some vendors' forms offer to indemnify for one type of intellectual property infringement (maybe patent) and not others. Other vendors' forms will indemnify for all types of infringement, but only if you've already lost a "final judgment." Given that infringement can only be the result of wrongful conduct by the vendor, what you want is to be indemnified against all costs from all forms of intellectual property infringement.

The vendor also generally wants to be able to stop you from using the product. That makes sense; the vendor wants to stop the infringement that's leading to damages. The problem, usually, is that the vendor not only does not offer to reimburse you for the disruption that this causes, but seeks to refund less than all of your money.

Boilerplate Ploys

Tucked away at the end of most vendors' forms is what many buyers call "boilerplate." It's a collection, generally, of innocuous-looking terms. Many buyers believe that they don't even need to read it; however, it can reverse some of your most critical assumptions. For example, it is often home to the following ploys.

Termination

A vendor's form will often give the vendor the right to terminate the contract if you breach, and to declare a breach if you make the slightest mistake. For example, a software vendor might have the right to cancel a software license if a payment is ten days late or if 101 users use a product for which you have a 100-user license. When the vendor terminates the license, the contract requires you to stop using the software. Often, you don't even have the right to notice and an opportunity to cure the default.

That's a draconian remedy, quite unlike the snake-oil remedies that the vendor's form gives you if the vendor fails to perform. Your entire business could rely on this software. As a result, the vendor can demand a ransom to "waive" its remedies (let you off the hook) for that default.

The Contract Is the Deal

You might think that you've beaten your vendor's contracting ploys by getting a proposal that makes some real promises. You check the proposal over and don't find any disclaimers, except that the deal is subject to signing a final contract.

Check that contract for a provision called "Integration" or "Entire Agreement." What it usually says is that the contract "is the entire agreement between the parties, and supersedes all other agreements, understandings, proposals, and statements." To a court, the word *supersedes* means eliminates, terminates, and washes away.

This provision allows the vendor to wash its hands of anything in the proposal unless the vendor warrants in the contract that what is in the proposal is true. You won't find that warranty in a vendor's form. Thus, the vendor has probably washed its hands of all the promises that it made even in a formal written proposal.

What about the oral promises that the salesperson makes when you sign the contract, or after you sign the contract? The contract eliminates those in the "Amendment" section. That section says that the contract "may be amended only by a written agreement of the parties." The bottom line is that the contract is the deal.

Use of Company Name

Some vendors' forms give the vendor the right to use the company's name in the vendor's lists of its clients. That means that the vendor can use your name to sell its products. Agreeing to that can jeopardize your trademark rights, and you are giving the vendor a license to use your name without being paid.

Even worse, this may mean that you'll have to field reference calls regarding the product. Even if you hate the product, you may feel a need to be at least noncommittal to get continued support from the vendor. Also, there is always the risk that the vendor may sue for defamation, business libel, intentional interference with business relationships, and so forth if you share your true feelings about a product you hate with potential customers.

Home Court Advantage

Very deep in the boilerplate there are often provisions called "choice of law" and "jurisdiction." The choice of law provision says which state's laws will govern the dispute. Your lawyers may have feelings about that. However, you can take comfort in the fact that the most important laws in this area are federal laws and relatively uniform state laws.

The "jurisdiction" provision is extremely important. It says where any dispute will be resolved. The vendor's form usually states that any dispute will be resolved in the vendor's own backyard. If you're not from those parts, you might have reason for concern about getting "local justice." You might also be concerned about the expense and difficulty of litigating a dispute in a faraway spot.

That's what the vendor wants. The vendor wants the difficulty of litigation, and the risk of getting a jury that roots for the home team, to scare you away from litigation. Thus, this is a critical clause that could have quite an effect on your leverage in a future dispute.

Right to Subcontract

The boilerplate might also give the vendor the right to subcontract its obligations. That means that the services may be provided by someone other than the vendor that you have selected so carefully. Often, the contract doesn't even give you a right to know when the vendor has made that switch.

This is particularly disturbing when you have selected a vendor based on its first-class hiring and training methods. The vendor might hire only A+ people, and that's what you want. If the vendor can subcontract, the subcontractor might hire B− people, and that's what you'll get.

The vendor's form may go further and disclaim any warranties of the subcontractor's work. Thus, the vendor may not be liable to you for its subcontractor's failures. And, because your company doesn't have a contract with the subcontractor, the subcontractor is not liable to you for its failures. Just as in a vendor's paradise, the vendor has made the sale and washed its hands of any obligation to perform.

Knowing the Deals

This chapter described the overriding themes in IT contracting:

- ▶ Whether the contract will leave you the flexibility to do what you want to do
- ▶ Whether the vendor is committing to meeting your needs or just to providing product
- ▶ Whether the vendor's obligations will be clear enough to enforce
- ▶ Whether the company will have meaningful remedies for vendor failure
- ▶ Whether the boilerplate will reflect or abort your expectations

The next step is to understand the key terms and issues of information technology deals. Chapter 11 describes a document that begins most important deals: the request for proposal, or RFP. An RFP is a document that a company sends to a variety of vendors to get proposals for deals. Often, this is the key document in starting information technology deals.

Next, Part Three describes three information technology acquisition activities:

- ▶ Licensing computer software (Chapter 12)
- ▶ Engaging consultants, generally to make the software work (Chapter 13)
- ▶ Buying computer hardware to use for running the software (Chapter 14)

Often, these activities are combined in a single deal or agreement. For example, a software vendor may provide consulting services, such as installation, conversion, and training. Or, alternatively, a consultant might sell you services and grant you licenses for the software produced as a result of those services. Hardware vendors often provide both installation services and software.

Outsourcing is another example of a combination of information technology software, hardware, and services. In outsourcing, an outside vendor takes over a traditionally internal information technology function. The vendor then provides IT services, such as processing data or operating and maintaining computer systems. Chapter 15 describes outsourcing issues.

Finally, Chapter 16 describes strategic alliances. In a strategic alliance, the company and the vendor (or another company) share the risks and rewards of operating shared assets. By understanding strategic alliances, you will be able to structure more creative deals and unlock opportunities that might not be possible with traditional deal structures.

Your deals will have idiosyncrasies and require special provisions. Ideas that make sense in most deals might not fit your deal. The discussion of key terms in this section should help you identify issues that may apply to your deals.

This part of the book will help you spot the right issues and understand what you want and what the vendor wants in each area. Whether your role is user, technical, financial, negotiating, or administrative, that will make you a better deal maker.

11
Request for Proposal

For larger, more complex IT acquisitions, a request for proposal (RFP) process is a valuable way to improve offers. In the development of an RFP, the user, technical, financial, negotiating, and administrative areas all work in close cooperation to create a detailed statement of the company's business requirements and distribute it to a number of vendors who are potentially able to provide a solution.

An RFP imposes a disciplined process for identifying needs. It forces vendors to formally make representations and commitments concerning the way they will meet those needs. It helps a company think through its request and obtain valuable information and commitment at the point in the process when its leverage is strongest. If done properly, the RFP will feed into the negotiating process, and the result will be a meaningful, administrable, risk-balanced contract tailored to fit the business needs of the customer.

The RFP should draw on all five roles: user, technical, financial, negotiating, and administrative. This team should be put in place to develop the RFP, select the list of vendors, review proposals, and negotiate and close the deal. The initial scope identified in the RFP may not be the scope of the final deal. Thus, this team must retain the flexibility to always pursue the right answer and not be forced into the scope established in the initial RFP.

The time and expense associated with developing an RFP can be significant. For this reason, it is worthwhile understanding when there is benefit to using this process. Normally, an RFP is prepared for one of the following reasons:

- ► A large amount of money is involved in the transaction.
- ► There is a complex business/technical need, and the vendor choice is not obvious.
- ► There are multiple vendors to be considered, regardless of the complexity of the project. This could mean that you have identified a group of relevant vendors, each with its own technical

solution to the business problem, from whom you want to solicit specific bids.

▶ The solution is unclear, and vendors may be able to provide "creative" recommendations to help the company find ways to solve the problem that it may have been unaware of.

▶ The customer seeks a bundle of services.

▶ Competitive bidding for pricing, product, and service levels could produce superior offerings from vendors.

▶ Government or other procurement requirements dictate the use of an RFP.

RFP Construction

Everything you state or ask in an RFP will send signals to the vendor about who you are, what your business problem is, and what you are looking for in a solution. The way you ask questions can determine whether you get a vague or a tight answer, an off-target or a focused response. After you frame questions carefully for the vendors, you get answers that are meaningful and comparable. The following commonsense questions should act as guiding principles in the development of questions and statements in an RFP:

▶ Will this question invite the vendor to give me the information I need to make a decision?

▶ Is the question clear?

▶ Am I providing all of the information the vendor needs in order to unambiguously answer my question?

Because the immediate goal of this step of the process is to elicit responses that are easy to compare, you should insist on consistency in RFP responses. Consistent responses will assist you enormously in determining which proposed solution is more appropriate and which deal more favorable.

The way you get consistent responses is by asking carefully crafted questions. If you merely ask for a response-time commitment, one vendor might offer a one-second *average* response time and another might offer a response time of one second or less at least 90 percent of the time. Those responses are not comparable. A carefully crafted question would ask, for example, for an *average*-response-time commitment.

All the roles (user, technical, financial, negotiating, and administrative) should work together to identify the key evaluation criteria by which responses will be judged. The exercise of deciding what is important to each constituency, not unlike the objectives prioritization exercise recommended in Chapter 7, "Negotiating," will clarify both the drafting of the RFP and the evaluation of responses.

One costly pitfall is an RFP that uses the sort of vague rhetoric often employed internally in marketing a project to the company's executives. For example, simply stating that a company is seeking to implement a "best-of-breed" or "world-class" solution is sure to produce meaningless assurances from all vendors that that is exactly what they provide. Terms like these mean different things to different people. As a result, they don't help vendors understand what you really need.

In fact, vague rhetoric often sends the wrong message. "Best in class," for example, could be interpreted by a vendor to mean either that you want to cherry-pick your favorite modules from a vendor's various solutions (thus depriving the vendor of its customary profit on a bundled solution), or that quality is so important to you that your requirement for the product is not price-elastic (and so the vendor can charge you an arm and a leg).

Generally, an RFP contains the following main types of information:

Company Information

▶ Financial information
▶ Industry information and company position
▶ Current technical environment
▶ Problem or need to be addressed
▶ Goals

Requirements

▶ Scope
▶ Service levels
▶ Timing
▶ Vendor commitment (personnel, quantities, releases)
▶ Implementation or transition plan
▶ Required terms and conditions
▶ Format of pricing

Questions

▶ Vendor financial information
▶ Vendor organizational information
▶ Vendor industry position

▶ Vendor solution
▶ Vendor reference accounts
▶ Vendor locations
▶ Vendor pricing
▶ Additional terms
▶ Optional services

Administrative

▶ Instructions on how to provide and format responses
▶ Instructions directing questions during the response period
▶ Time line for bidders' conference, questions, proposal due date, and company decision
▶ Statement that vendors will bear their own costs
▶ Statement that the RFP is subject to change by the company in its sole discretion and does not bind the company to buy any product from any company
▶ Statement that the contents of the RFP are confidential and (if applicable) subject to the confidentiality agreement between the buyer and the vendor

For an RFP to generate meaningful responses, these types of communications need to be in balance. Unfortunately, RFPs are often constructed with too many questions and too little factual information and requirements. These RFPs generate replies that tend to be difficult to compare in the evaluation stage, so that many clarifications with the vendors are needed after proposals have been submitted.

Identifying Vendors

Once you've written an RFP, you need to decide who to send it to. Deciding who to send it to is an externally focused process that complements the internally focused process of writing an RFP. Ideally, these processes are done at the same time and complement each other, with an increasing understanding of the company's needs helping and being helped by an increasing understanding of what is available in the market.

Initial Bid List

The initial list of vendors to be considered will come primarily from the user's market research. As discussed in Chapter 4, "The User," the user should have identified a range of options for solving the business problem. Where those options involve vendors, that list would have been developed.

Another source of information on relevant vendors is users or IT technical staff at peer companies. For example, a user who is manager of a claims area at an insurance company may be aware of a peer company that is realizing impressive savings through the use of a particular software product. That user will want to at least match, if not improve upon, the cost structure of his competitors, and so he will want to investigate the claims made by the vendor about that product's performance. Through contact with their peers at other companies (as well as attendance at trade shows, industry publications, vendor advertising, and vendor briefings), your team will have a high awareness of the technical tools that are currently being developed.

In addition, there are companies that offer as one of their primary services the identification of vendors of IT products for various business and technical needs. These information vendors have substantial research libraries that can be accessed and, for any topic that they have not already researched, they can provide analysts to work with you to uncover what's out there.

Whether or not you use one of the above means of identifying vendors, you may also be contacted directly by vendors who either are simply trolling for business or have some notion of what it is you're looking for. In fact, depending on the size of your company and your putative attractiveness as a potential customer, you may draw in most of the major players simply by letting it become known on the street that you are looking for a certain type of system.

Vendor sales reps are always out actively brokering the vendors' specific solutions to a world of customers with a variety of business needs. They want you to believe that they have no competition, which is why the team must look at impartial and objective sources to identify the full list of vendors who can meet the company's business need. Ideally, at the end of this process, you'll have a list of all of the vendors who could realistically be your best choice.

Winnowing the Bid List

Assume for a moment that the list of realistic potential vendors is about twenty vendors long. You may think that sending out RFPs to twenty vendors instead of to five would increase your chances of finding the best vendor, but there may be good reasons most of those twenty should be disqualified. Having twenty respondents will only cloud the evaluation process and require your team to deal with more paper, more responses, and more vendor sales reps. Additionally, the more vendors you include, the less incentive you give each of them to develop a truly competitive proposal. A vendor who is one of five will work harder to push to the top of the heap than a vendor who is only one of twenty.

The team should consider the following nine questions to reduce the number of potential vendors to whom you will publish an RFP:

1. Does what you know of the vendor's products meet your needs?
2. Are the vendor's products ranked highly by independent third-party reviewers?
3. Does your company have any direct experience with this vendor that would influence future dealings?
4. What is the vendor's financial strength?
5. Has the vendor grown so quickly that resources may be stretched?
6. What is the vendor's reputation?
7. Does the vendor serve your industry and companies of your size?
8. Does the vendor have experience solving your business problem?
9. Do the vendor's products or services generally match your company's strategic direction?

Often, these questions will allow the review team to winnow its list to a few key vendors, thus saving a great deal of unnecessary work for both the company's team and the vendors who are winnowed out.

Reviewing Responses

The RFP process should produce responses that assist the team in its decision making. The process of prioritization of objectives that is done as part of the RFP development provides the groundwork for this evaluation. This prioritization should give the team the basis for determining which proposal will win.

There are many scoring methods available to facilitate the evaluation of RFP responses. If the RFP is intended chiefly as a solicitation of bids on a commodity product in order to find the lowest price, the process of comparison will be simple. Often, however, the proposals from the vendors present a complex mix of seemingly incomparable attributes (e.g., price versus resource commitments versus product features versus performance versus market share).

A common approach to evaluating these mixes of attributes is a "rate and weight" methodology. Each criterion is assigned a relative weight, which is expressed as a percentage; these weights, in total, must sum to 100 percent for all criteria. The relative weights describe the importance to the team of each criterion. Price, for example, might be much less important than a vendor's ability to successfully implement a customized product in a timely manner. In this case, price might be assigned a weight of 15 percent and the criterion "quickly implement customized product" might be assigned a weight of 25 percent. Once all the key criteria have been assigned relative weights, the next step is to establish a uniform rating scale (usually 1 to 10) for how well each vendor performed on each criterion. Each vendor should be rated on each criterion. These ratings should then be tabulated and each multiplied by the weight for the criterion. The result will be a quantified comparison of the vendor offerings. Another benefit of this approach is that it can also help the team focus on the factors that will result in project success.

This description of a formal RFP process is not meant to suggest that a different thought process applies to smaller deals. The same thought process should apply to all deals. The difference is the level of formality.

12

Software Licenses

A software license is a conditional grant of rights to use software. Unlike a purchase contract, a software license does not give the company title to the software. Instead, the company merely obtains the right to use the software in limited ways under limited circumstances.

Because the vendor retains title to the software, the company and the vendor have an ongoing relationship. This is much more the case than under an equipment purchase agreement, where, once the vendor hands over a finished product, the company owns it free and clear. Under a software license, the company's right to use the software is conditioned upon its abiding by a set of conditions, some of which may be (at least as initially proposed by the vendor) quite onerous, inflexible, and difficult to administer. At its most threatening, this relationship can resemble that between a company and its first mortgage lender: The company needs the bank's consent for most of its significant business transactions.

This chapter will help you to navigate through a software license agreement, avoid the potential pitfalls, and conduct an informed and effective negotiation.

The Value Pricing Trend

Decades of negotiations between companies and vendors have brought about a number of changes in software licenses. On the one hand, license provisions that don't have revenue implications for the vendor have tended to become fairer over time. For example, in addition to giving companies the right to make a backup copy of software, vendor forms now often include the right to use a copy of the software for testing.

On the other hand, software vendors have been devising new and ingenious ways to ''value price'' their software to create the revenue streams that go far, far into the future. Value pricing is an effort by the vendor to price its software based on the value that the software provides to the company instead of setting a fixed price that must be low enough to appeal to companies that will obtain only a little value from the software. Vendors see some companies deriving a tremendous amount of value from their software, and they want a share of that value as revenue. Thus, for example, some software vendors charge a license fee based on the number of transactions processed by the software or the amount of information maintained by the software.

The value pricing trend has encouraged vendors to come up with various ways to limit a company's rights to use their software. Remember, software licensing is a relationship, memorialized by a written agreement. If you want to do something different from what you and the vendor initially agreed to, you are going to have to go back to the vendor for a consent or amendment to the license agreement.

Software vendors are not inherently interested in limiting the use of their software (except to the extent that unlimited use may affect their proprietary rights or reduce their opportunities to sell additional licenses). Most of the language in a vendor's proposed contract that limits a company's use of the software or sets rules and protocols actually just sets the stage for collecting more revenue from companies that make more use of the software.

Some increases in your company's use of software may affect a vendor's cost structure. For example, if you decided to install a vendor's software in fifty locations instead of just one and the vendor suddenly had to start taking telephone calls for support from all fifty locations, the vendor would have a reasonable basis for higher charges, probably in the form of an increase in the annual software maintenance fee.

Most increases in your use of software, however, do not affect the vendor's cost structure. For example, moving a mainframe software product from one model type to a larger model type machine would not increase the vendor's costs. Yet, companies have generally accepted the notion that software vendors should be able to charge more to companies that are running the software on a larger processor on the theory that those companies derive more value from the software. In fact, value comes from projects, not from software, and companies running software on smaller processors may in fact obtain more value from it than companies running the software on large processors because the small companies have projects that generate more value. Charging based on the number of users that are permitted access to software is another common approach. These sorts of limitations are merely proxies for value; they may or may not be appropriate for your company.

License Pitfalls

In general, companies should have only three basic obligations in a license agreement. They are:

- ▶ An obligation to pay
- ▶ An obligation to use the software only within the scope of use set forth in the license grant
- ▶ An obligation not to disclose the software or any of the vendor's confidential information

These obligations should be simple and straightforward. Nevertheless, vendors find contractual ways to multiply your company's obligations (giving them expanded opportunities for termination) and to multiply the limitations on your company's use of their software (giving them expanded opportunities for collecting revenue).

A common example of these limitations is the statement that the software must be run at a specific address. If the vendor discovers (usually while providing support) that the company has moved the software to a new location, the vendor can claim that the company has breached the contract and demand a "transfer fee." You might be able to fight this demand and win in court, but you are probably not in business to throw a lot of resources at resolving disputes with software vendors, and there is definitely a point at which simply capitulating to a vendor seems less costly than fighting over a transfer fee. This trade-off becomes particularly vivid when the software has become critical to your operation.

These limitations are pitfalls. They are often easy to miss in reading a software license agreement. They may not be expressed in clear language in a single area of the agreement. Instead, they are often hidden in ambiguities in contract language that *could* have a certain meaning but aren't explicit. These ambiguities must be identified and negotiated away by an IT attorney or other IT contract specialist.

When confronted during negotiations with a contractual ambiguity that looks like a pitfall for the company, the vendor's sales rep or attorney will often act amazed that you could have interpreted their words in that way or state that, "Well, of course, that's not what we were intending." Nevertheless, the burden is on you to find the hidden limitations and seal them up, one by one. Even if the relationship is cozy now, there may be a time down the road when the vendor sees a dwindling income stream from mature software and decides to cash in by getting creative about enforcing its various rights.

The Structure of Software License Agreements

The many contract terms in software licenses can be divided into the following categories:

- ► Setting context
- ► Granting the license
- ► Setting the rules and protocols
- ► Sharing risk
- ► Providing warranties
- ► Providing maintenance and service

The rest of this chapter describes the intent and typical contents of these provisions. Sample language is provided to illustrate how business points play out in contract terms. Although this sample language is not repeated in the chapters that follow, most of it is also found in the other types of contracts described in Part Three.

Setting Context

Recitals or ''Whereas'' Clauses

The recitals appearing at the front of the contract are a good place to record why the deal was done in the first place. The purpose of the recitals in a contract is to briefly describe the deal, the background of the deal, and what is to be found in the contract. The recitals can ease the administrative process because they allow people to quickly review the contract and understand its purpose and effect. Among other benefits, that process makes it more likely that the contract will wind up in the right file and that it will be reviewed when it ought to be reviewed.

Also, while not considered to be within the contract proper, recitals aid courts in interpreting the intent of the parties in entering into the transaction. Recitals can, as in the example below, be a way of establishing that, in choosing the vendor, the company relied upon the vendor's representations concerning its expertise. This can be particularly important if those representations were made during a formal RFP process.

Sample Provision

WHEREAS, Company is seeking to select and install a solution to automate its payroll process, Company submitted to Vendor a formal Request for Proposal ("RFP") setting forth in detail Company's requirements for its solution, including the functionality and performance of the requested solution as well as the various implementation services that Company requested the successful vendor to provide to support Company's desired implementation. The RFP also set forth various terms and conditions upon which each vendor was invited to submit a bid.

WHEREAS, based upon the results of the review and analysis of the RFP, Vendor prepared and delivered to Company a proposal entitled "Vendor's Response to Company Request for Proposal" ("the Vendor Proposal"), setting forth Vendor's responses regarding the appropriate software and service resources required to meet Company's business and technological needs and to effect Company's implementation in an expeditious and orderly manner.

WHEREAS, based on the information contained in the RFP and in the Vendor Proposal, and in reliance upon Vendor's knowledge with regard to Company's environment and unique operating issues and processes and in reliance upon Vendor's expertise in analyzing, designing, and engineering software systems, Vendor and Company agree that Vendor will provide a software solution for Company's environment and install and implement that solution subject to the terms and conditions set forth in this Agreement.

Granting the License

The heart of a software license is the grant of license. The grant of license provides the basic right to use the software as well as the what, how, by whom, for whom, for what, where, until when, and why of the software license.

You want the license grant to give the company unrestricted and flexible rights to use the software in the ways the company *needs* to use the software. A software license that, for example, restricts use to a single computer at a specific location may be perfectly appropriate, or it may be a pitfall that will end up in a costly renegotiation with the vendor in which you will have almost no leverage. It all depends on the company's needs.

Vendors regularly seek to limit use of their software in the following respects:

- ▶ To sites listed in an appendix
- ▶ To a single legal entity
- ▶ To legal entities listed in an appendix
- ▶ To a single enterprise
- ▶ To a specified number of authorized users
- ▶ To a specified number of simultaneous users
- ▶ To a specified number of computers
- ▶ To computers listed in an appendix
- ▶ To a certain group of people whose names are listed in an appendix

Sample Provision

GRANT OF LICENSE

Vendor hereby grants to Company a nonexclusive perpetual license to use the Software and related documentation at any Company location or the location of Company's Facilities Manager without any restrictions with regard to the number of copies or logical or physical regions, or to the number or location of CPUs. [Note: A vendor form might instead read "Vendor hereby grants to Company a nonexclusive, limited, nontransferable, revocable license to use the Software at the location and on the processor specified in Appendix X to process data for Company's XYZ department and for no other purpose.]

In addition to the grant made above, Vendor hereby grants to Company a nonexclusive, perpetual license to use any software programs developed hereunder and any modifications to the Software hereto which are developed and which modifications are made while Company has an active agreement for support for the Software.

TERM

The term of this Agreement shall begin on the Commencement Date and shall remain in force unless terminated pursuant to Section 16, Termination.

USE OF SOFTWARE

The Software shall be used only by Company or its Facilities Manager for Company's internal use only and will not be used in a service bureau environment or otherwise to process data for any third parties.

Company may not copy or otherwise reproduce the Software except (i) as is essential for Company's normal operation of the Software pursuant to the terms of this Agreement, or (ii) for system testing, system backup, maintenance, or recovery purposes.

Company agrees not to reverse-engineer the Software or any part thereof. Company further agrees not to incorporate any portion of the Software into any software it markets.

Source Code

Source code is the human-readable form of software. The source code for most business software is written in programming languages that are mostly made up of English words, and source code normally includes comments, in English, explaining what the source code is intended to do.

Source code is translated into object code using a program called a compiler. Object code is in machine language. Machine language is a series of 1s and 0s that mean quite a lot to a computer, but are difficult (at best) for humans to understand. Generally, the object code is what you run when you run software.

Software is extremely difficult to modify unless you have the source code. Most vendors provide only object code, thus preventing others from modifying the software or seeing how it works. With source code, it is possible not only to maintain the software, but also to develop a competing product. Thus, most vendors consider source code to be their "crown jewel" and avoid providing source code to companies.

In most circumstances, companies don't need source code for the software they license from vendors. They generally can rely on their vendors to modify the software as needed to correct errors and add new functions. However, it may be prudent to protect your company against the risk that a vendor becomes unwilling or unable to modify its software in the manner that your company needs. Also, of course, if your company intends to modify the software, it will need access to the source code.

There are two main ways in which companies obtain access to source code. First, the vendor can grant a license to the source code as a part of the main software license. Generally, vendors charge a substantial amount for a source code license. If you get source code as part of the initial license, you need to make sure that the vendor provides you with an update to that source code whenever it distributes an update to the software. Otherwise, the copy of the source code that you get could rapidly become outdated.

The other common method for providing access to source code is a source code escrow arrangement. Escrow arrangements are intended to protect licensees from having their businesses brought down when a vendor fails. Under a source code escrow arrangement, the vendor deposits the source code with an independent third-party escrow agent. The escrow agent is bound by an agreement that provides that under certain "release conditions," the source code will be provided to the company.

You want the release conditions to include all of the circumstances in which the company would need access to the source code. Common release conditions include the vendor's bankruptcy, insolvency, default, failure to maintain the software, or going out of business.

Every effort should be made to provide for an automatic release of source code upon a release condition, without the need for any sort of hearing or procedure. No matter what the escrow agreement says, even if a release condition has occurred, the vendor is likely to fight hard to prevent release of the source code. The source code is, after all, the vendor's crown jewel. Also, a vendor who can retain control of its source code when you need it may be able to extract a fee, which gives the vendor an incentive to prevent you from getting a copy of the source code.

The escrow arrangement also should give you a way to confirm the sufficiency of the escrow deposits. You want to know whether the vendor is updating the escrow account, instead of ignoring it or sending in blank diskettes. Large source code escrow agents have facilities to do technical verification of deposits, and to confirm that what is in escrow is the most recent release of the software. Also, you should demand that copies of all necessary technical documentation and related software be included with the escrow deposits.

Even with the best escrow arrangement, there is considerable risk. The copy of the software placed in escrow might be missing some sort of software key or password, without which it is of no value. The code may be difficult to maintain (perhaps explaining the vendor's failure to do so). Moreover, even under the best conditions, software is difficult to modify.

Sample Provision

SOURCE CODE

Vendor will maintain and will keep current, in a third-party escrow account with a reliable independent escrow agent, source code in machine-readable form for all the Software and all enhancements and revisions thereto ("Software Source Material"). The Software Source Material shall include all user and technical documentation, and all related software, required for a programmer of reasonable skill to modify the Software.

If Vendor: (i) dissolves; (ii) ceases to do business in the normal course; (iii) makes an assignment for the benefit of creditors; (iv) discontinues maintenance for any portion of the Software while Company has an active maintenance contract with Vendor; (v) becomes a party, voluntarily or involuntarily, to any proceeding under the Bankruptcy Code (except under Chapter 11 of Title 11) that is not dismissed within 60 days after the filing; or (vi) ceases to make payment for the maintenance of such third-party escrow account while any license between Company and Vendor remains in force such that the account is terminated by the third-party escrow agent, Vendor will, on Company's written demand, transfer the Software Source Material to Company to be used by Company only for the purpose of enabling Company to continue to use and support the Software without interruption and in accordance with this Agreement. Should Company take possession of the Software Source Material, Company's rights and obligations with respect to such Software Source Material shall be governed by the terms of this Agreement.

In connection with the execution of that escrow contract, Vendor also agrees to furnish Company with reasonable expedition:

a) A list describing all software components owned by Vendor to be used in operating the Software; and

b) A list identifying all software components not owned by Vendor that must be used in order to operate the Software, which list shall show the exact name, release designation, manufacturer, manufacturer's phone number and address, and purpose of the component; and

c) A list identifying all software and software modules that are required to develop, test, compile, and install the Software, which list shall show the exact name, release designation, manufacturer, manufacturer's phone number and address, and purpose of the component.

Setting Rules and Protocols

Terms setting rules and protocols make up the bulk of almost any software license contract other than a simple shrink-wrap license. While most of these terms are rarely controversial during negotiations, others are at the very core of the license arrangement and deserve attention. A selection of the important terms is presented here.

Introduction

The introduction identifies the contract by name and date and names the parties. This information is later used to identify the contract and who is bound by it.

Sample Provision

INTRODUCTION

SOFTWARE LICENSE AGREEMENT

THIS SOFTWARE LICENSE AGREEMENT is made as of [DATE] by and between THEIR CORPORATION ("Vendor"), a California corporation having an address at 123 Kangaroo Ct., PinkTofu, California 99999 and YOUR CORPORATION ("Company"), a Delaware corporation having an address at Company Plaza, Big Onion, Illinois 60606.

Definitions

The definitions section sets forth the meaning that a given set of words and terminology will have throughout the agreement. A definitions section may not be necessary for short agreements. However, as agreements become more complex or involve long negotiations, it is helpful to consolidate all of the defined terms at the beginning and to take more care in defining them. It is often the case that during negotiations, it will be necessary to create new terminology to capture the intent of the parties. Definitions also make agreements easier to administer. The following are some of the most important ideas to define.

Company

Define your company or the group of companies that will need to use the software. Define your company or enterprise as broadly as possible to provide flexibility for the future. If your company is one of a number of companies whose operations are consolidated under a holding company, name the holding company and include all subsidiaries. If the software will be used by one department of a company, avoid contracting in the name of the department unless the financial advantage of such a limitation is significant and you are sure the department will remain intact, with the same name.

Software

Define the software you are receiving under the license. Be sure to define it to include upgrades, updates, and revisions that are made available by the vendor from time to time.

Documentation

Define the user and technical specifications for the software. Attach them to the contract with a representation that the software conforms to them. Provide that specifications for any updates will be substituted from time to time.

Acceptance Criteria

Define the conditions under which you will accept the software and make payment to the vendor. At a minimum, these should include the Specifications. Ideally, they simply refer to the company's needs, as determined by the company in its sole discretion. A smart middle ground is defining detailed acceptance tests and the required results of running the software using the acceptance tests.

Facilities Manager

If the company has outsourced, or may outsource in the future, you need to provide language in the contract that makes it abundantly clear that the vendor's software may be operated by a third party, potentially on equipment controlled by that third party. For this definition, state that the Facilities Manager is a third party bound (or about to be bound) under a formal agreement to you who will operate the vendor's software pursuant to the terms of the license contract only on your behalf.

Site

Define the sites at which the software may be used. Ideally, you should be able to use the software at any site owned or controlled (including leased) by the company. Try to avoid agreeing to provide continuously updated lists of all install locations unless you can administer that requirement.

Acceptance

Acceptance provisions can be among the most valuable license provisions for the company. Acceptance is the point at which the company becomes obligated to take the software and pay the license fee. The more control the company has over acceptance, the less likely the company is to wind up with software that doesn't work in the company's technical environment.

The essence of an acceptance provision is that the software must be installed and must operate successfully in accordance with some set of criteria before you accept the software and pay for it. The best acceptance provision from the company's standpoint is one that allows the company not to accept the software for any reason. Most provisions, however, base a company's acceptance upon a more objective set of standards, such as whether the software conforms in all material respects to the user documentation or to a special acceptance test developed and agreed upon by both parties to simulate the software's actual use. An acceptance provision is meaningful only if you either hold money until the software is accepted or can get a full refund if the software doesn't pass the test. Because the criteria for acceptance are various, there are a number of ways in which acceptance periods can be drafted.

Sample Provision

ACCEPTANCE

The Software shall be deemed to be accepted by Company as of the 60th calendar day after installation unless Company notifies Vendor otherwise in writing that the Software fails to conform to any of the Acceptance Criteria. Any notification from the Company shall specify with reasonable particularity the areas in which the Software failed to conform with the Acceptance Criteria. If the Software is not accepted within said 60-day acceptance period, the acceptance period shall be extended an additional 30 days from the date of Company's notice to Vendor of its non-acceptance. If the Software is not accepted by Company by the last day of such extension, Company shall return the Software to the Vendor pursuant to the procedure specified in Section 16, Termination, and Company shall have no further obligation to pay any money due under this Agreement, and Vendor will then promptly return any money paid by Company. Company will not unreasonably delay or withhold any of the acceptance and notifications required in this Section.

Confidentiality

Another provision near the heart of a license agreement is the confidentiality provision. While there is often nothing controversial about confidentiality provisions, there are a few issues to consider.

First, if your organization employs consultants, you will need to expressly provide in any license you negotiate that your independent contractors (nonemployees) may have access to the vendor's confidential information. You may have to add that you will take reasonable steps to see that your independent consultants comply with the confidentiality provisions set forth in the contract or that you will bind any independent consultants in writing to hold all your information and the information of your vendors in confidence. Resist having to get consent from the vendor every time you may want to provide access to contractors. That creates an additional administrative burden. Note, also, that if you have outsourced your operations, or may do so in the future, you'll want to provide for access by your facilities managers to the vendor's confidential information.

Second, you want to avoid making the terms of the contract itself confidential. The vendor's concern here is that, if the terms of your deal are known, other companies may demand the same deal. However, agreeing to keep a contract confidential creates another administrative burden on the company by limiting its ability to review and administer the contract. You should agree to keep a contract confidential only if the vendor has given you substantial price concessions, and thus has something meaningful to protect.

Third, you want to avoid allowing vendors to "deputize" you by adding a term to the confidentiality provisions that states that you must notify them if you become aware of anyone else breaching the confidentiality of their software. This could obligate you to turn in anyone that you think might be out of compliance. Aside from the legal exposure that might result if you wrongly accuse a person or company, you should resist this provision because it's another way in which you can breach the contract and thus it gives the vendor another opportunity to terminate the license.

Sample Provision

CONFIDENTIALITY

The term "Vendor's Confidential Information," as used herein, shall mean the Software and all the documentation relating thereto, and any other nonpublic Vendor information clearly labeled by Vendor as confidential.

The term "Company's Confidential Information," as used herein, shall mean all nonpublic Company information, including but not limited to information of a business nature such as Company's business plans, policies and practices, computer software programs and associated documentation and material that are

proprietary to Company or to which Company is under an obligation to prevent disclosure, software and documentation that Company has licensed that Vendor comes to know during the
performance of its duties under this Agreement, as well as any
information clearly labeled by Company as confidential that Vendor or its employees come into possession of during the performance of its duties under this Agreement.

Each party agrees that it will use the same standard of care
(and bind its employees, consultants, and facilities managers to
such standard) to prevent disclosure of the other's Confidential
Information to third parties (other than Company's consultants,
independent contractors, and facilities managers), as it uses to
protect its own confidential information and trade secrets. Each
party further agrees that it will use reasonable precautions to see
to it that such employees and consultants observe the covenants
of this Agreement.

Company shall have the restricted right to disclose Confidential Information to Company's third-party consultants or facilities managers. Prior to Company disclosing or making available
any Confidential Information to any such third-party consultant,
Company agrees to bind such third-party consultants to confidentiality in writing with respect to such disclosures.

Termination

Termination by Vendor

Make sure that a vendor cannot lightly terminate your software
license. If the vendor will have the right to terminate the license upon
a breach of the contract, make sure that this right is limited to a
breach of one of the *material* terms of the contract and that you have
a period of time in which to cure the breach or to demonstrate that
you are making a reasonable effort to do so. Ideally, the vendor
should never be able to terminate as long as you are making a diligent
effort to cure the breach. As stated before, you as licensee should
have three material obligations: to pay, to use the software within the
bounds of the license grant, and to keep the vendor's information
confidential.

Termination by Company

Unlike companies, vendors have many obligations in a software
license. The vendor's fulfillment of these obligations can be critical to
you. For example, the vendor can be obligated to deliver software by
a certain date, to guarantee that the software will operate according

to specifications, and to support the software and quickly restore function in the event of an error. In negotiating the agreement, when you are determining the vendor's critical obligations, remember that you want to hook your right to terminate to the vendor's breach of any of those provisions.

Because companies grow to rely on software, terminating a software license is rarely something a company wants to do. Vendors know that. In order for there to be any credible threat to a vendor flowing from your right to terminate, you want the right:

- ▶ To stop a contractually stipulated flow of payments to the vendor
- ▶ To require the vendor to refund money
- ▶ To obtain liquidated damages

Sample Provision

TERMINATION

If either party breaches a material term of this Agreement, and does not cure such breach within 30 days after receipt of notice of such breach from the nonbreaching party, or if such breach cannot be cured with due diligence within such 30-day period, then, following an additional 30-day period granted upon written request from the breaching party to the nonbreaching party (which request shall not be unreasonably withheld), then the nonbreaching party may terminate this Agreement by providing the breaching party 30 days' notice of its intention to terminate.

Upon termination of this Agreement as set forth in this Section, Company shall immediately stop all use of the Software and immediately either return or destroy the Software and documentation and certify its destruction to Vendor in writing.

Upon termination of this Agreement by Company for Vendor's breach, Vendor shall return all payments made by Company hereunder for the license of the Software.

Payment

While it may seem like a mundane detail, payment is one of the primary obligations of the company and therefore deserves some attention. Payment provisions should meet four minimum standards:

1. They should be easy to administer.
2. They should provide a protocol for correction of billing errors while maintaining the vendor/company relationship.

3. They should correspond with the timing of the flow of value to the company (e.g., if you are taking delivery of a few copies of the software now but will only be ramping up use for a full rollout twelve months from now, then the payment stream should reflect that pattern).
4. They should create incentives for the vendor to perform (e.g., payments should be contingent upon the vendor's delivery of a module or your acceptance of software).

Sample Provision

PAYMENT

All payments hereunder shall be made in U.S. dollars.

An Initial Payment of 30% of the Total License Fee shall be made by Company to Vendor after execution of this Agreement within thirty (30) days after receipt of an invoice.

A Second Progress Payment of 30% of the Total License Fee shall be made upon delivery of the Software to Company within thirty (30) days after receipt of an invoice.

The Third Progress Payment of 40% of the Total License Fee shall be made upon Company's Acceptance of the Software as defined in Section X, "Acceptance" within thirty (30) days after receipt of an invoice.

All other payments required hereunder shall be made by Company to Vendor within thirty (30) days after receipt of an invoice.

Vendor may change the charges for the Maintenance Plan hereunder after the Initial Contract Period, provided that, in no event will any increase in such charges hereunder exceed by more than 5% the annual Maintenance Plan charge for the immediately preceding annual period.

Company shall pay all nondisputed amounts as they become due in accordance with the time frames set forth above. In the event Company disputes any amount on any Vendor invoice, Company and Vendor agree to use reasonable efforts to resolve such disputes as soon as possible within 90 days after Company provides written notification to Vendor. Vendor agrees to provide full supporting documentation concerning any disputed amount or invoice to Company within 30 days after Company provides written notification of the dispute to Vendor. Provided that Company furnishes written notification of the dispute to Vendor within 30 days after Company receives the disputed invoice, Company shall have no obligation, during the 90-day period specified above, to pay any amount that Company reasonably disputes hereunder.

Except for disputed amounts, as defined above, in the event that any sum due to Vendor from Company is not paid in full within 30 days after Company receives written notice that such payment is past due, at Vendor's sole discretion, Vendor may assess a penalty for the period the amount remains unpaid after the expiration of the 30-day period on the unpaid portion thereof in an amount equal to 1.5% each month the overdue amount remains unpaid.

If any services under this Agreement are to be performed at a location other than Vendor's place of business, then Company will reimburse Vendor for its travel-related expenses according to the standard Company Travel Expense Policy, a copy of which is attached hereto as Appendix Q.

Most Favored Nation

A most favored nation (or most favored company) provision states that the vendor will treat your company as well as the vendor treats anyone else in terms of the price and contractual provisions. The contractual "teeth" in a most favored nation provision will provide that in the event that the vendor offers more favorable terms to another company, those terms will also be offered to your company. Vendors are reluctant to offer these provisions and will take pains to explain that each deal they do is idiosyncratic and so cannot be compared with other deals.

What most often winds up happening is that the most favored nation clause becomes qualified with words to the effect that the vendor will not offer a better deal to companies that are like yours. The more qualified the clause becomes, the less value it has. For example, vendors often seek to have the most favored nation clause apply only to deals with companies that are similarly situated with respect to use of the software, volume, size, complexity, location, types of data, type of industry and type of equipment. (Are there any?)

As a practical matter, most favored nation provisions are among the most difficult provisions to draft and negotiate to produce a meaningful result. Vendors view them as a challenge to their sovereign right to make whatever deals they need to make in circumstances neither they nor you can anticipate. Vendors also state that they would be unable to administer such a provision because they have no tracking system in place that would allow them to do this. (Why would they?) Nevertheless, it's important that you at least try to get the vendor to commit itself to treating you fairly in the future, if only to force a dialog concerning where the company stands with the vendor. Often, that dialog can bring some reality to participants who have been swept away by a vendor's "trust me" patter.

Sample Provision

MOST FAVORED NATION

Vendor hereby represents to Company that the prices set forth in this Agreement for software, maintenance, and other services are no higher than the prices Vendor has charged or is currently charging any other companies that are comparable in size and in the character and complexity of their technical environment to Company for the same software, maintenance, and other services.

In no event will Company be charged for future software, maintenance, or other services at a rate higher than any future Vendor company of comparable size, and of comparable character and complexity of its technical environment.

Vendor agrees that it will provide the same level of service and enhancement development to Company as is provided for the same price to any other company or organization that has or in the future will have a material ownership or controlling interest in Vendor. Vendor further agrees that it will continue to provide such performance for the Software for as long as Vendor provides such performance for the Software to any other company. It is the express intent of the parties that Vendor shall not disadvantage Company by changes in the level of service, enhancement development, or design of the Software.

Assignment; Binding Effect

There are two sides to the assignment provision. Most software licenses, nevertheless, routinely permit the vendor to assign the license and forbid the company to assign it. As you are probably aware, there has been, and will continue to be, a lot of merger and acquisition activity in the software industry, and, naturally, software vendors want their contracts to be transferable to their new owners.

Sample Provision

BINDING EFFECT

This Agreement shall be binding upon and shall inure to the benefit of the parties and their respective heirs, successors, assigns, and legal and personal representatives.

Vendors fairly argue that you should not have the right to transfer the license to a third party. If you could transfer your license freely, you might transfer your license to a company that, under the vendor's value pricing scheme, should pay much more for it.

However, companies need the right to assign in the event that they are acquired by a new owner or wish to sell off a line of business and have the license for the software that supports that line of business travel with the sold line of business. Signing an agreement that prohibits your assignment of the contract could significantly constrain your ability to implement strategy for your organization.

Sample Provision

ASSIGNMENT

This Agreement, and all rights and obligations of Vendor hereunder, may be assigned, pledged, transferred, or otherwise disposed of, by Vendor either in whole or in part, with written notice to Company. No such assignment will affect any of Company's rights under this Agreement.

Company may assign this Agreement to any successor in the United States or in Canada; provided that Company gives written notice to Vendor within 30 days following such an assignment.

It should be noted under this topic that under most outsourcing arrangements, you will not be asked to assign your software agreements to the facilities manager. The more usual arrangement is to simply obtain a consent from the vendor for the facilities manager to run the software and to "suspend" maintenance until the outsourcing relationship ends.

Entire Agreement

The entire agreement provision states that whatever promises the vendor might have made to you during the sales cycle (even written promises) are not part of the deal unless they are included in the contract.

Sample Provision

ENTIRE AGREEMENT

This Agreement represents the entire agreement between the parties with respect to the subject matter hereof, and supersedes any and all prior or contemporaneous understandings, representation, proposals, contracts, and agreements. This Agreement may be amended only by a written instrument expressly amending this Agreement and executed by the parties hereto.

The entire agreement clause means that software buyers need to get all representations about the software's performance in writing and then to attach those representations to the agreement. This should be the company's approach throughout the negotiations.

Sample Provision

INCORPORATION OF RFP AND PROPOSAL

Company's RFP Letter and the Vendor Proposal and additional correspondence, clarifications, and materials as attached are attached as Appendix A to this Agreement and are specifically incorporated by reference into this Agreement. In the event of a conflict between the terms and conditions of this Agreement and the terms of any of the material in Appendix A, the terms of this Agreement will control.

Use of Name

Vendors often want to use your company's name as a reference in their marketing. If your name is prestigious, or associated with wise decisions, vendors will be particularly interested in using it.

Whatever your position is with respect to the use of your company's name and the issue of implied endorsements, you should not automatically grant this right to vendors without getting some benefit from it in the negotiation. The vendor is asking to trade on your company's good name. Your company has probably invested a great deal of its resources building up the goodwill associated with its name.

If you give a vendor the right to use the company's name in its marketing, the use should be subject to provisions that protect the company's trademark rights and do not permit the vendor to imply any affiliation, sponsorship, or endorsement by the company of the vendor or the software.

Sample Provision

USE OF NAME

Vendor shall not use any of Company's names, marks, or logos in any of its advertising or promotional literature.

Quiet Enjoyment

Quiet enjoyment provisions state that as long as your company is using the software as permitted by the license grant, and is not otherwise in material default, the vendor will not disrupt your operations. This provision has become more important, as vendors are now attempting to negotiate more restrictive licenses, demanding the right to audit your company for compliance more frequently, and embedding devices in software that the vendor can remotely trigger to hamper the software's operation in order to gain leverage in disputes or negotiations.

Sample Provision

QUIET ENJOYMENT

Vendor shall not disturb the Company's quiet and peaceful possession of the software and the unrestricted use thereof for its intended purpose by Company according to the license granted hereunder. Vendor shall not at any time activate any time bombs or any other devices designed to disable or prevent operation of the Software.

Sharing Risk

For a vendor, the ideal license agreement is one in which the vendor agrees to deliver its software to the company, and the company accepts the software "as is," with no recourse if it doesn't operate, let alone if it doesn't meet any particular business needs. That, while seeming extreme, is not that far from the basic risk position that you will find embodied in most vendors' form license agreements. One of the most difficult jobs in negotiating a license agreement, therefore, is to introduce the spirit and the words that reflect a fairer approach to sharing risk.

Because you as the software licensee will be integrating software into your operations with the consequence that your operations could either succeed if the software works or fail if the software becomes inoperable, you will always be taking a greater risk than the vendor. There are, however, several risk areas for which it has become standard in the industry for software vendors to provide you with a measure of protection.

Infringement Indemnification

If the vendor's software is found to infringe upon the proprietary rights of some third party, you could be named in an infringement suit simply by virtue of your having used the software. Because you have absolutely no control over whether a vendor's software infringes on a copyright, patent, or other proprietary right of a third party (unless the vendor developed the software from your specifications), you should take none of the associated risk.

Sample Provision

INFRINGEMENT INDEMNIFICATION

Vendor warrants that it is the sole owner of the Software, or that it holds contractual marketing rights to said Software, and has full power and authority to grant the rights granted in this Agreement without the consent of any other party. Vendor warrants that the software hereby furnished or to be furnished does not infringe upon or violate any patent, copyright, trade secret, or any other proprietary right of any third party. In the event of any claim by any third party against Company, Company shall promptly notify Vendor and Vendor shall defend such claim, in Company's name, but at Vendor's expense and shall indemnify Company against any loss, cost, expense, or liability arising out of such claim, whether or not such claim is successful. If Company is prevented from using the software as the result of such claim, Vendor will either a) return to Company, prorated on a five-year straight line basis, all amounts paid hereunder by Company; or b) at no additional cost to Company obtain usage rights for Company; or c) at no additional cost to Company modify the Software(s) so as to cure the infringement or violation.

Indemnification and Insurance

If the vendor is going to come to your site to install the software, test the software, train your personnel, or perform maintenance on the software, you should probably require a basic indemnification from the vendor with respect to any bodily injury, death, or property damage that may arise out of the performance of these services. In addition, you should require the vendor to hold prudent levels of insurance in order to avoid a situation in which you have to go after the vendor's assets in order to collect on a loss. While a sample indemnification is included, the levels of insurance you may want to require should be determined by your risk manager.

Sample Provision

INDEMNIFICATION AND INSURANCE

Without limitation as to amount, anything to the contrary in this Agreement notwithstanding, Vendor hereby fully indemnifies Company, assumes the defense of, and saves and holds Company harmless from any and all liability, claims, demands, damages, and costs of every kind and nature for injury to or death of any and all persons, including without limitation, employees or representatives of Vendor and for damage, destruction, or loss to or of any and all property, real and personal, including, without limitation, property of Company or of any person or persons (but excluding software and databases), arising out of the Vendor's performance of its services under this Agreement.

Requirements—Vendor agrees to keep in full force and effect and maintain at its sole cost and expense the following policies of insurance during the term of this Agreement:

(a) Workers' Compensation and Employer's Liability Insurance:

—Statutory Workers' Compensation including occupational disease in accordance with the law.

—Employer's Liability insurance with minimum limits of $500,000 per employee by accident/$500,000 per employee by disease/$500,000 policy limit by disease.

(b) Commercial General Liability insurance covering services performed under this Agreement providing limits of not less than:

—Bodily Injury and Property Damage Liability: $1,000,000 per occurrence.

—Personal Injury and Advertising Injury Liability: $1,000,000 per person or per organization.

—Medical Payments: $5,000 per person.

—General Policy Aggregate: $1,000,000.

—Software/Completed Operations Aggregate: $1,000,000.

(c) Commercial Business Automobile Liability insurance including coverage for all owned, nonowned, and hired vehicles providing coverage for bodily injury and property damage liability with combined single limits of not less than $1,000,000.

(d) Professional Liability insurance covering acts, errors, and omissions arising out of Vendor's operations or services in a limit of not less than $1,000,000 per occurrence/$1,000,000 aggregate.

Approved Companies—All such insurance shall be procured with such insurance companies and in such form as shall be acceptable to Company. Such insurance companies shall maintain a rating greater than B^{++} and be at least a Financial Size Category

VII as both criteria are defined in the most current publication of Best's Policyholder Guide.

Endorsements—Vendor's liability policy as required herein shall be endorsed to name Company and all of its subsidiaries, affiliates, officers, directors, agents, servants, and employees as Additional Insureds for any and all liability arising at any time in connection with Vendor's performance under this Agreement. Such insurance afforded to Company shall be primary insurance and any other valid insurance existing for Company's benefit shall be in excess of such primary insurance. Vendor shall obtain such endorsements to its policy or policies of insurance as are necessary to cause the policy or policies to comply with the requirements stated herein.

Certificates—Vendor must provide Company with certificates of insurance signed by authorized representatives of the respective carriers for each year that this Agreement is in effect. Upon request, Company may inspect Vendor's original insurance policies. Each certificate of insurance shall include a statement that the issuing company shall not cancel, nonrenew, reduce, or otherwise change the insurance afforded under the above policies unless 30 days' notice of such cancellation, nonrenewal, reduction, or change has been provided to the Company.

Limitation of Liability

Vendors naturally try to limit their liability. For infringement, bodily injury, death, and property damages, there should be no limit on the vendor's liability. To cover other types of risks, it is common for vendors to exclude consequential damages (most commonly, lost profits resulting from an inoperable system) and retain only liability for direct damages. For other possible types of loss, you need to determine, based on the risks that you, your attorney, and your negotiating team can envision, what the minimum acceptable limit is for those exposures. If the software is run on a stand-alone PC and doesn't interface with any of your other systems, and if the vendor will never set foot on your site, as long as there is no limit on infringement indemnification, you can probably accept the vendor's commonly proposed limit of the cost of the software. Very often, however, the cost of the software bears no relation to the exposures you suffer by installing and implementing software. In the below provision an absolute dollar limit was put on other types of vendor liabilities.

Sample Provision

LIMITATION OF LIABILITY

IN NO EVENT SHALL EITHER PARTY BE LIABLE FOR LOST PROFITS OR ANY OTHER INCIDENTAL, CONSEQUENTIAL, OR EXEMPLARY DAMAGES, NOR

SHALL VENDOR BE LIABLE FOR ANY OPERATING DIFFICULTIES RESULT-
ING FROM (i) ANY MODIFICATION TO THE PROGRAM PRODUCT MADE
BY ANYONE OTHER THAN VENDOR, (ii) ANY ERRONEOUS, IMPROPER, OR
INCOMPLETE DATA IN DATA FILES OR ANY INPUT STREAM, (iii) ANY
HARDWARE, FIRMWARE, OR OPERATING SYSTEM MALFUNCTIONS, OR (iv)
ANY MODIFICATION TO THE ORIGINALLY INSTALLED OPERATING SYS-
TEMS OR TO THE ORIGINAL CONFIGURATION OF THE COMPUTER. EACH
PARTY'S LIABILITY TO THE OTHER UNDER THIS AGREEMENT SHALL IN
NO EVENT BE GREATER THAN $1,000,000. EXCEPT IN THE CASE OF (i) NEG-
LIGENCE, WILLFUL MISCONDUCT, OR STRICT LIABILITY; (ii) LIABILITY OF
VENDOR UNDER WITH RESPECT TO INFRINGEMENT, BODILY INJURY, OR
DAMAGE TO TANGIBLE PERSONAL PROPERTY; OR (iii) LIABILITY OF COM-
PANY FOR THE LICENSE FEE.

Warranties

The warranty, obligation, and responsibility provisions state what
the vendor and the company will do under the agreement. Vendor
warranties under a license agreement can be very significant, particularly if the software is mission critical to you, and there have been
complex negotiations during which the vendor has made many representations about the software's performance, about the way the
vendor will support the software, about the resources the vendor will
commit to developing the software in the future, and so forth.

Sample Provision

WARRANTIES

Vendor warrants that it is the sole owner of the Software hereby
furnished or to be furnished, or that it holds contractual marketing
rights to said Software, and has the full power and authority to
grant the rights herein granted without the consent of any other
party.

 Vendor warrants that, beginning with the first complete delivery of the Software, the Software will perform according to any
applicable Vendor-published specifications for a period of one (1)
year. During this period, if Vendor is unable to correct any devia-
tion from the above specifications within 10 days after written notification from Company, Company shall return the specific
uncorrectable Software to Vendor and Company shall have no further obligation for payment of any money otherwise due under
this Agreement. Vendor will then promptly return any money
paid by Company for that Software it is unable to make operate
as specified in the Vendor-published specifications.

The time service standards for such warranty work will conform to "The Vendor Support Services Escalation Procedures" attached hereto and made a part hereof as Appendix L.

During the Warranty Period, Vendor will make all new releases of the Software available to Company at no charge.

Vendor warrants that the Software will be, at installation, and remain, for a period of five (5) years after implementation, provided Company is currently enrolled in the Maintenance Plan hereunder, compatible with Company's environment as that environment is defined in "Company Operating Environment" attached hereto and made a part hereof as Appendix M. Company may notify Vendor of a change in its operating environment by publishing to Vendor a new Appendix N and making a formal request to restore compatibility with Company's operating environment and Vendor will use diligent efforts to restore compatibility with Company's operating environment if it is commercially reasonable for Vendor to do so, at Vendor's sole discretion. "Diligent Efforts" as used in this Section shall mean the expeditious and persistent application of effort and resources by Vendor to promptly act upon such notification to restore compatibility of the Software with Company's operating environment.

Vendor warrants that maintenance will be available for the Software for a period of five (5) years.

Vendor warrants that it will provide adequate staffing levels to support ongoing support and service.

Vendor warrants that all services will be performed in a professional and workmanlike manner.

Vendor warrants that the Software correctly processes and will not produce incorrect results in processing dates after December 31, 1999.

Vendor warrants and represents that it will use its best efforts to ensure that any data or programs provided by Vendor to Company shall be free, at the time of shipment, of any computer Virus. In the event that the Software is contaminated by Virus, Vendor will immediately replace the Software so contaminated.

Vendor warrants that, other than as may be explicitly provided for in this Agreement, Vendor will not imbed in the Software any device or capability to disrupt or terminate its operation, or take any action to invoke such device or capability.

OTHER THAN THE WARRANTIES EXPRESSLY MADE IN THIS AGREEMENT, VENDOR DISCLAIMS ALL WARRANTIES, INCLUDING, BUT NOT LIMITED TO, ANY IMPLIED WARRANTIES OF MERCHANTABILITY OR FITNESS FOR A PARTICULAR PURPOSE.

The vendor may take the position that the company has various responsibilities to fulfill in order to make the software a success. Be careful about accepting these responsibilities, since they tend to dilute the vendor's warranties. One common example of a responsibility the company may be given that affects the warranty and many of the company's other rights under the agreement is the responsibility to install the current version of the vendor's software. Many large companies with hundreds of installed software packages have difficulty in tracking all of the new software updates that a vendor releases, and so this could pose a very real risk to you. A recommendation for this particular responsibility is to relax the requirement and provide six to eighteen months to install any new release.

Another example of how the company's responsibilities might affect warranties is the case of software under development. If there are milestones and deliverables for the vendor, the vendor will want to add language to the agreement stating that if you cause a delay in the delivery of the software, the vendor will have no liability. At most, these exceptions should apply to the extent to which the company's failure directly causes the vendor's failure.

Providing Maintenance and Service

Normally, software licenses include provisions for maintenance of the software. At a minimum, you should get commitments from the vendor to provide phone support and bug fixes, as well as a commitment to distribute new releases when they are generally made available.

You'll want to carefully define "bugs" as, perhaps, failures to conform to the specifications or to published documentation. Vendors have been known to refuse to fix "bugs" on the basis that they are merely undocumented features. One vendor went so far as to ask for an additional license fee for "undocumented features" that were causing a company significant downtime.

If the availability and operability of the software is important to your enterprise, you may want to set forth detailed time service standards for response to or resolution of reported problems based upon defined severity levels. Many vendors actually have internal policies for how quickly they escalate and attempt to resolve problems, and often vendors are not averse to simply attaching these policies as an exhibit to the agreement. Naturally, you'll want to make sure that the policy meets your requirements. Some vendors will offer "premium" support for a higher fee.

Sample Provision

MAINTENANCE PLAN

Vendor will maintain the Software to operate in Company's environment, supply technical bulletins and updated user guides from time to time, supply Company with any bug fixes, improvements, modifications, or enhancements to the Software, and operate a Telephone Support Service, which is made available hereunder pursuant to the terms of the Vendor Support Services Escalation Procedures attached hereto and made a part hereof as Appendix M. Bug fixes, improvements, modifications, or enhancements to the Software will be supplied as printed listings or as tapes, as Vendor deems appropriate.

In addition to the above, Vendor will provide reasonable general technical assistance on use and application of Software. Vendor senior staff will be reasonably available by telephone to consult with users on how Software can best be used for new applications and in new areas to meet Company's needs in the most effective possible way. Maintenance will be provided only to those portions of the Software or their replacements that incorporate all program corrections and enhancements delivered to Company. No maintenance shall be provided if any physical form or part of the Software shall have been abused, misused, or modified other than by Vendor, by or on behalf of Company. If any error, bug, or defect in the Software shall be due to Company modification, error, or negligence, Company shall reimburse Vendor for the services provided by Vendor to determine and/or correct such error, bug, or defect at the then-current Vendor service rate, and for the reasonable expenses incident to such services. Should Company omit payment of the annual maintenance fee, maintenance can be reinstated by payment of all previous annual fees.

Vendor will provide training and installation services as required by Company. For a minimum period of three (3) years after execution of this Agreement, Vendor will make additional training available as requested by Company. The services mentioned in this paragraph will be performed by trained personnel at a mutually agreeable site. Phone support of the installation of the Software will be provided at no additional charge to Company.

Conclusion

A software license is a complex agreement that, because title never passes to the company, involves the company in an ongoing relationship with the software vendor. Because of the ongoing nature of the contractual relationship, software licenses should be negotiated carefully. The above guidelines and sample language should help you successfully navigate through the negotiating process and successfully negotiate a software license.

13

Consulting

Companies hire consultants to do work that cannot be done by employees, or because they see an advantage in having the work done by people who are not employees. Information technology creates special needs for consultants. This chapter discusses the consulting relationship generally, and also addresses the special issues that make hiring IT consultants both difficult and necessary.

The Benefits to the Company

A consultant is an independent contractor hired to do something specific. The thing to be accomplished may be a one-time task, such as a specific programming project. It may be a type of service, such as installation. It may be a defined deliverable, such as a research report or feasibility study. Whatever the specific task is, it defines the relationship. When the task has been accomplished, the consultant's role ends. Defining this task up front is the way to maximize this benefit.

When the definition is done well, the company knows what it is paying for. Unlike an employee, whose job description defines broad duties and responsibilities, the consultant has something specific to do and knows that all her efforts are to be applied to that single end.

When special skills are needed for a single task, it is probably easier for a company to find a consultant who has these skills than to hire or assign a full-time employee. Single tasks should never last forever. Employees are usually hired permanently. Hiring a permanent employee to accomplish a time-limited task is a mismatch. Hiring a consultant to do such a task gives the company the flexibility to seek a person with the single set of skills needed to accomplish the task. It also allows the company to stop paying for those skills when they are no longer needed.

Not only does the company avoid paying for a permanent solution to a temporary problem, but it also avoids unnecessary employment costs while the problem is being solved. Because consultants are independent contractors, they are ineligible for health benefits, retirement plans, and other employee fringe benefits. With consultants, there is no employer contribution for Social Security, or for unemployment taxes or workers' compensation. These usual costs of hiring an employee are avoided.

Locking In the Benefits of Consulting

None of the benefits discussed in this chapter will accrue unless the consultant and the company agree on the terms of the arrangement in advance. The consulting agreement must clearly delineate the work to be done and the price to be paid for that work. If it is to be an instrument of a successful relationship, it must also treat other important issues.

Defining the Work Product

The primary advantage of using consultants is their dedication to a specific accomplishment. Therefore, defining what is to be accomplished is vital to the success of the association.

The accomplishment, or work product, must be spelled out in the consulting agreement in complete, detailed, unambiguous specifications. Nothing should be assumed. Nothing should be left out because it seems to be understood.

If the consulting project includes interim deliverables, they should be spelled out in as complete, detailed, and unambiguous a manner as the overall project. These interim deliverables, which may include weekly status reports, time sheets, project plans, or flow charts, are the company's best means of monitoring the consultant's work. Additional milestones might include company approval of the result of one phase of the project before continuing to the next phase.

Having a Plan

While not every plan needs a consultant, every consultant needs a plan. If the need for a consultant is so vague that no plan or justification can plausibly be written for it, something is wrong. Even when consultants are hired to fill a gap in a company's normal IT operations because of extraordinary demand in a certain area, there still needs to be a plan explaining the need and justifying the choice of consultants to fill it.

The plan should also spell out applicable testing procedures (if any), such as test databases to be used, boundary conditions to be tested, and results to be obtained to verify accuracy, freedom from errors, and efficiency before the consultant's deliverable is accepted.

The Benefit of Predictable Costs

One of the most important benefits of using consultants is being able to predict and monitor project costs accurately. When a project is to be carried out using company employees, it is very difficult to determine the portion of their salaries and benefits that should be allocated to the project. They will probably be doing other things while they are working on the project. The proportion of their time that they spend on the project will not remain constant. Because company employees have skills that match position descriptions and not project descriptions, they may not perform the project work as efficiently as they do their regular jobs. All these factors make estimating project personnel costs difficult.

With consultants, costs are estimated and agreed to ahead of time. Because the consultant's role is defined in terms of a specific task or project, there can be no question of apportioning costs. Because the consultant's fee is defined in the consulting agreement, the project can be planned with greater accuracy.

To make sure this benefit is achieved, the company should structure the consultant's compensation in a way that admits of no ambiguity. If the compensation is unclear, the agreement is risky.

There are two smart ways to pay for consultants. One smart way is to have a fixed price for accomplishing fixed objectives by fixed dates. If the consultant doesn't achieve the objectives, the consultant doesn't get paid. The other smart way is to pay the consultant on a time-and-materials basis, but to monitor progress closely and have the right to stop the consultant, or change the consultant's objectives, quickly.

Consultants often argue for mixed versions. For example, consultants would like to be paid their time-and-materials rates for achieving fixed objectives. The more time they spend, the richer they get. The company winds up paying too much. Other vendors want a fixed price for undefined work. In that case, the less effort they expend, the more profitable the fixed fee becomes. The company winds up getting too little. Smart companies reject both of these mixed versions.

In this era of "partnering," when everyone from long-distance telephone companies to office supply stores claims to be a participant in a company's business success, there is a temptation to write consulting agreements with compensation provisions that are contingent on achieving business goals. Don't do it. Unclear compensation terms are invitations to disputes.

Suppose a consultant asks for a fixed percentage of any savings achieved as a result of the project. Such a compensation provision seems to have "win-win" written all over it. The consultant has a stake in the project's success. The company pays part of its consulting bill with what can (albeit erroneously) be looked at as found money. Why not proceed? Because the day of reckoning the savings will be nearly as full of weeping and gnashing of teeth as the biblical Day of Reckoning. Disputes are inevitable.

The consultant is almost certain to argue for the most liberal definition of the savings achieved by the project. The company will have to decide whether, if savings were achieved, they can be attributed to the project the consultant worked on, or have some other cause.

Tracing this cause-and-effect trail is difficult. For most purposes, calculating savings does not need to be done with a high degree of precision. But if a consultant's compensation depends on its precision, disputes will probably result.

Even if savings are easily calculated to the satisfaction of both parties, it is a mistake to tie the consultant's compensation to them. Such a linkage forces the company to accept a cost that may not be commensurate with the service provided.

Suppose a project results in verifiable savings of $1.5 million for the first year. The consulting agreement might include a provision that awarded part of any savings to the consultant as follows:

- ▶ 10 percent of first-year savings up to $1,000,000
- ▶ 15 percent of first-year savings from $1,000,001 to $2,000,000
- ▶ 20 percent of first-year savings over $2,000,000

How does the company analyze the cost of the consultant before the project begins? The fact that the fee is a function of savings does not absolve finance of its responsibility for assessing costs. Nor does the fact that costs will be lower as a result of the successful completion of the project. Stripping away the nonessential, finance must conclude that the consultant's pay could be very small or very large, and that it is impossible to predict which it will be. What if the actions that result in year-one savings cause unforeseeable increased costs in year two? Will the consultant refund the money?

If you trade in a gas-guzzling car for a more efficient model, your fuel costs are likely to go down. Suppose the car dealer who sells you the more efficient car suggests that you pay extra because of all the money you'll be saving on fuel. Is that a fair request?

Not really. While the car dealer helped you to achieve lower fuel costs, you may be paying a price for those savings in other areas. You might have sacrificed the smooth ride of a luxury car for something less comfortable. You might be buying more airplane tickets because the new economy car makes long drives too uncomfortable. You might be spending more time on the road because the new car doesn't go as fast as the old one. In short, you might be incurring other costs that counterbalance the money you're saving on gasoline.

Even if the request were fair, how would you go about establishing a baseline for your old fuel costs? Sure, you're driving a gas-guzzler now, but that's only because you don't think it's worth the money to replace the engine. Your average fuel costs for the last five years may be lower than the projected costs of operating your new fuel-efficient car, even though your current-year mileage is poor. What if you drive fewer miles than predicted next year because you carpool? Which number do you use to establish a baseline?

Projects never exist or function in isolation. Their success, and thus their imputed savings, is always contingent on the systems and operations with which they are interwoven. Measure their success in those terms. Plan them on the basis of predictable costs and realistic benefits. Don't build unnecessary uncertainty into the planning process by instituting a variable fee structure for the consultant.

The Benefit of Staffing Flexibility

Companies often need expert IT help for short periods of time. The cost of hiring permanent employees for short-term needs is unacceptably high. Similarly, reducing permanent staff takes a toll on a company's management and morale and results in high termination costs.

Consultants provide staffing flexibility. Hiring them when short-term needs arise makes perfect sense. In the short term, they often cost less than employees. They can be chosen for their fitness for the special need, rather than for the qualities that full-time employees must possess. If the consulting agreement is properly written, they can be replaced quickly and easily.

When Good Consultants Go Bad

Even in consulting companies, some employees are better than others. When the people the vendor supplies leave more than a little to be desired, the company buying their services must have the ability to make a change.

The cost of using a vendor that churns consultants through an assignment can be great. Every consultant requires some on-the-assignment training. These ramp-up costs can be burdensome, especially when it is considered that the company pays for new consultants at the same rate that it pays for fully acclimated and productive consultants. The more often the vendor reassigns individual consultants, the higher the ramp-up costs, the lower the productivity of the consultants, and the less likely it is that the project will be concluded successfully and within budget.

The company therefore needs to protect itself against bad workers being assigned to it by the vendor, and against excessive turnover.

Replacement of Consulting Personnel

The company should make sure it has the right to get rid of any consultant who isn't performing satisfactorily. The consulting agreement should solidify this right with language similar to this:

Sample Provision

Vendor agrees that Company shall have the right, in its sole discretion, to require Vendor to immediately remove any Consultant from performing services under this Agreement. In such event, Vendor shall, upon Company's request, furnish a replacement Consultant with the requisite skills, training, and experience within one (1) business day or as otherwise agreed by the Parties. Company's exercise of any of its rights under this paragraph shall not in any way limit the obligation of Vendor to perform its obligations under this Agreement.

If the relationship between Vendor and any of its Consultants performing services under this Agreement terminates, Vendor shall so notify the Company Project Manager and, if Company so requests, replace such Consultants within one (1) business day or as otherwise agreed by the Parties. If any of the Consultants are absent for more than three (3) consecutive business days during which they were to perform services under a Statement of Work, Vendor shall, upon Company's request, replace such Consultants within one (1) business day or as otherwise agreed by the Parties. Upon the occurrence of either of the events described in this paragraph, Company shall be entitled to comparable services at no charge for the lesser period of one (1) month or the period Vendor personnel performed services under the Statement of Work. Any failure by Vendor to comply with this paragraph shall be deemed a material breach of this Agreement.

Marketing by Consultants

Many consultants are born marketers. They are often compensated on the basis of how much business they create for the vendor. As a result, if you're not careful, you can find that a consultant whom you've hired to perform real work is instead out marketing additional work. Policies to avoid this need to be in place and enforced. Also, you may wish to expressly prohibit marketing activities by consultants who are billing their time to you. A sample provision follows.

Sample Provision

MARKETING BY PERSONNEL

Except for a single marketing representative designated in writing by Vendor to Company (the "Vendor's Marketing Representative"), none of the Consultants shall conduct any marketing activities at Company; provided that each Consultant shall have the right to report potential marketing opportunities to the Vendor's Marketing Representative. Vendor and Company have agreed that it will harm Company if any of the Consultants are engaged in marketing instead of performing services under this Agreement and that such harm will be impossible to accurately assess. As a result, if any Consultant personnel other than the Vendor's Marketing Representative is found conducting marketing activities at Company, Vendor shall automatically grant a credit to Company in an amount equal to five times the daily rate (or forty times the hourly rate, if time is billed hourly) for the Consultant found to be in violation of this Section. The parties agree that this amount is a reasonable estimate of such harm.

Hiring Restrictions

Just as a vendor's employees can be unacceptably bad, they can also be unbelievably good—so good, in fact, that the company may wish to hire them away from the vendor. Similarly, the vendor may find just the person it's been looking for among its contacts within the company.

Allowing employee swapping undermines the consulting relationship. The consultant becomes reluctant to send its best people to the raiding company. The company becomes reluctant to hire the best consulting firms for fear of exposing its own employees to too much temptation.

The wisest course is to prohibit cross-hiring with a provision in the consulting agreement:

HIRING RESTRICTION

Except with the prior written approval of the other Party, each Party agrees that it shall not hire any person employed by the other and performing services under this Agreement, unless when the offer of employment is made such person either (i) has not performed any services under this Agreement for at least one (1) year or (ii) has not been employed by the other Party for at least six (6) months.

Terminating the Agreement

If using consultants is all about flexibility, the company must ensure that it allows itself the ultimate flexibility—the freedom to terminate the consulting contract with or without cause. The terms of disengagement must be fair to the vendor, of course, but they must be flexible enough to allow the company to enter into the consulting contract without feeling hemmed in or losing the core benefit that led it to choose consultants in the first place.

Here is a sample termination clause:

TERMINATION

The Company shall have the right, with or without cause, to terminate a Statement of Work by giving Vendor notice of termination. If Company so terminates, Company shall pay Vendor (i) all amounts due to Vendor as of the effective date of termination, as identified in such notice of termination, under such Statement of Work plus (ii) all demobilization costs reasonably and actually incurred by Vendor as a result of the early termination of the Statement of Work, provided that Vendor shall use reasonable efforts to minimize such demobilization costs and that such demobilization costs shall not in any event exceed the fees payable to Vendor for the thirty (30) days prior to the date when Company gave such notice of termination.

Who Owns the Work?

The consulting agreement should determine the ownership of any software or other work created under the agreement. This is often a hotly contested issue.

Why Ownership Is Important

Vendors may want to own what they create so that they can sell it again to other customers. Some consulting vendors have built their entire business around the idea of being paid to create software, then using that software on the next job. Of course, they refer to it as their "knowledge capital," not as "other people's software."

Why would a company ever agree to pay a vendor to develop software if the vendor will own the work? There are two reasons. First, companies want to deal with vendors with a lot of "knowledge capital." Second, the economic deal may reflect the value that the vendor will retain. That is, the vendor may be willing to sell you services for less money in anticipation of making more money down the road with other clients.

The company may want to own what the vendor creates. Owning what the vendor creates means never having to ask the vendor for permission to use it. This is particularly critical if what the vendor is doing is making changes to the company's software. In that case, the company would lose control over its own software if a vendor owned threads that run through that software.

Owning all rights in the created work is a business necessity if the software or other work contains the company's trade secrets or otherwise provides a competitive advantage. Otherwise, the vendor could (and probably would) quickly sell your company's trade secrets or key competitive advantage to your competitors.

Finally, owning all rights may be worth money. If the company hires the vendor to implement something particularly clever, the company can market that work. Alternatively, the company can let the vendor market it, but charge the vendor a royalty. Either way, the company, rather than the vendor, gets the benefit of the company's cleverness and creativity.

What Happens Without a Written Contract

What would happen if you hired the vendor on a handshake? You might think that if you paid for the development, you'd own the work. Not true.

In the United States, copyright ownership is determined by the U.S. Copyright Act. That act provides that, absent a written agreement designating what the consultant does as a "work made for hire," the person who creates the work owns the copyright.

This makes sense when you think about the origin of the Copyright Act. The Copyright Act was designed to protect authors of books, not owners of software. The people who drafted the Copyright Act were looking out for authors (the little people) and figured that buyers (big companies) could look out for themselves. The way you look out for yourself is a written agreement.

This is just a hoop you've got to jump through in order to have your company be the "author" of the work under the Copyright Act. You need a written contract, it has to have the magic words in it, and it has to be signed before the software is created. There are also other statutory requirements. Otherwise, the vendor is the author and owns the work at creation.

Of course, if the vendor owns the software, the vendor can assign ownership to you. For a few legal reasons, that's not as good as a work-made-for-hire, but it's close. However, it also requires a written contract. Good consulting agreements use both alternatives, so that if the work turns out not to be a work-made-for-hire, the work is assigned to the company.

Sample Language

The following language is designed to give the company what it wants, while protecting the vendor's rights in its existing intellectual property. Sample language giving the vendor all rights can be found in any consultant's form.

Sample Provision

WORK-MADE-FOR-HIRE

Vendor shall promptly disclose all Work Product to Company. All Work Product, including all applicable rights to patents, copyrights, trademarks, and trade secrets, inherent therein and appurtenant thereto, shall constitute work-made-for-hire belonging exclusively to Company. To the extent that any Work Product does not constitute work-made-for-hire owned by Company, Vendor hereby assigns and transfers all of its right, title, and interest in such Work Product to Company. Company shall have the right to obtain and to hold in its own name patents, copyrights, trademarks, and trade secrets or such other protection as may be appropriate to the subject matter, and any extensions or renewals thereof. Vendor agrees to provide to Company, or any party designated by Company, all assistance reasonably required to evidence and perfect Company's rights.

VENDOR PROPRIETARY MATERIAL

Company does not under this Agreement acquire any ownership rights in software, documentation, or other material that is proprietary to Vendor ("Vendor Proprietary Material"). However, if Vendor incorporates any Vendor Proprietary Material in any of the Work Product, or any of the Work Product requires Vendor Proprietary Material in order to operate, Vendor hereby grants Company a nonexclusive, royalty-free, fully paid, perpetual, irrevocable license, without right to sublicense, to make, use, sell, copy, and display the Vendor Proprietary Material.

Confidentiality

Consultants often have access to both a company and its competition. Were they to share information, inadvertently or otherwise, considerable harm could be done. For this reason, the company must protect itself with comprehensive confidentiality provisions in the consulting agreement.

The sample provisions shown here may seem unnecessarily exhaustive. But even a document as innocent-seeming as an internal telephone directory can do considerable harm if the wrong people have access to it. Ask any company that has lost a competitive advantage because an internal document was shared with its competition, and you'll quickly learn how important it is to enforce confidentiality.

Sample Provision

CONFIDENTIAL INFORMATION

The term "Confidential Information" shall mean (i) the software, systems, procedures, business plans, business strategies, internal organization, internal telephone directory, designs, flow charts, plans, product and component drawings, specifications, manuals, supplier lists, customer lists, customer data, cost and price data, marketing information, and other data and information relating to the existing or planned business, software, or information technology systems of the Company; the Work Product, and any other confidential information or trade secrets respecting the business affairs or property of the Company that Vendor may acquire or develop in connection with or as a result of the performance of its services under this Agreement; (ii) the terms of this Agreement and any other agreement entered into by the Company; and (iii) all notes, analyses, compilations, studies, or other material containing any information described in clauses (i) and (ii). Such information shall be deemed Confidential Information, whether or not such information is provided in writing and whether or not such information is marked confidential.

CONFIDENTIALITY OBLIGATION

Vendor acknowledges and agrees that all of the Confidential Information is confidential to Company. Vendor shall keep the Confidential Information secret, and Vendor shall not sell, transfer, publish, disclose, display, or otherwise make available any Confidential Information to any person other than an employee of Vendor with a need to know such information in order to provide services to Company under this Agreement without the prior written approval of the Company Account Manager. Vendor shall use the same standard of care as it uses to protect its own confidential information and trade secrets (but not less than reasonable care), and shall bind its employees, agents, or representatives to such standard, to prevent disclosure of Confidential Information.

Keeping Consultants Independent

In order to avoid paying employment taxes on consultants and paying employee benefits to consultants, companies need to treat consultants as consultants, not as employees. That's harder than you might think.

Independent Contractor or Employee?

The Internal Revenue Service watches how companies use IT consultants carefully. Independent contractors who perform services for a single company in the course of a tax year may have their status challenged by the IRS.

People are considered employees if the company that hires them has the right to control the way they do their work. It doesn't matter whether the company actually exercises this right. All that matters is that the company has such a right. If it does, the IRS considers that the independence of a contractor has been taken away and replaced by a de facto employer-employee relationship.

The IRS uses a twenty-factor test to determine whether someone doing work for a company is an employee or an independent contractor. In their view, you are most likely an employee if more than a few of these factors apply to you.

1. Someone tells you when, where, and how to work.
2. The business trains you to perform services in a particular manner.

3. Your services are part of the business operations because they are important to the success of the business.
4. Your services are rendered personally.
5. The business hires, supervises, and pays workers.
6. You have a continuing relationship with the business.
7. The business sets your work hours.
8. You are required to work or be available full-time.
9. You work on the premises of the business, or on a route or at a location designated by the business.
10. You perform services in the order or sequence set by the business.
11. You submit reports to the business.
12. You are paid by the hour, week, or month.
13. The business pays your travel and business expenses.
14. The business provides your tools, materials, and other equipment.
15. You have no significant investment in the business.
16. You don't make a profit or suffer a loss from the business.
17. You normally work for one business at a time.
18. You don't offer your services to the general public.
19. The business has the right to fire you.
20. You have the right to quit without incurring liability.

Consider this example from the training manual the IRS developed for its own auditors:

> A computer programmer is laid off when Company X downsizes. Company X agrees to pay the programmer $10,000 to complete a one-time project to create a certain product. It is not clear how long it will take to complete the project, and the programmer is not guaranteed any minimum payment for the hours spent on the project. The programmer does the work on a new high-end computer, which cost the programmer $5,000. The programmer works at home and is not expected or allowed to attend meetings of the software development group. Company X provides the programmer with no instructions beyond the specifications for the product itself. The programmer and Company X have a written contract, which provides that the programmer is considered to be an independent contractor, is required to pay federal and state taxes, and receives no employee benefits from Company X. Company X will file a Form 1099.

According to the IRS, one factor suggests that the person might be an employee, some are neutral, and several indicate independent contractor status. There is no clear resolution.

Vendor Employee or Company Employee?

When consultants are provided by a large consulting firm, there should be no ambiguity about their employment status. They work for the vendor. But to avoid confusion on the part of either party (or the IRS), the consulting agreement should contain language similar to this:

Sample Provision

Employees of Vendor assigned by Vendor to perform services under this Agreement shall at all times during such assignment be and remain employees of Vendor and not of Company. Vendor shall be solely responsible for paying its employees' entire compensation earned in connection with the subject matter of this Agreement and any related taxes, expenses, holidays, sick time, vacations, and benefits and shall indemnify and hold Company harmless against any claims by any of the Consultants for employment benefits from Company with respect to services performed under this Agreement.

At all times during this Agreement, all of the Consultants shall clearly identify themselves as personnel of Vendor and not employees of Company. This shall include any and all communications, oral, written, or electronic. Each of the Consultants shall wear a badge indicating that he or she is a guest, and not an employee, of Company. It is the responsibility of Vendor and the Consultants to avoid any confusion regarding whether the Consultants are employees of Company. Any breach of this paragraph shall be a material breach of this Agreement.

Projects by the Hour: The Consulting Paradox

Consultants and the companies they serve are always at cross-purposes in at least one area. Consultants sell time; companies buy accomplishments.

It may be unenlightened self-interest, but it is self-interest nevertheless that motivates consulting vendors to sell as many hours as the company is willing to buy. Conversely, the company wants to spend as little as possible, preferably in the form of a single prequoted price, to accomplish its project.

If the company fails to define its project adequately, the consultant will have plenty of leeway to meet her goal of generating the maximum number of billable hours.

On the other hand, if the company does a good job of defining deliverables, it keeps the consultant oriented to that task and eliminates the opportunity for excessive billing.

Consultants are an important part of most companies' information technology strategies, especially in the downsized nineties. It is easy for a company to become too dependent on them and lose the ability to accomplish its IT goals without outside help. For these companies, the realization that they cannot run their IT departments without consultants usually comes too late.

To avoid such dependence, companies must have the discipline to define the goal of every consulting relationship in a comprehensive work product statement and consulting agreement. Companies must also have the discipline to define exit criteria and require consultants to exit when they are no longer needed. Only in this way can companies achieve the benefits of using consultants without becoming victimized by overbilling or overdependence.

14

Equipment

To get the full benefits of software, companies need a dizzying array of computer equipment that receives, processes, stores, transmits, prints, and displays data. This chapter describes the key issues that face companies as they buy, maintain, and lease computer equipment.

Buying Equipment

Equipment is purchased under sales contracts. In most ways, these contracts are very similar to software licenses. The key provisions describe what the company will get for its money, how the company will pay, and the warranties and indemnities that the vendor will provide. Clauses regarding limitation of liability, insurance requirements, infringement indemnification, and so forth read the same way and have the same meaning as they do in software licenses.

However, there are also important differences between buying equipment and licensing software. Perhaps the most important is that equipment, unlike software, is not merely an electronic copy. Producing equipment involves significant time and expense. Thus, for example, unlike software vendors, hardware vendors do not have a legitimate concern about things like scope of use and copying.

Another key difference is that equipment, unlike software, rapidly becomes obsolete. It has parts that wear out. Also, vendors regularly bring out equipment that is so much better, faster, and cheaper than prior models that it is worth replacing even fully functional equipment. The accelerating pace of technological improvements is steadily decreasing the amount of time between when a model comes out and when smart companies replace it with a newer model.

Ordering

Buying equipment begins with placing an order. The company needs the order to define exactly what it will get. To avoid ambiguity, each product should be described both in the vendor's language (usually product numbers) and in plain English.

The order must set forth, in detail, what you are ordering. Any ambiguity is an opportunity for the vendor to supply something less than, or other than, what the company needs. Nothing is implied on an equipment order—not even absolutely necessary cables. Thus, the technical role must sign off on whether the order specifies the right combination of the vendor's products (or, in IT jargon, the right "configuration").

The order must also specify exactly what the company will pay for the equipment. Often, equipment vendors both state that the price will be the vendor's list price (perhaps less a discount) and have a pricing system so complex that the company has no choice but to simply trust the vendor's calculation of the price. This is not a heathy situation.

In addition to pricing clarity, the company may want price protection. The company might want to ask for the benefits of price decreases by the vendor at any of the following points:

▶ Before the vendor delivers the equipment
▶ Before the company accepts the equipment
▶ Before the warranty expires

Finally, the order should specify any charges for taxes, shipping, site preparation, installation, training, and so forth. These items are easier to negotiate before the equipment is ordered than after it is installed and working.

The Wait for Delivery

After ordering equipment, companies want to know when it will be delivered. Because software doesn't work without equipment, equipment delivery dates are often on a project's critical path. If a project includes, for example, a nationwide rollout for new equipment, there may be dozens or even hundreds of critical equipment delivery dates.

Your project plan may require your vendors to deliver on exactly the predetermined delivery dates. One vendor's equipment may be required for another vendor's work. To avoid delay and finger pointing, you may want each vendor to have a separate delivery date.

Vendors can't produce equipment instantly. In fact, vendors often have substantial backlogs, and are unable to provide equipment for months after receiving your order. In those cases, getting delivery commitments from the vendor can be critical to achieving your project plan.

While you're waiting for delivery, there is a reasonable chance that you'll want to change your order. Equipment vendors regularly announce new or upgraded models. Companies' understanding of their needs continues to evolve. Also, another vendor might make a more attractive offer if you have more time. Thus, you want the purchase contract to allow you to adjust or cancel your order, perhaps up to thirty days before delivery. At a minimum, you want the right to cancel if the vendor cannot deliver when promised.

Also, while you wait for equipment, the vendor might produce a new model or cut its prices. Because of the rapid increases in the price/performance ratio for equipment (it generally doubles every eighteen months for processors), this is a very real possibility. You want to get the benefit of the better equipment and lower prices announced while you wait. That is a reasonable requirement, particularly given that you are agreeing to order equipment far in advance only because of the vendor's decision not to increase capacity enough to meet the demand for its products on a timely basis. To get the benefit of upgrades and price decreases, you'll probably need the right to be notified by the vendor if the vendor announces any upgrade to the equipment you order.

Vendors, of course, want to lock you into the model you order. One reason is that committed orders make production scheduling easier. Another reason is that if you are locked into one model and want a different one, the vendor can charge an upgrade fee for allowing you to make that change. Needless to say, vendors hate to give you the right to cancel because that creates a risk that you will go somewhere else to take a better deal.

Site Preparation

Before the equipment is delivered, you need to prepare the site. At a minimum, you'll need power and communication cables routed to the spot where the equipment will be used. However, some equipment requires considerably more site preparation. For example, mainframe computers often require a raised floor, air-conditioning, special fire suppression gear, elimination of strong magnetic fields, uninterruptible power supplies, and very complex cabling.

Site preparation can be expensive and time-consuming. On the other hand, it is beyond annoying to be unable to install an expensive piece of equipment for days because you lack a particular cable.

You may be able to obtain site preparation services from the vendor, perhaps at a considerable discount. In any event, prior to delivery, you should seek to have the vendor confirm that your site is adequately prepared. Otherwise, when the equipment doesn't work, you risk having the vendor blame your site preparation.

Delivery

You might expect that "delivery" occurs when you accept the equipment. In fact, delivery often means delivering equipment to a shipping company at the vendor's shipping dock, even when the vendor picks the shipping company.

The difference is important if the equipment is lost or destroyed after it is delivered to the shipping company but before it gets to your computer room. Before delivery occurs, the vendor bears the risk of loss. After delivery occurs, the company bears the risk of loss. (This result may, of course, be changed by contract language.)

There are two things you can do about this. One is to get the vendor to accept the risk of loss until the equipment is safely installed. The other is to have insurance coverage for the equipment from the time the risk of loss passes.

Installation

Installing mainframes and other complex computer equipment is difficult technical work. Generally, the vendor or some other expert installs complex computer equipment. As a result, you need to have the purchase contract include installation services. In this context, the vendor acts as a consultant, and thus many of the issues raised with respect to consultants apply.

The purchase contract should commit the vendor not just to installing the equipment, but also to installing the equipment on a particular schedule. When the equipment is installed is as important as (or more important than) when it is delivered because the machine will not function until it is installed. Committed installation resources can be invaluable.

Depending on the consequences of an installation delay, the company may want the contract to spell out reductions in the purchase price of the machine that apply if the installation dates are missed. To avoid having these credits be considered penalties and thus be unenforceable in the courts, these credits should be reasonable estimates of the actual harm that the company would suffer in the event of an installation delay and be characterized as liquidated damages.

Training

Unless you are currently using the type of equipment you are buying, your people may need a substantial amount of training in the use, care, and feeding of the new equipment and any related software. Training can be a substantial component of cost, and poor training can impose significant additional downtime, retraining, and other costs.

Training contracts are generally highly negotiable, particularly to the extent that any custom training or small-group training is involved. Here are a few things that may be worth negotiating:

► Where and when the training will be done
► The content of training materials and curricula
► Whether the company can reject trainers
► Whether people from other companies will be trained at the same time
► How many copies of the training materials the company can make
► Whether the company can make and use videotapes of training sessions
► The grade level at which the training will be presented
► What exit tests the vendor will conduct
► Who will pay for retraining of people who fail the exit tests

Acceptance

Once equipment arrives, you can accept or reject it. If you reject it, you don't pay for it. If you accept it, you must pay for it. If you accept it and it doesn't work, your remedy is generally limited to having the vendor try to repair it. Thus, accepting equipment substantially reduces your leverage. You don't want to accept equipment unless it works.

Vendors' forms often state that the company will automatically accept equipment when the vendor has installed the equipment and it has passed the vendor's acceptance test. The value of that to the buyer is, well, open to question.

What you want is the right to have your technical people test the equipment for a reasonable period of time before you accept it, using their own acceptance tests. It's very smart to use your own data to do this testing. If you use the vendor's data or made-up data, you haven't tested to see if the equipment is going to work for you with the data you actually use.

As a part of this testing, the company might verify both that the equipment works on its own and that the equipment works properly with other equipment. The company's systems integrators are often the source of these types of tests.

Vendors generally agree to reasonable and specific acceptance tests, so long as their right to be paid is not extended indefinitely. Also, vendors reasonably ask for notice of what failure caused you not to accept the equipment and a reasonable period to correct that failure. There's no harm in agreeing to this; you'd have that conversation anyway.

Warranties

Warranties From Manufacturers

The vendor's warranty should include a promise by the vendor that the company is getting what it expects when it buys the equipment. Vendors generally offer a warranty that the equipment when installed will conform to the vendor's published specifications for a period of time, generally thirty or ninety days.

You, of course, want considerably more. The vendor's specifications will rarely have sufficient specificity and clarity to enable you to determine whether the equipment will meet your business needs. As a result, you may want to obtain warranties from the vendor that:

- ▶ The company will receive good and marketable title to the equipment, free and clear of any liens or encumbrances.
- ▶ The equipment will be free from defects in materials, design, or workmanship.
- ▶ The equipment will process the expected amount of data with the expected response time.
- ▶ The configuration set forth on the order is sufficient to allow the system to work properly.
- ▶ Each component listed on the order is properly sized with respect to the other components, and will not limit the speed of the other components.
- ▶ The equipment conforms to its specifications.
- ▶ The vendor's proposal and specified advertising literature accurately describe the equipment.
- ▶ The equipment is compatible with specified equipment and software.
- ▶ The equipment is new, not used.

▶ The equipment is in good working order, and has all engineering changes installed.

Essentially, what you want to do is to require the vendor to stand behind the representations that induced you to purchase the equipment. You may need to think creatively about that. For example, if the vendor won your business with a prototype machine, you would want a warranty that the equipment works in the same way as the prototype.

Disclaimers

Generally, you will need to make sure that the warranties you want appear in the contract. Most vendors' forms disclaim all warranties that are not expressly stated in the contract and provide that the contract supersedes any other understandings. Thus, absent fraud or misrepresentations, you're probably limited to the warranties in the contract.

Vendors are almost universal in their desire to disclaim the implied warranties of merchantability and fitness for a particular purpose. In the United States, those warranties are provided by the law of contracts embodied in the Uniform Commercial Code. Without a contract, the company gets those warranties. Thus, it is important for negotiators to understand those warranties both to determine whether the company is better off buying equipment without a contract and to be able to use them to gain the moral high ground in negotiations.

The implied warranty of merchantability is a warranty that the equipment is fit for the ordinary purposes for which it is purchased. This warranty is breached when defects in the goods purchased prevent their proper operation.

The implied warranty of fitness for a particular purpose is a warranty that the equipment is fit for the company's specific purposes. This warranty is breached when all of the following occur:

▶ The vendor has reason to know the company's particular purpose in buying the equipment.
▶ The vendor has reason to know that the company is relying on the vendor's skill or judgment in purchasing the equipment.
▶ The company in fact relies on the vendor's skill or judgment.

Don't those warranties sound reasonable? Sure they do. You probably do expect the equipment to be free of defects. You probably are relying on the sales rep's judgment in buying the equipment. Disclaiming these warranties means that you are taking the risk that the product will be defective (though still conforming to specifications) or that the vendor's sales rep sold you a product based on his commission structure instead of your needs.

Although it is common and perhaps beyond reproach to allow a vendor to disclaim these implied warranties, negotiators must be vigilant to avoid disclaimers of other warranties. For example, some vendors seek to expressly disclaim the contents of their proposal or even of their printed descriptions of the equipment's capabilities.

Exclusions

The sales contract also might exclude certain problems from the warranty and acceptance provisions. What the vendor is saying, in effect, is that these problems are not the vendor's fault and thus are not covered by the warranty.

For complex systems, it is common to exclude any problems resulting from using the equipment in the wrong environment. By environment, the vendor refers to such things as appropriate power supplies, absence of magnetic fields, proper air-conditioning, and so forth. Basically, vendors' forms say that if you don't give the equipment a good home, it's going to misbehave. As noted above, it's smart to demand that the vendor certify the site before delivering the equipment. However, that certification helps only as long as you do not change the environment.

It is also common to exclude problems caused by the way you use the system. For example, installing memory boards from another manufacturer might void the warranty. The warranty might be void simply because you attempt to repair the system without calling an authorized service person.

Warranties From Resellers

If your vendor is merely a reseller, without the ability to service the equipment, you will need warranties directly from the manufacturer. You can get those warranties directly from the manufacturer or on a pass-through basis. If you are offered warranties on a pass-through basis, you need to verify that your vendor has the right to pass warranties through. You will not have any legal right to require a manufacturer to stand behind warranties unless the manufacturer made these warranties to you, either directly or by authorizing a reseller to pass them through.

A manufacturer will generally refuse to provide warranty service unless it made the warranty directly. The reason that manufacturers refuse to provide warranty service, even on new equipment, is to control "gray market" sales. In a gray market sale, a company uses its substantial buying power to obtain low prices on equipment, ostensibly for internal use. It then resells the equipment, undercutting both the manufacturer and authorized resellers.

Remedies

The value of a warranty depends on the remedies the sales contract gives you when the equipment does not perform in accordance with the warranties. Vendors' forms generally limit that remedy to next to nothing. For example, a vendor might state that the company's only remedy is for the vendor to use its reasonable efforts to repair or replace the defective part of the equipment.

What you want, of course, is to have the vendor on the hook for any damage to you because the warranty was incorrect. You also want the vendor to try to fix the problem, but that would happen anyway if the vendor was liable for any damage to you. Interestingly, that is pretty much the result under the law of contracts. If you buy equipment without a contract, you get the implied warranties and the right to sue for unlimited damages. Any vendor's form sharply limits that right. Think about that.

A second-best, but more commercially reasonable, alternative is to include in the contract a list of all the bad things that could happen and, for each bad thing, what the vendor must do if it does happen. For example, if equipment that is needed for production fails, the vendor might agree to provide a loaner system within twenty-four hours if the problem has not been fixed.

A third-best, but very realistic, objective is to obtain the rights described under the heading "Maintaining Equipment" later in this chapter. For example, you might require the vendor to respond to service calls within a defined period of time and with defined efforts. In that case, the warranty essentially provides nothing more or less than a period of free maintenance.

Even with this third-best option, you should seek a "lemon clause." Some machines have flaws that are hard to find. As a result, they may fail repeatedly within the warranty period. The vendor's service people will temporarily repair a problem, but the vendor seems unable to find and eradicate the root cause. To protect the company, a lemon clause provides that if, during the warranty period, the equipment fails an unreasonable number of times, the vendor will replace it with a new machine at no charge.

Maintaining Equipment

Equipment needs care. It has tiny little parts that get dirty and wear out. Then the equipment fails. Equipment that is well cared for doesn't fail as often. You want the vendor to take care of the equipment and fix it quickly when it fails. That service is generally provided under a separate maintenance contract.

You should negotiate a maintenance contract before you buy the equipment. Generally, only the vendor can keep its equipment running. Thus, your leverage disappears as soon as you buy the equipment. You have no choice but to buy maintenance if you need the equipment.

There are a couple of exceptions to this. For some types of equipment, multiple vendors provide maintenance. For other types, it's cheaper to just replace the equipment that fails than to have a maintenance agreement. Finally, very sophisticated companies can maintain equipment on their own. However, the general rule is that you don't want to buy equipment unless you've contracted for maintenance or have a reasonable maintenance or post-warranty replacement plan.

What Is Included in Maintenance?

Vendors generally charge an annual fee for a defined base set of maintenance services. Any services beyond those base services are provided on a parts-and-labor basis. Needless to say, the smaller the set of base services, the more money the vendor makes. You want as much as possible included.

The base services generally include preventive and remedial maintenance. Preventive maintenance means inspecting and lubricating moving parts, cleaning the machine, installing engineering changes, and replacing worn parts. Remedial maintenance is repairing failed hardware.

You'll need to carefully review all of the exclusions from maintenance. What is reasonable depends on what kind of equipment is being maintained. Vendors' forms commonly exclude service required as a result of abuse, use of the equipment other than for the purposes for which it was designed, accident, improper environmental conditions, and similar matters.

The most troubling exclusions relate to problems caused by user error, software error, and other vendors' systems. Unless the vendor is required to demonstrate that the equipment is not at fault, these provisions invite vendors to point fingers instead of solve problems.

When Will the Vendor Provide Maintenance?

Maintenance contracts generally offer three types of maintenance. The first type is standard maintenance. With standard maintenance, you have the right to expect the vendor to take your calls and dispatch a technician during business hours. The base charge covers that.

Most vendors also offer extended maintenance service or warranty uplift. For an additional charge, the vendor will take your calls for additional hours each day. For example, standard maintenance might be from 8:00 A.M. to 6:00 P.M. Monday through Friday, while extended maintenance would be from 4:00 A.M. to midnight, Monday through Saturday. Emergency service might be available at off-hours for an additional fee.

There are two things you want here. First, you want remedial maintenance to be available during the times when you need your equipment. Second, you want preventive maintenance to be done only during your off-peak hours. It's worth negotiating a contract clause that prohibits the vendor from shutting down your equipment during your peak hours to do preventive maintenance.

How Quickly Will the Vendor Provide Maintenance?

If your equipment fails, you want it fixed as soon as possible. Unfortunately, it's impossible to specify in a contract how quickly a problem will be repaired because that depends, in large part, on what the problem is.

One common contracting approach is to specify a required response time. Response time is the time between your call to the vendor to report an equipment failure and the arrival of the vendor's technician at the equipment's location. A response-time provision should be combined with a requirement that the technician use diligent and continuous efforts to solve the problem, and perhaps a requirement to send expert technicians to assist if the problem is not solved promptly.

Another contracting approach is to control some of the factors that affect the time to a completed fix. You could, for example, obtain a warranty as to the number of technicians the vendor will employ in your city and their level of familiarity with your equipment. Similarly, you could require the vendor to maintain a parts inventory for your equipment, ideally at your site in a locked cabinet under the vendor's complete control, to make sure that a missing part will never keep your equipment down. Large data processing shops often contract for a dedicated, on-site technician for their key systems.

A third contracting approach is to build financial incentives into the maintenance contract. If the vendor fails to meet service levels for response time or repair time, the company could have the right to:

► Liquidated damages
► Additional months of maintenance at no extra charge
► Maintenance service from a third party at the vendor's expense
► Termination for breach with a refund of prepayments

How do you choose among these approaches? First, conduct a user and technical analysis of the potential cost of equipment failure and the potential benefits of the more expensive maintenance options. Second, prepare a cost-benefit analysis. The cost-benefit analysis will indicate which types of maintenance are worth purchasing for which types of equipment.

Term

The initial term of a maintenance agreement is almost always one year. Renewal terms are almost always one year. The problems spring from the renewal provision.

Vendors' forms generally state that the maintenance agreement will automatically renew at the vendor's then current price unless either party cancels at least, say, thirty days in advance of the expiration.

You could easily find yourself paying too much for maintenance. Once you've purchased equipment, you have little choice but to continue to maintain it. Unless you have some contractual protection against price increases, the vendor might take advantage of its superior leverage to rapidly increase its maintenance prices. Such protection needs to include both a price protection clause and a right to renew. If you don't have the right to renew, the vendor can evade the price protection clause by cancelling the contract.

Another risk with the automatic renewal provision is that you find yourself automatically renewing maintenance for equipment that's in a landfill. That's costly. Careful administration of disposal is the best (and perhaps the only) way to solve the problem. Administration should maintain a full and complete asset inventory and a database of maintenance contracts and their renewal provisions.

Billing Disputes

A detailed asset inventory and database of maintenance terms is not easy to make or keep up to date. Most companies are maintaining hundreds of pieces of equipment, and some are maintaining tens of thousands. As a result, it's likely that you'll find yourself in billing disputes with maintenance vendors.

Vendors' forms generally provide that the company is in default if it does not pay whatever is written on the vendor's invoice within the stated period. Then, upon a default, the vendor has the right to terminate maintenance.

If a vendor terminates maintenance, and that vendor is the only realistic source of that maintenance, the company faces a terrible choice: Either it can slink back to the vendor and offer to pay whatever the vendor asks, or it can buy new equipment from another vendor. As a result, it is important to structure the contract so that the company is required to pay only undisputed amounts.

In addition, you should demand effective procedures for disputing a vendor's bills. For example, demand provisions that require the vendor to:

- ▶ Maintain detailed maintenance records.
- ▶ Provide those detailed records to the company.
- ▶ Specify, on each invoice, what machines are being maintained.
- ▶ Permit audits.
- ▶ Refund any money paid for maintaining equipment that the vendor knows that the company isn't using.

Leasing Equipment

Computer equipment can be leased under operating or capital leases. An operating lease, or true lease, is a lease that covers substantially less than the economic life of the equipment and provides a buyout option at fair market value. Companies enter into operating leases because they need equipment for only a few years, because they wish to lay off the risk of obsolescence on a leasing company, because they don't have the capital, or because they don't want to have the equipment as an asset on their books.

A capital lease is a lease that covers the full economic life of the equipment and provides a buyout for a nominal fee. In its economics, a capital lease is very similar to obtaining a bank loan to buy the equipment.

For tax and accounting reasons, companies often seek to structure operating leases that look very much like capital leases. The dividing line between the two is subtle and is a question for the company's tax and accounting experts.

Hell-or-High-Water Clause

Most leases will contain a clause stating that the obligation to make the lease payments is absolute, "come hell or high water." Thus, even if the equipment doesn't work, the company will have to pay for it. When the financing source is a passive investor, this clause is generally nonnegotiable. The lessor doesn't know or care what the equipment is or what it does. Instead, the lessor views this as a purely financial transaction.

If the company will have to pay for the equipment whether or not it works, it's important for the company to make sure that the equipment works. Most companies solve that problem by obtaining maintenance directly from the manufacturer.

Note, again, that a manufacturer will generally provide warranty service only to companies that purchase from the vendor or from an authorized reseller. If the lessor is not an authorized reseller, the company may find itself without warranty support. The solution to this problem is called a sale and leaseback—all at the same time, the company buys the equipment from the manufacturer, the company sells the equipment to the lessor, and the lessor leases the equipment to the company. Properly done, a sale-and-leaseback transaction creates the direct relationship required to provide warranty rights to the company.

Quiet Enjoyment

The company needs the right to quietly enjoy the leased equipment. Most lessors' forms permit the lessor to repossess and sell the equipment upon a payment default. Imagine, for example, a lessor electing to take your company's mainframe computer one day. You'd probably be out of business. Thus, it's important to limit or delay the vendor's right to repossess.

Fair Market Value Buyout Rights

Operating leases generally provide that the company may purchase the equipment at fair market value. Because of the cost, risk, and difficulty involved in replacing equipment, equipment that is in place and working is often worth far more than its "fair market value" to the company. That gives the vendor the opportunity to negotiate for a fair market value well above the actual fair market value of the equipment.

There are two good ways to protect yourself from that risk. One is by establishing in the lease appropriate mechanisms for determining fair market value based on an objective, third-party standard. The other is to have the right to return like-kind equipment to the vendor in lieu of the exact leased machine.

Another piece of leverage that's worth negotiating out of vendors' forms is the obligation to deliver the leased machine to such location as may be specified by the lessor. Shipping computer equipment across the country can be expensive, at least relative to the value of used computer equipment. That gives the vendor extra leverage in negotiating the fair market value buyout price.

Tax Indemnification

Leasing is often a way of transferring the tax benefits of ownership of leased equipment. The price of the lease will reflect these tax benefits. Lessors generally take the position that these tax benefits are part of the deal. Thus, they expect you to indemnify them if they lose the tax benefits because of something you do (such as using the equipment outside of the United States) or because of changes in tax laws. What you need to be careful about is that you aren't indemnifying the lessor against a loss of tax benefits resulting from something the lessor does.

Disposal

Some computer equipment contains environmentally hazardous materials. The disposal of such computer equipment is regulated by environmental laws. Your company can face substantial penalties if it (or its contractors) improperly disposes of computer equipment. As a result, it is critical to make sure that any equipment you dispose of is handled in accordance with all applicable laws.

15

Outsourcing

In the world of information technology, the term *outsourcing* refers to turning over responsibility for an internal information technology function to an outside vendor. In addition to taking over responsibility for the function, the vendor may purchase the assets, license the software, and/or hire the people that the company uses to perform the function.

The outsourced function could be the entire information technology department. More often, though, the outsourced function is only part of the information technology function—for example, running the data center or a help desk, developing software, providing telecommunications, or maintaining desktop computers.

This chapter describes outsourcing. It first describes, from the company's perspective, the reasons to outsource, or not to outsource, a function. It then describes the perspective of an outsourcing vendor. The remainder of this chapter describes key issues in outsourcing: scope of services, pricing, people, sale of assets to the vendor, use of intellectual property, communication, liability, and duties upon termination.

An outsourcing arrangement involves a great deal of consulting. Thus, although they are not repeated here, the points raised in Chapter 13, "Consulting," apply to outsourcing. Also, an outsourcing arrangement is a type of strategic alliance. Thus, Chapter 16, "Strategic Alliances," also applies to outsourcing.

Analyzing Outsourcing

Outsourcing is a much bigger decision than hiring a consultant. When a company hires a consultant, it gets a temporary boost to its skills. When a company outsources, it gives up people with key skills. After outsourcing, the company may no longer know how to perform the outsourced function. The difficulty of reversing the decision to outsource means that it requires careful analysis.

Reasons to Outsource

Improve Financial Results

An outsourcing vendor may offer to perform a function for less than it costs the company to perform that function itself. Also, the vendor's fee structure can be either more stable or more closely related to the company's revenues than the cost of running an internal function. Those advantages can improve the company's income statement.

Outsourcing can also improve a company's balance sheet. Because the vendor is providing services that the company used to provide internally, the company does not need some of its assets. The vendor often is willing to pay cash for those assets. The company can use the cash proceeds to reduce debt, pay dividends, or otherwise please its stockholders. Also, the sale takes assets off the company's books. By reducing its total assets, the company boosts its return on assets (ROA) ratio.

Focus on the Company's Core Competencies

In today's tough competitive environment, your company needs to focus on its core competencies. Running an information technology function can distract from that focus. With outsourcing, those distractions will be handled by the vendor.

Get Better Performance

Information technology isn't a distraction for the vendor. It's the vendor's core business. More often than not, information technology is the vendor's core competency. As a result, the vendor may be able to hire better people. At the outsourcing vendor, the function is a line job. The career path leads to the CEO's chair.

Another result is that the vendor may have the scale and the focus required to perform the outsourced function effectively. The vendor might be making research and development investments. It may have fixed assets that make sense only with a huge base of business. It may just mean top management attention to that function.

Ideally, outsourcing gives the company the best performance available, even in staff areas. At the extreme, the company becomes a "virtual corporation." It does what it does best and outsources the rest. With world-class performance in every area, its speed, efficiency, and capabilities increase rapidly.

Reasons Not to Outsource

Loss of Control

Before a company outsources a function, it has direct control over that function. Management can choose the people, perform the function, and set their pay. After a company outsources, it needs to manage through a contract. The company's control over the outsourced function is limited to the control rights included in the contract. Those rights will never be as extensive as the control the company has over employees. If the company just signs a vendor's form, those control rights can be very limited.

Loss of Flexibility

Outsourcing contracts generally have long terms. Ten-year terms are not unusual. During this period, the company's needs may change dramatically. However, the vendor may not elect (or be able) to change its offerings to meet the company's new needs. If the vendor is willing to change its offerings, it may charge the company a steep price for doing so. If the outsourcing arrangement is exclusive, the company may be locked into inferior service from a vendor.

A short contract term gives the company more flexibility. However, rebuilding an internal function or moving to a new vendor is never easy. As a result, the company faces the risk of being locked into the outsourcing relationship regardless of the stated term.

Dependence on the Vendor

The company may transfer a mission-critical function to the vendor. If the vendor stops performing that function, or performs it poorly, the company may suffer greatly. Even with the right contract terms, this will give the vendor tremendous leverage over the company.

Service Taxes

When a company outsources, it replaces an internal cost with out-of-pocket fees. In a growing number of jurisdictions, these fees are taxable. If these fees are taxable, the tax is a new cost for the company.

The Vendor's Position

Outsourcing vendors tend to be very sophisticated. They are generally expert in the function that the company is outsourcing. That's why the company turns to them.

However, more than in other transactions, these vendors face substantial risks. They often agree to take on people, assets, and responsibilities based only on the company's promises. The people might be terrible. The company's equipment might be little better than junk. Real estate could expose the vendor to staggering environmental cleanup costs. Unanticipated events might make the function far more challenging than the vendor assumed when it set its prices.

Moreover, these vendors often make up-front investments. To provide lower costs over the term of the outsourcing contract, outsourcing vendors invest in cost-saving technology, retrain employees, and add new processes. They hope to recoup these investments over the term of the contract. That's why the long terms make sense.

Outsourcing vendors' sales costs can be relatively high. They often need to understand the existing internal function in order to price their services. They interview the providers and the users. They review documents. They may send an army of analysts to assess existing service levels. They generate ideas for improvement. All of that takes time and money.

As a result, by the time an outsourcing vendor offers firm pricing, that vendor has a good deal of sunk costs to attempt to recover. The vendor does not want to lose the deal and thus lose its sunk costs. Therefore, the company's leverage may grow until the moment when the company commits itself to an outsourcing vendor.

Services

The description of services is the core of the outsourcing contract. Defining the services well is critical to getting what the company needs from the outsourcing vendor. Well-crafted rights enabling the company to require a change in the services and to obtain services from other vendors are essential to making the outsourcing arrangement a success over the long term.

Defining the Services

Outsourcing contracts generally describe the services as some combination of making resources available, handling tasks, and completing projects. If the contract calls for making resources available (such as 50 gigabytes of disk storage or 10,000 programmer hours/year), the company can use this resource as it pleases. If the contract calls for handling tasks, the vendor completes the tasks with whatever resources are required. Projects, such as developing a new software application, may be defined in the contract or after the contract is signed.

In theory, all services can be defined as making resources available, handling tasks, and completing projects. In reality, things get missed.

Think about your own job. Could you write a complete list of all the things you do? How about a list of everything the company will need you to do next year? How about in the next ten years?

Companies and vendors take two approaches to the things that get missed. The company prefers to have the vendor take responsibility for the entire function. With this approach, the vendor would agree to do everything that the internal function is currently doing. Alternatively, the vendor could agree to do everything closely connected with the services described in the agreement.

Vendors, of course, do not want to agree to perform unknown services that have unknown costs. Vendors prefer to agree on a well-defined set of services, then do the things that get missed as additional services for additional compensation. That approach is fair only if the price will be fair.

Service Levels

Service levels are the numbers and dates that make the obligations meaningful. They define how well, how quickly, or how comprehensively the vendor must perform a service. Without good service levels, the service obligations are of little comfort to the company.

Service levels must be measurable. The company cannot enforce the vendor's promise of two-second response time without being able to measure actual response times. Thus, the company's systems integrators can play a key role in determining service levels.

Service levels must also be meaningful. They need to be tight enough to influence vendor performance. They need to measure the characteristics of the services that are important to the company.

To define service levels, analyze the service levels being achieved internally. If the company has not measured its existing service levels, service levels can be set after the contract is signed. However, the service levels may well be tighter if they are set during negotiations. When the company signs, its leverage declines.

Changes in the Services

It is, of course, impossible to specify all the services for a ten-year outsourcing contract. The world will change. The company will change. Technology will change. As a result, the services will have to change.

Some changes can be anticipated in general terms. For example, the contract could require the vendor to update its technology every two years to "$n - 1$" technology (the second-best product available). Alternatively, the contract could require the vendor to use whatever technology is used by the company's key competitors.

Not all changes can be anticipated in this fashion. The contract needs to spell out a procedure for changing the services to be performed. The procedure should give the company the right to propose changes and receive a fair price proposal for these changes. If the company and the vendor cannot agree on a proposed change, the company must have the right to get the services it needs from another vendor.

Exclusivity

Vendors want the exclusive right to provide the services, and any new related services, to the company. Exclusivity gives a vendor a reliable revenue stream, full control over the outsourced function, and the chance to provide additional services at attractive rates.

Companies prefer to have the right to obtain services from other vendors. This right can give a company the leverage it needs to enforce service levels or renegotiate a bad deal. Also, if the vendor does not maintain the capabilities required by the company, this right may be essential to getting the right services for the company.

Even if the company lacks the leverage to avoid exclusivity, good compromises are available. The vendor could have a right of first refusal to provide the new services on the terms offered by any competing vendor. The company could commit to purchasing a minimum quantity of services. The contract could be exclusive for a limited time, or exclusive as to some services but not to others.

Pricing

The pricing for services in outsourcing transactions usually includes base fees and variable fees. The base fees are the same, regardless of how much the company uses the vendor's services. The variable fees are per-unit prices based on how much the company uses the vendor's services. The company may be able to change the base fees in special circumstances. In addition, the fees may change based on the level of service that the vendor provides. These changes can give the vendor another incentive to perform well.

Base and Variable Fees

Base fees must be paid, regardless of actual usage. They compensate the vendor for making a service available to the company. For example, the contract could provide a fixed annual fee for making available a help desk to handle all user questions about desktop software.

Variable fees, by contrast, are fees based solely on usage. For example, instead of a base fee, the help desk vendor could charge $10 per call for help desk services. This type of pricing is sometimes called *metering*.

Many outsourcing contracts combine base and variable fees. The base fee may cover the basic operation, with a variable fee for volume beyond that assumed in the vendor's base pricing. Continuing the help desk example, the contract could call for a base fee of $10,000 per month for up to 1,200 calls, plus $10 for each call over 1,200 and a reduction of $5 for each call under 1,200. The increase is larger than the decrease because the vendor needs to keep enough people available to handle the full 1,200 calls.

Different companies prefer different pricing structures. Companies that turn to outsourcing to make their costs more predictable often prefer fixed fees. Other companies turn to outsourcing specifically to make their costs more variable. By doing so, they tie their costs more closely to underlying business activity and revenues.

Although various companies use different mixes of base and variable fees, some patterns are clear. Base fees are generally used for services that involve large fixed costs or are difficult to measure in increments. Variable fees are generally used for services that are easy to measure, such as the number of calls to the help desk.

Adjustments to Base Fees

Outsourcing is a long-term arrangement in a rapidly changing world. When the world changes, base fees that looked right when you signed the contract can look very wrong. As an outsourcing buyer, you want to be able to change the base fees when the world changes. That can give you competitive pricing throughout the term of the contract.

Periodic Revisions

One protection that companies obtain in outsourcing transactions is the right to increase or decrease the level of services that are priced with base fees. For example, let's say that the contract requires the vendor to provide 10,000 programmer hours per year on some task. There is a base fee for that, plus variable fees for hours over 10,000. The company might have the right to increase or reduce the number of programmer hours and pay a different base fee.

Why is an adjustable base fee different from a variable fee? For one thing, the base fees generally can be changed only occasionally, perhaps once each year. Also, the change will take effect only after a notice period, perhaps three months. The notice period gives the vendor time to move people on or off the project. The vendor cannot do that instantly. Finally, the size of the change is usually limited, perhaps to 20 or 30 percent per year.

Major Events

The right of periodic revision can give a company good protection against gradual changes in its business environment. However, when a major event changes the company's business, the company may need a major change in the services and the base fees. For example, if the company sells a division that consumes 20 percent of the services, the company will want to reduce the base level of services by something like 20 percent.

Changes in the Vendor's Costs

Over the term of the contract, the cost of providing the services may change significantly. Often, the vendor is the first to point this out. Vendors commonly ask for an adjustment to their prices based on any future increases in the Consumer Price Index (CPI) or the Employment Cost Index (ECI). (You'll need to make sure that these cost-of-living increases apply only to costs that increase over time, such as salaries. The cost of technology generally decreases over time.)

Similarly, the company should have the benefit of reductions in the cost of computing technology. For example, imagine that you have outsourced your mainframe processing to a vendor for a ten-year term. Your outsourcing deal assumes that mainframe prices will fall by 10 percent in the first year and that a new IBM mainframe will be purchased in the second year. The first year, IBM drops its mainframe prices by 30 percent. Unless the pricing mechanism reduces prices to reflect the reduced cost, what would have been a windfall for the company (before outsourcing) becomes a windfall for the vendor. If the vendor is getting a fair margin, there is no reason to give windfalls to the vendor.

Of course, not all reductions in cost are windfalls. Some of them come from the vendor's working very hard to identify cheaper ways to perform the services. You want to give the vendor an incentive to do that. As a result, you may want to share the benefit of cost-saving ideas implemented by the vendor. To do that, you will need to be able to define baseline costs from which the savings can be measured.

Changes in Market Prices

Locking into a long-term deal doesn't have to mean locking yourself out of market pricing. You can at least pursue the objective of having market pricing throughout the term of your deal. Most favored customer, benchmarking, and right to rebid provisions are designed to help you do that.

A most favored customer provision states that the company will be the vendor's most favored customer. Thus, if market conditions require the vendor to offer better terms to its new clients, the company also gets those terms. As a result, the contract stays close to the market throughout its term.

There are problems with most favored customer provisions. First, you might not start out as the vendor's most favored customer. Second, your vendor's best customer might also be paying high prices. Third, because outsourcing deals can have dozens of prices, it may be impossible to determine whether one outsourcing deal is better than another. Finally, vendors tend to see their pricing as highly confidential and are loath to reveal it to you to enforce your most favored customer clause.

A benchmarking provision adjusts pricing based on how an independent expert sees the pricing in your transaction. The independent expert compares your transaction to a large database of similar transactions with other vendors.

Benchmarking clauses are designed to overcome the problems with most favored customer clauses. You don't have to be the vendor's most favored customer, just in some percentile of outsourcing deals. Maybe you are in the best 30 percent. The comparison is with all vendors, not just your vendor. Thus, it is effective even if your vendor's prices are high for all of its customers. Comparing outsourcing deals remains complex, but the independent benchmarking company has expertise in doing so. Finally, the vendor does not have to disclose its pricing for other deals for the analysis to go forward.

Benchmarking also has difficulties. For benchmarking to work, some independent expert must have a representative sample of other existing deals. Otherwise, the benchmarking firm will be unable to state, with sufficient confidence, how the pricing on your deal compares with the market price of other, similar deals. There may be no such database. Also, even if the benchmarking analysis tells you that your pricing is high, it doesn't tell you precisely how it should be adjusted.

A right to rebid provision is often used in tandem with a benchmarking clause. A right to rebid provision allows the company to bid the services out again. The vendor might have a right of first refusal. The benefit of a right to rebid clause is that it allows the company to go back to the market to discover a market price. The right to rebid might be triggered by poor results in benchmarking, by the passage of time, or by another significant event.

Financial Incentives

There are many carrots motivating vendors to perform well in outsourcing arrangements. Good performance may lead to additional business and renewal at the end of the term. A happy customer is a good reference account. There is pride in a job well done.

However, it hardly hurts to wield a few sticks. The company's big stick is the opportunity to declare a breach of contract and terminate the contract. That would deprive the vendor of the profits it expects over the term. In those transactions where the vendor has made a substantial investment in the hope of large profits in later years, this can be a substantial incentive to perform.

However, this big stick is of only limited value. Terminating the contract is costly for both the vendor and the customer. Also, termination is available as a remedy only when the company can prove by objective evidence that the vendor has breached the contract and failed to cure within a reasonable time. The vendor's performance can be lousy for a long time without ever permitting a termination for breach.

Thus, you may want to have some little sticks. In outsourcing agreements, the little sticks are usually service-level credits. Service-level credits reduce the fees payable to the vendor if the vendor fails to meet the required service levels. They give a lagging vendor a bit of pocketbook pain. Thus, they reduce the risk that the vendor may try to increase its profits by providing service that is just good enough to avoid a termination for breach.

Vendors rarely propose service-level credits in their contracts. However, they rarely reject the concept. Instead, they try to make payment more unlikely by proposing that the service levels apply only:

- ▶ After repeated breaches
- ▶ If not cured within a certain period
- ▶ If not earned back by subsequent superior service
- ▶ If the company notifies the vendor of the failure within a short period
- ▶ If not solely the fault of the vendor

Another approach often taken by vendors is to accept the idea of service-level credits but insist that the contract also include service-level bonuses. A service-level bonus is an additional amount payable to the vendor if the vendor provides performance above and beyond what is required.

Service-level bonuses make sense only when superior vendor performance provides business value. If 98 percent CPU availability is what the company needs to get its processing done, 99 percent CPU availability might be of no further benefit. Thus, the company should avoid paying bonuses for 99 percent CPU availability.

Invoicing

Invoicing seems mundane—maybe too mundane to even define in a contract. However, in outsourcing, the way in which the invoice is crafted can make a real difference in the success of the outsourcing effort. For example:

▶ The invoice needs enough detail to permit chargeback. Chargeback systems ensure that the company's business units want the services enough to pay for them.

▶ Direct invoicing of foreign subsidiaries may have tax advantages. The subsidiary's payments under the outsourcing arrangement may be deductible for VAT (value-added tax) purposes.

▶ The way items are described may have important tax effects. Is an item a taxable service or a license? Will the cost be capitalized or expensed for tax purposes?

▶ Is the invoice specific enough to permit the company to verify the vendor's charges?

▶ What currency will be required for payments? Who bears the currency exchange costs and risks?

Audit

The company should have the right to audit the vendor's books and records supporting its charges. Also, to provide the right incentives, the outsourcing contract should require the vendor to bear the cost of the audit if the audit reveals that the vendor overbilled the company by some percentage.

The Company's People

The people issues are the most critical and the most emotional in outsourcing deals. The company has people who are performing the functions that will be outsourced. Most of those people will be transferred to the vendor or laid off. The people who are laid off may sue the company. The people who remain may be demoralized.

Layoffs

Layoffs are painful. When people get fired, morale drops and work slows or stops. The company should use experienced human resources professionals to minimize these problems. Depending on the company's existing policies, outplacement and severance plans may reduce the pain.

The company's ability to lay off its current employees may be restricted by:

▶ *Plant closing laws.* These laws require anything from prior notice to employees who may be laid off to governmental consent to laying employees off. These laws are best known for protecting factory workers, but they often also apply to information technology employees.

▶ *Union agreements.* Union agreements may prohibit layoffs or impose costly procedures.

▶ *Antidiscrimination laws.* In the United States, a layoff creates legal risk if it has a disparate impact on protected classes of employees. It is always prudent to work with specialists in these issues when planning a layoff.

The company may continue to need the laid-off employees for a transition period. During the transition period, the vendor may need to transfer these employees' knowledge to the vendor's staff. The vendor may also need these employees until it can move the company's processing to its own facility. At a minimum, it needs them to be happy enough not to do mischief to the company's systems.

As an incentive to stay through the transition period, companies usually offer the laid-off employees a "stay bonus." A stay bonus is a bonus that will be paid only if the employee continues to perform throughout the transition period.

Transferred Employees

Some employees of the company may become employees of the vendor. Those employees are often referred to as "transferred employees."

The transferred employees are not really transferred. A company does not have the power to simply transfer its employees to another company. Instead, the vendor offers these company employees a job. If an employee takes such a job, that employee has "transferred" to the vendor.

The company generally wants certain employees to join the vendor. These employees provide continuity. They know the company's operation and can assist in ways that other employees cannot. To get these employees to take a job with the vendor, companies may:

▶ *Shut other doors.* These employees may be told that they cannot transfer to other departments within the company. At the extreme, the company may terminate their employment.

▶ *Offer comparable compensation.* The company may require, in the outsourcing contract, that the vendor offer designated employees salary and benefits comparable to those currently provided by the company.

▶ *Ensure job security.* The company may require, in the outsourcing contract, that the vendor retain these employees for a minimum period of time.

▶ *Provide favorable treatment under benefit plans.* For example, the outsourcing contract could require the vendor to waive preexisting conditions under its health insurance plans. It may require the vendor to credit the employee's years of service with the company as years of service under the vendor's benefit plans. Employer loans may be transferred.

Severance benefits can raise difficult issues. Companies generally do not want to pay severance to terminated employees; however, it may be required by law. Also, the company may want certain employees to join the vendor, but those employees may not join if it means forgoing severance benefits.

The vendor's hiring decisions can also raise difficult issues. In the United States, various laws prohibit discrimination in hiring decisions. These laws make hiring decisions risky. The vendor may prefer to have the company select the employees who will transfer to avoid that risk. Equally, the company may want to make sure that the risk stays with the vendor.

Retained Employees

The company should retain certain key employees to manage the vendor relationship and set strategies. For this purpose, the company will need to retain employees who understand the function involved. Otherwise, the company may be unable to maintain control of the outsourcing relationship. Thus, companies that lay off or transfer all the employees who understand the outsourced function may find that their cost-cutting zeal has actually increased their costs.

When to Announce

When the company announces that it is considering outsourcing, employees may begin to look for other jobs. Valuable skills may walk out the door. Thus, companies worry about when to announce the outsourcing to their employees.

Some believe that the announcement should be made as soon as possible. The cat will get out of the bag eventually. Employees will respond better if they hear from management rather than through the grapevine. Also, if the employees know about the outsourcing, they can help in defining the services. Finally, the employees who are not involved in the outsourcing will cease to trust management if they are not informed.

Others believe that the outsourcing should be kept secret until the signing. If employees know about the outsourcing, they may leave the company. Also, there is no deal until the contract is signed. If the contract is never signed, the company will have given a false alarm. In this view, it's better to wait.

Vendors generally favor early announcement. This may be because leverage shifts to the vendor when the announcement is made. This is certainly true if key people leave the company when they learn they will be transferred to the vendor. In that case, the company's only practical solution is to outsource.

Vendors also gain by being able to better understand the operation before they take it over. After the announcement, they can talk honestly and openly with employees. Also, after the announcement, the employees may work harder for the vendor because they think of the vendor as their future employer.

The Vendor's People

The issues involving the vendor's personnel who will provide the services can be equally difficult and emotional. The vendor might dump its worst employees on the company's account. The vendor might churn employees so quickly that none of them understands the company's business.

The company may ask for contractual protections against dumping and churning. This seems fair. However, the vendor has a vital interest in making the most productive use of its people. The vendor also wants to keep its people happy. That may require moving them to new accounts. Without its people, the vendor cannot survive.

Companies commonly request the following contract provisions to protect their interests in this regard:

- ▶ The right to name the vendor project manager and key vendor employees
- ▶ Minimum periods of service with the company, perhaps a year or two, before the vendor transfers any account manager or other key vendor employees
- ▶ The right to approve changes of the vendor's account manager
- ▶ The right to require the vendor to replace unsatisfactory employees assigned to the company
- ▶ Full-time commitment of the vendor's account personnel to the company
- ▶ Prohibition on using key vendor employees to provide similar services to competitors

▶ No restriction on hiring the vendor's employees used to provide services to the company upon termination of the outsourcing contract

Information Technology Assets

Running an information technology department requires a lot of assets—computers, printers, cables, software, real estate, contracts. When the company turns over the function to the vendor, the company no longer needs these assets. The vendor might need them. The vendor may even buy them just to make the deal work.

Software

The vendor will need a license to use the software that the company owns. The company should continue to own its software so that it can use that software when the contract ends. The license should have the sort of terms that vendors generally ask for from customers. Those terms are described in Chapter 12.

The software that the company owns free and clear is easy to handle compared to the software that the company merely licenses from third parties. Almost all software licenses prohibit outsourcing. For example, the scope of use clause in a license usually says that only the licensee can use the software, perhaps only on a machine owned by the licensee. Also, the confidentiality provision prevents the licensee from disclosing the software to a third party, such as an outsourcing vendor.

Could you assign the license to the vendor, making the vendor the licensee? Probably not. Most software licenses prohibit assignment. Even if the company could assign the license to the vendor, the vendor probably could not use the software for the company's benefit. Most licenses prohibit running the software for a third party. For good measure, software licenses also tend to prohibit using the software in a service bureau.

If the company has the luxury of time, it can obtain the right to outsource from its software licensors when it buys software and thus enjoys maximum leverage. Most companies lack that luxury. They are negotiating with an outsourcing vendor long after they signed their software licenses. Thus, they need to seek consents from their software licensors.

Getting consents is a time-consuming chore. It can also be expensive because many vendors charge for these consents. The outsourcing contract needs to allocate the work and the cost of obtaining the required consents. The company and the vendor both have value to add to the process of obtaining consents, so sharing both the financial and the administrative burdens often makes sense.

Real Estate

The company is running its operations somewhere. The vendor may want to take over that location. If the company owns the location, it will need to sign a lease with the vendor. The company will be the lessor and the vendor will be the lessee. Leases need to include provisions dealing with who will pay for utilities, improvements, security procedures, and so forth.

If the company is leasing the location, it will generally need a sublease or an assignment of the lease. Either one may require consents from the property owner(s). Either way, the parties need to think about who will bear any liability for environmental damage, who will seek and who will pay for consents from the property owner, and whether the company will need access to the space taken by the vendor.

Equipment and Other Hard Assets

The vendor may also agree to acquire certain equipment or other hard assets of the company. The company generally has the right to sell its equipment without asking permission (unless the equipment is collateral for a loan). The vendor may be concerned about the condition of the equipment. Usually, though, the only issue is the price to be paid. The company should not declare victory if it gets a high price. The vendor will trade off the price paid for the equipment against the price of the services.

If the company leases equipment, the leases may prohibit assignment or outsourcing. If they do, the outsourcing contract should allocate the work and cost of obtaining the necessary consents.

The company could continue to hold the title or lease to the equipment and allow the vendor to use the equipment to provide services. In that case, the outsourcing contract needs to allocate responsibility for maintenance, insurance, upgrades, damage, and similar items.

Intellectual Property

The Company's Intellectual Property

Generally, the vendor will need access to some of the company's confidential information in order to perform the services. The company may have copyright, patent, trade secret, or trademark rights in the data and other information it provides to the vendor. The company wants the vendor to:

- ▶ Keep the company's confidential information confidential.
- ▶ Keep the company's confidential information secure against hackers and other information thieves.
- ▶ Correct any errors that the vendor creates while manipulating the company's data.
- ▶ Return the company's data on demand.

The Vendor's Intellectual Property

The vendor may use its own software and other intellectual property to provide services to the company under the contract. If so, the company needs a license to use that intellectual property that continues through the term of the contract and for a period after termination. Otherwise, the company may find itself unable to continue its business after termination.

The vendor's software may be crucial to processing the company's data. If so, the company may want the vendor to provide a copy of its software to the company. The company may also want the source code placed in escrow.

Third-Party Software Used by the Vendor

The vendor may also use licensed software. The vendor will be unable to simply grant the company a license because the vendor does not own the software. However, the company has the same concern about being able to run its business upon a termination. It will need that software if it ever reverses the outsourcing.

What should the company do if the software is not readily commercially available? One approach would be for the company to obtain a separate license to the software. That is the most flexible but the most costly approach. Another approach is to require the vendor to obtain a consent to transfer the license to the company upon termination. If both of these are too costly, perhaps the company should have a right of approval over the software that the vendor uses. The company can use that right of approval to require the vendor to use only readily available software.

Communication Mechanisms

Day-to-Day Communication

Outsourcing is an intimate relationship. The vendor and the company must communicate well and regularly to stay in sync. The contract may help this communication by providing for the following:

- A designated vendor account manager and company account manager to act as day-to-day liaisons.
- Annual technology and financial plans and other reports.
- Periodic meetings of a management committee composed of vendor and customer personnel and a designated vendor executive and company executive.
- Plans for communication with the company's information technology department and with its internal customers. The vendor's role and the company's role should be clear to avoid conflicting signals to end users.
- The vendor's obligation to coordinate its activities with those of the company and the company's other service providers.

Dispute Resolution

Courts are rarely the best way of resolving outsourcing disputes. Courts act slowly. Litigation is costly and contentious. Judges and juries know little about outsourcing. The process is public and thus may be embarrassing or require disclosure of highly confidential information.

Outsourcing contracts usually include various alternative dispute resolution mechanisms. Some outsourcing contracts include all three of the following mechanisms:

1. *Escalation.* Any dispute will first be referred to two midlevel executives of the parties. If they are unable to resolve the dispute, it will be referred to two high-level executives for resolution. The theory here is that higher-level executives have broader perspectives and superior dispute resolution skills.

2. *Mediation.* The parties meet with a third party who is an expert in bridging differences. They use a defined process to seek resolution. The process is confidential. The results are not legally binding unless the parties sign a written agreement.

3. *Arbitration.* The parties hire one or more people to act as judges. These people can be experts in outsourcing or information services. The parties can write their own rules, or use rules developed by arbitration experts. The process is confidential and legally binding.

Lawyers should define the desired procedures in detail in the contract. Otherwise, there may be disputes over the way a dispute will be resolved. The last thing a troubled outsourcing relationship needs is more disputes.

Liability

If something goes wrong, who will pay? In outsourcing, the answer often depends on what went wrong.

Breach of Contract

If the vendor breaches the contract, the company will not get the right service. The company may need to buy a replacement service from someone else immediately. The cost of the replacement service is called direct damages.

A replacement service may not be enough. The company may lose profits or suffer business interruption. These are called consequential damages. Courts can only guess at the amount of consequential damages.

The vendor will want limitations on its liability for damages from breach of contract. These typically include:

- ▶ Limiting direct damages to an amount equal to a few months' base fees
- ▶ Excluding consequential damages
- ▶ Excluding any damages from events beyond the vendor's control

What the parties negotiate is an allocation of risk. The vendor generally claims that its thin margins do not permit it to take on all of these risks. The company argues that these risks must fall to the vendor to give the vendor the right incentives not to breach. The vendor argues that a few months' fees are its entire profit and thus quite enough incentive.

Harm to Persons and Property

Damages may result from negligence or willful misconduct. People may get hurt. The hurt may be physical or of the type remedied by employment discrimination laws. Property may be damaged. Intellectual property may be infringed.

These liabilities are different from breach of contract. Instead of a failure to provide a service, they involve a wrongful act. There is a stronger argument that the perpetrator should indemnify the wronged party. Thus, these damages are often handled separately in outsourcing contracts.

Termination

Termination provisions cover two topics:

1. When can the outsourcing relationship be terminated?
2. What obligation will the vendor have to assist in the transition?

The termination provisions may be the most important in the outsourcing relationship. The right to terminate is the biggest stick that the company can carry, and, without a smooth transition to a new provider, the company will not be able to stay in business.

When the Company Can Terminate

Outsourcing contracts generally have long terms. The vendor often needs at least three years to recoup its initial investment. The company often desires a long commitment from the vendor. Ten-year contracts are by no means unusual.

The company generally may terminate either for cause or for convenience. "Cause" means a good reason other than just wanting to move to a more profitable arrangement. Such reasons may include the following:

▶ Material breach by the vendor that is not cured within the cure period or resolved by dispute resolution
▶ Ongoing failure to achieve service levels
▶ A *force majeure* event that lasts more than a defined number of days
▶ Changes in tax laws or other external circumstances that have a material adverse effect on the economics of the outsourcing relationship
▶ Significant business changes, such as mergers, acquisitions, and divestitures
▶ Bankruptcy or other indicators of insolvency
▶ Change in control of the vendor (perhaps only if the vendor is acquired by a competitor of the company)
▶ Price/performance below agreed-upon standards, as indicated by independent third-party benchmarking

The company should not need a good reason to terminate. Instead, the contract often allows termination for convenience. However, there is usually a termination fee for termination for convenience.

The termination for convenience fee gives the vendor the benefit of its bargain. The size of the fee should be defined in the contract. It covers (at least) the vendor's unamortized upfront costs and investment and may (at most) cover the vendor's anticipated profit from the outsourcing relationship.

The termination rights give the company some leverage with the vendor. After all, the vendor does not want to lose a customer. However, this leverage is very limited; both sides know that a termination would entail a great disruption and risk to the company.

When the Vendor Can Terminate

Generally, the vendor's rights to terminate are far more limited than the company's rights to terminate. Why? Because the outsourcing relationship is critical to the company's survival, but not to the vendor's. Thus, the company needs more control. However, the vendor at least has the right to terminate upon a material breach by the company.

Transition Assistance

When the contract terminates, the company must move its work from the vendor's control to internal control. The company must either rebuild the internal function or make a transition to a new vendor. A rough transition could cripple the company's business.

Unwinding the relationship may be harder than forming it. When the vendor and the company form the relationship, they are building trust and looking to the future. In the unwind, the trust is gone and the future is short.

All this means that the contractual provisions for the unwind may be the most important in the contract. They need to be careful and complete. And they still need to work after five years of changes. The company should consider the following provisions:

- ▶ A minimum period during which the vendor will continue to perform base services.
- ▶ Transition services to be provided by the vendor, such as training, data conversion, and software procurement. These services should be detailed with great care.
- ▶ Prices for such transition services. If the prices are not in the contract, the vendor may ask a ransom.
- ▶ The right to extend the termination effective date if the company is not ready for a transition.
- ▶ The right to hire the vendor's personnel who perform services for the company.
- ▶ The right to purchase the assets that the vendor is using to provide the services.
- ▶ The right to obtain data and other intellectual property.
- ▶ Licenses for software used by the vendor to provide the services.

Summary

Outsourcing is a very complex process. It takes a long time to put in place and a long time for all of its implications to play out. There is great opportunity and great risk. To succeed, the company must keep its eye on the key issues, namely:

- ▶ Services and service levels
- ▶ Pricing
- ▶ The company's people
- ▶ The vendor's people
- ▶ Assets

- ▶ Intellectual property
- ▶ Communication mechanisms
- ▶ Liability
- ▶ Termination

16

Strategic Alliances

An innovative and powerful way to work with a vendor is through a strategic alliance. In a strategic alliance, the company and the vendor share the risks and rewards of creating, using, or marketing software. In a well-designed strategic alliance, sharing risks and rewards gives the vendor a strong incentive to act only in the company's best interest.

How do companies decide to form a strategic alliance? One last play might answer that question.

ACT I

Scene: A conference room.

Company: Well, what do you think of my idea for the enhancement to your product?

Vendor: It's fabulous. It's a great idea. Anyone in your business would love to have this system. It's the perfect addition to our base software.

Company: Have you costed it out?

Vendor: Yeah. It's going to be about $5 million.

Company: I was afraid you'd say that. My finance guys did a cost-benefit on this thing, and it's worth about $1 million to us. I can't justify more. But I really need this software. There's $1 million of real value there, and there's probably a promotion in it for me personally.

Vendor: Could you make $5 million by licensing it?

Company: Easy. At $500,000 a pop, I could sell twenty licenses with my hands tied behind my back. That's $10 million.

Vendor: So, do we have a deal?

Company: No. We're not going to be a software company. It's not our strategic direction, and more than that, our culture is all wrong. We'd screw it up. But you're a software company. You're small, but you're good. Why don't *you* build this thing and license it?

Vendor: I wish I could. It would be a big break for us. But we don't have $5 million.

Company: Why not use venture capital? Or a bank loan?

Vendor: If only it were that easy. Banks don't want to lend when there aren't any hard assets to foreclose on. Getting venture capital takes months of time and lots of luck, and would mean spreading your idea all over the street. Also, I'm not willing to give up equity in my company.

Company: Is money the only problem?

Vendor: No. Even if we had the money, we don't have the credibility that you have. This thing would sell because your company is behind it.

Company: Then my dreams have turned to dust.

Curtain falls.

ACT II

Scene: Company is alone in a room filled with straw, sobbing. As the curtain rises, a small, energetic, brightly dressed man enters.

Man: What is amiss here? Why so gloomy?

Company: I have a brilliant idea for software that would solve all the key problems in my department. I've found the best software company to write the code.

Man: But why so glum when all is so well?

Company: This software isn't worth building for me alone. It would have to be sold widely. My company won't do that. The vendor can't afford to build it. Even if the vendor could build it, it doesn't have the credibility to carry it off.

Man: Who does?

Company: We do. We have what they need, they have what we need.

Man: Cheer up, your troubles are over. Rumpelstiltskin's my name, deals are my game. I have the answer.

Company: You're the Rumpelstiltskin who spins straw into gold?

Rumpelstiltskin: That's me. But I'm out of that business. Now I spin business ideas into large bank balances.

Company: Your fee, if I recall, is a first-born child?

Rumpelstiltskin: Nah, I'm out of that, too. The collection problems were terrible. Now I'm just looking for cash, like any other consultant.

Company: Sold. What's your answer?

Rumpelstiltskin: An alliance.

Curtain falls.

ACT III

Scene: Lunch at a four-star restaurant.

Vendor: So what's this new idea of yours?

Company: An alliance.

Vendor: Tell me more.

Company: You've got what we need. We've got what you need. Let's put those together.

Vendor: You're proposing a merger?

Company: Nothing like that. We're not going into the software business. Here's the deal. We'll invest $5 million in your company. We'll get equity. And board seats. And control rights. You'll develop the software. You'll sell the software. We'll get our $5 million out of our equity interest. What do you think?

Vendor: It's a good start, but my answer is no. I'm not giving up equity in my company. I've got a better idea. You give me $5 million. I'll enhance my software. You'll get a royalty on every sale of the enhanced software. You'll be a co-developer, reference account, and champion. It's a different alliance, but it's still an alliance. What do you say?

Company: I say no. My company does not buy royalty interests in software. We invest in companies. We buy equity.

Vendor: What about the rest of my idea?

Company: I like the rest of your idea.

Vendor: OK, let's be creative. We'll set up a 50/50 joint venture company. You'll put in your $5 million for equity in the JV. I'll put in my existing software for my equity. The JV will contract development and marketing out to my company. We'll both have two directors. The JV will develop the software. You'll still be co-developer, reference account, and champion.

Company: I like it.

Vendor: Do we have a deal?

Company: We have a deal.

As the curtain falls, Vendor and Company shake hands and dance out of the restaurant.

Key Issues

Although negotiations for strategic alliances are generally cooperative, the parties to an alliance may negotiate some issues fiercely because their interests are diametrically opposed. Of these issues, these four are key:

1. What will each ally contribute?
2. How will control be shared?

3. How will risks and rewards be shared?
4. How will this end?

Contributions

The right alliance partner is one that needs what you have and has what you need. Because alliances are ongoing relationships, the allies may be required to make contributions both immediately upon signing the contracts and throughout the alliance. For contributions at the signing, the contracts generally specify what is to be contributed in detail. For contributions to be made in the future, alliance contracts may take the approach of detailed specifications or the approach of providing broad parameters, with the details to be filled in by the allies by mutual consent after the contracts have been signed.

Cash and Hard Assets

The most straightforward type of contribution is cash or hard assets at the closing. However, the allies generally do not want to contribute capital until it is needed by the alliance. If capital contributions are to be made after the closing, the following issues should be addressed in the contracts:

- ▶ How will the size and timing of calls for additional capital contributions be determined?
- ▶ Will an ally be able to block a capital call?
- ▶ How long will the process take?
- ▶ Will there be upper limits on required capital contributions?
- ▶ Can the call be for hard assets or only for cash?
- ▶ If one ally makes a required capital call and another does not, what preferential rights or exit rights will the ally that makes the required contribution have?

Intellectual Property

Intellectual property can be contributed to the alliance by either an assignment (a transfer of all rights) or a license (an authorization to take certain actions, with intellectual property rights retained by the ally who provides the license).

The following issues often arise when intellectual property is licensed within an alliance:

► The scope of the intellectual property rights to be licensed.

► Permitted uses of the licensed intellectual property.

► The territory (geographic area or vertical market) where the intellectual property may be used.

► Exclusivity or, in lieu of exclusivity, restrictions on licenses to others.

► The right to sublicense.

► Rights to intellectual property developed after forming the alliance.

► Valuation of intellectual property contributions for purposes of determining the relative rights of the allies to share in profits. This issue is particularly difficult when the alliance is formed to exploit intellectual property that is so new, or so specialized, that there is no basis for assessing a market price.

► Rights to register intellectual property rights and obligations to enforce intellectual property rights against infringers.

► How to transfer trade secrets and know-how (e.g., training, consultation, classes, exchanges of personnel, or facility visits).

Technology or Products to Be Developed

An ally's role in the alliance may be to contribute technology or products that it has yet to develop. For example, large companies often form alliances with entrepreneurial software vendors. The large company contributes the capital required to design, develop, and test new products, along with a variety of management skills and a powerful distribution system. The small company contributes development effort.

When an ally is contributing development effort, the contracts should specify the tasks to be completed to develop the product, the target dates for completing those tasks, whether the developer's obligation is absolute or simply to use its best (or reasonable) efforts to complete the tasks by the target dates, what consequences there will be if the tasks are not completed by the target dates, and what reasons for the developer's failing to complete the tasks by the target dates might be acceptable and so not lead to these consequences.

Because alliances are generally formed to compete in rapidly changing markets, the contracts should also allow the allies to change the tasks and target dates. The contracts should specify a procedure for proposing such changes, the standards for determining how these changes will affect the payment and other obligations of the other allies, the effect of failure to agree, and whether the allies are obliged to act reasonably in discussing these changes.

Market Access

An alliance with a well-established distributor, wholesaler, or retailer can be the fastest, least risky, and most cost-effective way to gain access to a new market. However, the contracts must give the distributor, wholesaler, or retailer strong enough incentives to market the product effectively in its home market. Otherwise, particularly in an exclusive arrangement, the alliance can do more harm than good. Thus, the following issues often arise in negotiating for market access:

- ▶ Obligations of the ally providing market access to promote the products, such as a general "best efforts" obligation or a series of carefully described obligations
- ▶ Minimum sales obligations, backed up by termination rights or dramatic reductions in commission rates if the minimum sales obligations are not met
- ▶ Royalties structured to encourage diligent sales efforts, such as the use of upfront payments, minimum royalties, increasing or decreasing royalties, and royalty obligations that expire before the license expires
- ▶ Restrictions on sales of competing products by the ally providing market access

Due Diligence

Although a strategic alliance is fundamentally a relationship of trust, each ally should conduct a due diligence examination of each of the other allies and its ability to make the contributions it has agreed to make. Due diligence needs to consider not just whether another ally can perform at the closing but whether it will be able to perform throughout the term of the alliance. Thus, for example, one needs to consider whether an alliance partner has sufficient long-term financial strength, skills, market access, and rights to relevant intellectual property.

Control

A strategic alliance is an ongoing, collaborative relationship in which each ally retains its chain of command and the allies share control over pooled resources. The contracts must resolve how two or more chains of command will share control over the pooled resources. The competing considerations here are, on the one hand, each ally's desire to control, or at least influence, decisions, and, on the other hand, the need for rapid, consistent, and efficient decision making.

Control Rights

There are three key control rights that you can apply to each key decision.

The Right to Make Your Ally Do Something

This approach is often used when one ally has special expertise or a particularly strong interest in the decision. For example, the ally who is doing the software development might control key development decisions. Also, this approach is used when the allies believe that the alliance needs rapid, consistent, efficient decisions in order to succeed.

The contract may require the ally who can make the decision to consult with the other ally before making the decision. This approach is similar to the first approach but sacrifices some speed and efficiency in order to foster the communication that is vital to successful long-term relationships.

The Right to Prevent Your Ally From Doing Something

The contract can require that the decision be made only with the consent of all (or some majority) of the allies. This approach requires more discussion and is more difficult and time-consuming than the others. However, the discussion may produce better decisions. When one ally has a right to make decisions, it may dominate decision making and put its own interests above those of its ally or, for that matter, of the joint venture itself. Both partners may be worse off as a consequence.

The Right to Discuss a Decision Before It Gets Made

The contract can require an ally to consult with the other allies before making some decisions. This sort of right is very much in the spirit of an alliance, allowing good communication to produce good decisions. However, if the alliance is fraying, the discussion is likely to be perfunctory.

Control in Joint Venture Entities

One way to share control over pooled resources is through a joint venture entity. With a joint venture entity, control over most of the day-to-day activities of the joint venture can be delegated to a joint venture management team whose single focus is the success or failure of the joint venture. In that fashion, day-to-day decisions can be made efficiently and without the need for consultations between the allies.

In a joint venture entity, decisions of a strategic or long-range nature can be decided by a board of directors or similar governing body, ensuring that all views are considered. Each ally generally is represented on the governing body, and decisions generally require the consent of most or all of the allies. An ally can be given the right to discuss, but not make, a decision—for example, by giving the ally one board seat on a five-member board.

The following are examples of the types of decisions that are often reserved to the governing body:

- Purchase or sale by the joint venture entity of significant assets or technology
- Licensing of material proprietary rights by or to the joint venture entity
- Admission of new allies or sale of additional securities
- Appointment or removal of accountants, legal counsel, and key officers for the joint venture entity
- Compensation of the management of the joint venture entity
- Material changes in pricing or manufacturing policies
- Borrowing or lending significant amounts, or giving loans or guaranties
- Distributions from the joint venture entity to the allies
- Transactions with the allies and their affiliates
- Adopting or changing the joint venture entity's budgets or long-range plans
- Changing the governing documents of the joint venture entity, such as the articles of incorporation or the partnership agreement
- Entering a new line of business, using a new trademark, or announcing a new product
- Termination of any line of business of the joint venture entity
- Material government filings and other public announcements

Other Control Mechanisms

Other control mechanisms are required in a direct alliance. In a direct alliance, there is no separate joint venture entity and no shared governance structure. Thus, decisions on control are decisions on how the alliance partners themselves will act. The contracts can obligate an ally to do something if the other ally requests it, or prevent an ally from doing something if the other ally objects.

Some contracts provide that an ally must act reasonably in using its right to object. The problem with this compromise approach is that it does not automatically produce a clear result. If one ally makes a proposal and another ally objects, the allies may dispute whether the objection was reasonable. Because alliances are generally used to chart new territory, there will rarely be a well-accepted course of dealing or judicial precedent to resolve the debate.

Dispute Resolution

None of these control mechanisms prevents disputes. Disputes will continue to arise over what new markets to enter, what products to develop, and which people to hire. The value of these approaches is that they give the alliance a way to make a decision in spite of a dispute.

Disputes over what to do next should be distinguished in the contracts from disputes over contractual provisions (that is, disputes over who gets what). Courts and arbitrators are skilled and have hundreds of years of experience in resolving disputes over who gets what. However, courts and arbitrators generally act too slowly and have too little insight to offer to be the right way to resolve disputes over what to do next.

For disputes over what to do next, even when the control mechanism provides clear results, contracts often give the ally who disagrees with the decision prescribed by the contracts the right to force a reconsideration. One way to do this is by providing for escalation of the decision. An escalation provision might function as follows:

▶ If a project manager disputes a decision of another project manager, and the dispute is not resolved within a stated period after a notice of dispute is given, then the project manager may refer the dispute to senior executives of the allies.
▶ If the senior executives are unable to resolve the dispute within a stated period, any of the senior executives may refer the dispute to the chief executive officers of the allies.
▶ The chief executive officers of the allies will meet within a stated period and use their reasonable (or best) efforts to resolve the dispute.

This approach is effective only when the alliance is being managed by people at least two levels down in the corporate structure of each ally, and the number of allies is small.

Another effective approach is to designate a third-party decision maker. Some industries are blessed with skilled consultants with well-respected skills in making certain types of decisions. Those consultants can be brought in to resolve disputes over what to do next.

Finally, a dispute over what to do next could be an exit trigger and permit an ally to use an exit procedure.

Sharing of Risks and Rewards

Forming alliances is often referred to as *partnering* because, much as in a partnership, the sharing of risks and rewards is central to alliance transactions. The sharing of risks and rewards is generally a hard-fought negotiating issue. Each ally seeks to bear the least possible amount of risk and have the maximum opportunity for reward.

Ideally, the way in which risks and rewards are shared will give each ally the right incentives. Control provisions, by and large, are simply efforts to avoid the effect of perverse incentives that are built into the sharing of risks and rewards. The better the incentive structure created by the sharing of risks and rewards, the less need there will be for control provisions.

There are three primary methods for sharing the ongoing risks and rewards from an alliance: profit sharing, royalties, and transfer pricing. An alliance can involve one or more of these elements. In addition, the contracts often contain warranty disclaimers, limitations on liability, and exclusion of consequential, special, and incidental damages.

Profit Sharing

In a profit-sharing arrangement, the allies share the alliance's net profits. Corporate dividends and partnership distributions are shared in accordance with the relative ownership percentages of the allies. Profit sharing aligns the interests of the allies, because each of them seeks to maximize the alliance's profits.

Sharing profits implies sharing losses. Depending on the structure of the alliance, each ally's potential losses may be limited to the ally's contributions, or the losses may be unlimited. An ally facing unlimited losses should demand the right to terminate the alliance if it becomes unprofitable.

Profit-sharing arrangements generally include provisions giving each ally veto rights over large expenditures and over any arrangements by which profits could be transferred from the alliance to one of the other allies.

In a direct alliance in which an ally is obtaining a share of the profits of another ally, the allies should carefully define how net profits will be calculated. The calculation method should first define revenue, specifying what revenue from what products and related products will be included and in what fiscal period, and whether related payments such as business interruption insurance will be included. The calculation methodology should then define the deductions from revenue in calculating net profits. These deductions may or may not include such items as taxes, overhead, depreciation, and royalties paid to the ally receiving a share of the profits. These deductions are influenced by accounting decisions such as allocation of overhead, depreciation and amortization schedules, and allocation of shared costs.

Royalties

In a royalty arrangement, an ally pays a percentage of its revenues to another ally. As in a profit-sharing arrangement, the allies share the risks and rewards of high and low sales. However, in a royalty arrangement, the allies do not share the risks and rewards of high and low costs. Instead, those risks and rewards are allocated to the ally paying the royalties. This is appropriate if the ally paying the royalties has primary control over the costs.

The key economic issue in a royalty arrangement is the royalty rate. The following factors are relevant in determining a royalty rate:

▶ The incremental contribution to the product's anticipated gross margin that is made by the ally receiving the royalty
▶ The product's stage of development
▶ Funding by the ally receiving the royalty
▶ Degree of risk
▶ Market exclusivity
▶ Whether the product will be sold directly or through distributors and sublicensees; that is, whether the total revenues from the product exceed those of the ally paying the royalty
▶ Whether the product will be sold "bundled" with other products
▶ Whether there will be additional royalties owed to third parties

Royalties can be based on sales revenue or on the number of units sold. The risks shared under these arrangements differ. A royalty based on sales revenue shares the risks and rewards of both a high or low prevailing market price and a high or low number of units being sold. A royalty based on the number of units sold allocates all of the risks and rewards of a high or low prevailing market price to the ally selling the product and shares the risks and rewards of a high or low number of units being sold.

Royalty structures also allocate the risk that the value of the contribution justifying the royalty drops. To allocate that risk to the ally receiving the royalty, the contracts would provide that, for example, the royalty will be reduced if patent claims are invalidated, if technology protected as a trade secret enters the public domain, if the product is found to infringe the intellectual property rights of third parties, or if a competing, noninfringing product comes to market.

If the royalty will be based on revenues instead of units sold, the ally receiving the royalty should consider control provisions to avoid the product's being used as a loss leader or being sold inexpensively with a bundle of other products to reduce the royalty obligation. These control provisions must be based on the particular products and technologies involved and must be tailored to avoid applicable restraints on resale price maintenance. To support these control provisions, the ally collecting the royalty must receive regular reports on the level of sales and have the right to conduct an audit to verify the level of sales.

Transfer Pricing

If one ally will handle manufacturing and another ally will handle distribution, some of the risks and rewards of the alliance can be shared through transfer pricing. The transfer price is the price at which the ally that manufactures the product sells the product to the ally that distributes the product. The key issue is how the transfer price will be set.

Percentage of Resale Price

A transfer price based on a percentage of the resale price is similar to a royalty arrangement in that it shares the risks and rewards of high and low prevailing market prices. The manufacturer's concern with a transfer price based on a percentage of the resale price is that its profits depend on the prevailing market price, a factor that is largely out of its control. Thus, the manufacturer should consider bargaining for some control over the process by which the prevailing market prices will be set.

Cost Plus

A transfer price based on the cost of production plus a percentage margin allocates the risk of high manufacturing costs and the reward of low manufacturing costs to the ally that purchases the product. Further, it rewards the manufacturer for high costs and punishes the manufacturer for low costs by increasing the manufacturer's profits as its costs increase. As a result, purchasers under cost-plus contracts generally demand provisions to control manufacturing costs.

Fixed Price

A fixed transfer price allocates all the risk of manufacturing cost to the ally that manufactures the goods and all the risk of changes in market prices to the ally that purchases the goods.

These three transfer pricing approaches are often combined. For example, a common way to combine the fixed-price and cost-plus methods is by providing for a fixed price that escalates with the increase in the Consumer Price Index. The percentage of resale-price and fixed-price mechanisms could be combined by defining the transfer price as a fixed price plus a percentage of the resale price, or as a fixed price that is adjusted based on the percentage change in the prevailing market price of the product.

Exit Strategies

Most alliances terminate. Some terminate because they run into trouble. Some terminate when they succeed. Some outlive their purpose.

Exit strategies are a key issue in negotiating the contracts. Although it may seem pessimistic, or even counterproductive, to discuss how the alliance will end before it even begins, it is tremendously valuable for all of the allies to know that they have a clear path out of the alliance if need be and to know what will become of the shared assets if an ally exits the alliance.

The two key issues to negotiate are (1) what events, or exit triggers, will give an ally the right to exit the alliance, and (2) what procedures will be available to each ally upon an exit.

Exit Triggers

Each ally wants the right to exit quickly from an alliance. Each ally wants to be able to rely on the alliance as a part of its strategy. Each ally wants the other ally to depend on and invest in the alliance. As a part of balancing these conflicting objectives, the allies generally agree on the events that will trigger exit rights. Common exit triggers include the following.

Failure to Achieve Objectives

Alliance contracts often permit the allies to exit if the alliance fails to meet the economic goals set forth in the initial business plan. For example, the allies may be able to exit if the alliance is unable to raise sufficient capital or develop a key technology before a certain date, or if the alliance does not achieve revenue or profit projections. This protects the allies from being locked into an ill-conceived or unprofitable alliance.

Expiration of Term

Alliance contracts are often set for a fixed term of years. At the end of the fixed term, the alliance will end unless it is extended by mutual agreement. Another similar provision is a voluntary time "window" during which any ally may terminate the alliance.

Adverse Action by Government Entities

Contracts may give the allies the right to exit if specific governmental approvals are not received. For example, the allies may condition the alliance on obtaining all required governmental licenses and consents. Contracts may also give allies the right to exit if a relevant governmental authority takes actions such as adversely changing tax laws, imposing currency controls, failing to protect technology, or declaring material terms of the contracts to be void or illegal.

Default

Contracts often permit an ally to exit the alliance upon a material default by another ally. However, if the alliance is a critical element in an ally's business strategy, making default an exit trigger may create an unacceptable level of risk for that ally. At the same time, the right to exit the alliance is often a useless remedy for the nondefaulting ally because the nondefaulting ally continues to need what the defaulting ally has to offer. Thus, the allies should consider other remedies for defaults, such as monetary damages or shifts in control of the alliance.

Disputes

If a dispute over what to do next cannot be resolved within a reasonable period of time using the dispute resolution mechanisms contained in the contracts, an exit right may be appropriate. However, such an exit right should be drafted with caution. Otherwise, this exit trigger creates a right to terminate for convenience by advocating an unacceptable course of action.

Change in Control

Alliance contracts often permit one ally to exit if there is a change in control of another ally. Strategic alliances are, by definition, more than simple relationships between a buyer and a seller. Having the right partner is key to succeeding in an alliance. Thus, an ally often argues that, just as personal services contracts generally may not be assigned, a strategic alliance must terminate if there is a change in control of an ally. An argument against providing this as an exit trigger is that, although there may be a change in control of an ally, the ally still has the skills, market access, and capital that made it the right partner.

Success

Alliances with well-defined objectives often terminate when those objectives are attained. For example, an alliance to create a particular piece of software may terminate when development has succeeded.

Exit Procedures

Exit procedures are the rights that an ally will have if an exit trigger occurs. Before designing the exit procedure, the allies should consider what they will need to do if the alliance terminates. For example, if an alliance involves outsourcing a critical function in an ally's value chain (such as research, development, production, manufacturing, marketing, or distribution), that ally will need to replace the alliance upon termination. That ally will need either the right to purchase the shared assets required to perform that critical function internally or sufficient time (perhaps a year) to create a new alliance to handle the function. However, if the alliance involves an independent business structured as an entity joint venture, termination of the contracts upon thirty days' notice may be appropriate.

The exit procedures that will be available to an ally may differ based on the exit trigger. An ally whose exit trigger is a default by the other ally might be entitled to more rights than an ally that exits for other reasons. Alliances that succeed might terminate in a flurry of cross licenses to intellectual property, whereas alliances that end in failure are more likely to end with a reversion of intellectual property rights to the original contributor.

Finally, each ally must consider what technology it will need in order to continue its business. If an alliance involves jointly owned intellectual property, each ally may need a license to that intellectual property in order to continue its business after the alliance terminates. If an ally contributes key technology to the alliance, it might require a purchase option to obtain control of the technology.

Exit Procedures for Entity Joint Ventures

The following exit procedures are commonly employed in alliances structured as entity joint ventures.

Transfer of Equity Interest to Third Party

An easy way to permit exit is to permit an ally to sell its interest in the joint venture entity to a third party. As noted above, however, the allies are often reluctant to allow an ally to replace itself with a stranger. As a result, the allies commonly protect themselves against a transfer by placing one or more of the following restrictions on transfer:

- ▶ Interests may be transferred only with the consent of the other allies, which consent will not be unreasonably withheld.
- ▶ No ally may transfer any interest to any competitor of any other ally.
- ▶ Any transfer will be subject to a right of first refusal; that is, the transferring ally, before transferring its interest, must offer to sell its interest to the other allies at the price offered by the proposed transferee.
- ▶ Any transfer will be subject to a right of first offer; that is, the

transferring ally must, before offering the interest to any third party at a price, offer to sell it to the other allies at that price.
► If any ally is transferring its interest, the other allies will have "tag along" rights—that is, the right to participate in the sale.

The alliance agreement also may give the transferring ally "drag along" rights—that is, the right to require the other allies to participate in the sale.

Sale of Entity to Third Parties

An ally might have the right to require a sale of the joint venture entity to third parties. The ally may also have the right to require that the sale be conducted in a particular way, such as an auction, a private sale managed by an investment bank whose compensation is expressed as a percentage of the sale price, or the registration of the joint venture entity's securities for public sale. A similar right would require that the joint venture entity's assets be sold and the proceeds distributed.

Sale of Interests to an Ally

An alliance may terminate with one ally buying out another ally's interests in the joint venture entity. An ally that requires the pooled assets in order to continue its business after the termination of the alliance may obtain a call right, that is, the right to purchase another ally's interest in the joint venture entity. An ally who would prefer not to have an equity interest in the joint venture entity if another ally has departed may obtain a put right, that is, the ally would have the right to require its interest to be purchased by another ally.

If one ally will sell its interest to another, the contracts must describe how the price for the interest will be set. The price is often set using one of the following approaches:

► *An appraised price.* The contracts should specify whether the appraisal will be based on a discounted cash flow, market comparables, or liquidation value model; how the appraiser will be selected; the assumed time frame for the sale; which will pay the expenses of the appraiser; and whether the value will be based on a continued alliance with all allies or on ownership by the ally expected to purchase the interests.

► *A formula price.* The formula might set the price of the interest based on the historical balance sheets and income statements of the joint venture entity. For example, the price might be set at book value or a multiple of the profits for the prior fiscal year.

▶ *A price set in a buy/sell offer.* In this alternative, one ally names a price and offers to either sell its interest in the entity to the other ally at that price or buy the other ally's interest at that price. The other ally then has the right to decide whether to buy or sell at that price. An ally has an incentive to name a fair price because the other ally has the option to either buy or sell at that price. This procedure may be unfair if, for practical or economic reasons, one ally is in a better position to purchase the other's interest.

Sale of Interests to the Entity

The contracts may grant an ally a right to put its interest in the joint venture to the joint venture. This exit right takes many forms. A preferred stockholder in a corporation might have a redemption right. A general partner in a partnership may have the right to withdraw and be paid the balance of that partner's capital account. This procedure is appropriate only where the entity is likely to have, or be able to obtain, the liquid assets required to purchase the interest.

Withdrawal Without Compensation

In alliances that are not directly intended to generate profit, such as a consortium to develop an industry standard, the allies often have the right to withdraw without compensation.

Dissolution

The contracts could give an ally the right to cause the alliance to dissolve and distribute the shared assets.

Exit Procedures in Nonentity Alliances

If the alliance will not be structured as an entity joint venture or involve an investment by one ally in another ally, the range of termination procedures depends primarily on the form of the alliance. The following are examples.

Licensing Arrangements

When a licensing arrangement terminates, the licensor generally continues to own the licensed intellectual property. The licensee should consider whether it will need some license rights to meet its own obligations. For example, if the licensee will incorporate some of the licensed intellectual property in its own products, the licensee may need a continuing license to allow it to grant sublicenses that go beyond the term of the alliance or to maintain products sold to customers before the alliance terminates. The licensee may also seek a right to purchase a perpetual, royalty-free license for some defined price upon a termination.

Marketing, Distribution, and Franchise Arrangements

Generally, the manufacturer, distributor, or franchisor in a marketing, distribution, or franchise arrangement retains its manufacturing facilities and intellectual property rights. In these arrangements, the manufacturer or franchisor generally obtains contractual provisions for return of its intellectual property. The marketing agent, distributor, or franchisee often obtains sufficient transition time to phase out inventory and, perhaps, find a replacement manufacturer or franchisor. Both allies may need continuing audit rights for tax and other reasons.

Research and Development Alliances

When a research and development alliance terminates, the contracts generally specify which will own or have the right to use the intellectual property of each ally and the jointly developed intellectual property.

Equity Investments

When one ally has made a substantial equity investment in another ally, the termination procedure may be for the investor to purchase the remainder of the other ally. As described above under "Sale of Interests to an Ally," the price for the remainder of the other ally could be an appraised price, a formula price, or a price set in a buy/sell offer. However, a buy/sell offer is rarely appropriate in this type of alliance because the investor generally has considerably more economic power than the other ally. The other mechanisms described above for joint venture entities should also be considered.

Closing Off Other Exits

Contracts are also subject to general provisions of law that, unless dealt with, provide other exit triggers and exit procedures. These must be closed off if the intent of the allies is to limit exit rights to the provisions set forth in the agreement. What these other exits are often depends on the form of the alliance. Under partnership and similar laws, general partners may have a right to withdraw or to call for a dissolution. Under Section 272 of the Delaware General Corporation Law, either shareholder in a joint venture corporation where each of them owns half of the shares may call for and receive a court-ordered termination. Bankruptcy laws may also create what amount to termination rights.

Negotiating Technique

Be Cooperative

Negotiating strategic alliances requires a cooperative approach. The allies may be working together for a long time; they cannot afford the ill will that a confrontational approach creates. Mutual respect and trust are essential.

In negotiating an alliance, extreme positions are likely to backfire. The allies are often similarly situated, and thus each ally is likely to find itself giving to the other ally any provision that it obtains for its own benefit. That puts a premium on reasonableness.

Be Creative

Strategic alliance negotiations, almost by definition, involve tremendous opportunities to "expand the pie." These opportunities will be lost unless the allies work together creatively to uncover them.

Expect Some Ambiguity

In negotiating license agreements, you properly strive to nail down every contingency and specify in detail what the vendor will supply upon signing. In negotiating alliance agreements, the allies must adapt to a far different need: the need to write contracts that make sense in a long-term business relationship that must change as rapidly as the markets in which the allies compete. That will require more ambiguity, and more key issues will need to be worked out as the alliance continues.

Summary

In negotiating strategic alliances, the issues of contributions, control, allocation of risks and rewards, and exit strategies generally require substantial negotiation. If the allies approach that negotiation creatively and work cooperatively to consider a variety of options, provisions can be negotiated that provide acceptable protection to all allies and support a common strategy. The allies can then work together in their mutual best interest to succeed at a common objective.

Index

acquisitions, 33, 112
  benefits of, 70–71
  roles in, 34–36
administrative function, 99–110
  and acquisition process, 35
  standards, 99–100
  support of other roles, 117
alternatives, awareness of, 81–82
anchoring in negotiations, 81
arbitration, for outsourcing dispute, 228
"as available" product, 130
assignment contract clause, 126
  in software license, 164–165
audit, of outsourcing vendor books, 220

bait and switch, 25–26
  by customer, 96
base fees for outsourcing, 215
  adjustments to, 215–218
benchmarking clauses, 217–218
benefits
  of acquisition, 70–71
  change and analysis of, 72
  vs. costs, 63
bid list, 142–144
binding effect of software license, 164–165
boilerplate contract, 134–137
book basis, vs. cash flow analysis, 66–67
breach of contract, 228
bugs, 173
buying, rules for, 101–103

capital lease, 205–206
cash flow analysis, vs. book basis, 66–67
change
  and benefit analysis, 72
  and deal reassessment, 49
  and status quo, 12–13
client/server system, 10
clients, as vendor references, 47
commission plan, for sales reps, 89
commitment, 82, 85
communications, 22, 48, 91–93
company name, vendor use of, 135–136
confidentiality in contract, 125–126
  and consultants, 159, 187–188

consequential damages, 228
consultants, 125, 177–191
  absence of written contract and ownership,
    185–186
  benefits to company, 177–178
  confidentiality and, 159, 187–188
  flexibility from, 181
  hiring restrictions for, 183–184
  independence of, 188–190
  marketing by, 183
  plan for, 178–179
  projects by the hour, 190–191
  replacement of, 182
  terminating agreement, 184
consulting agreement, 178–187
  ownership of work, 184–187
  vendor or company employee, 190
  work product definition, 178
contracts, 85, 123–138
  assignment clause, 126
  auditing compliance with, 109–110
  automatic renewal, 102
  boilerplate, 134–137
  confidentiality in, 125–126, 159
  damages in, 132–133
  enforcement of, 103–105
  and industry standards, 130
  intellectual property indemnities, 133–134
  "jurisdiction" clause, 136
  obligation clarity, 131
  product or meeting needs, 127–129
  reasonable efforts, 132
  refund rights, 132
  remedies, 131–133
  restrictions in, 124–127
  rules and tracking, 101–103
  scope of use in, 126–127
  signing, 48
  standard form or nonstandard, 94
  subcontract rights, 136–137
  technical ideas in, 58
  termination, 135
  vague obligations, 129–131
  vendor's form, 123–124
  waiver and estoppel, 107–108

control
  in negotiations, 83–86
  and outsourcing, 211
  in strategic alliances, 238–242
Copyright Act, 104, 185–186
core competencies, and outsourcing, 210
cost-benefit analysis, 66–72, 76–77
costs
  vs. benefits, 63
  confidentiality and, 125
  of incompatible systems, 15
  monitoring, 106
  one-time project, 67–69
  ongoing, 69–70
  predictability for consultants, 179–181
  project or transaction, 73–77
  of technology implementation, 18
customer ploys, 95–97

damages, in contract, 132–133
database, of technology contacts, 102–103
Deal Wheel, 33, 36–41
  business problem in, 36, 38
  deal formation, 38–39
  deal negotiation, 39–40
  deal signing, 40
  performance monitoring, 40
decentralization, and integration, 55
decision maker, ego of, 22
delivery of equipment, 196
  wait for, 194–195
demos, 18
direct damages, 133, 228
disclaimers, for equipment warranties,
      199–200
discounts, vs. savings, 63
dispute resolution, 227–228
  in strategic alliances, 241–242
  documentation, of performance, 108–109
  due diligence, in strategic alliances, 238

economies of scale, loss of, 15
enforcement, of contracts, 103–105
"Entire Agreement" provision, 135
equipment, 193–207
  acceptance, 197–198
  disposal, 207
  installation, 196
  leasing, 205–207
  maintaining, 202–205
  order cancellation, 195
  ordering, 193–194
  and outsourcing, 225
  site preparation, 195–196
  testing, 197–198
  training for use, 197
  wait for delivery, 194–195
  warranties, 198–201
escrow arrangement, for source code, 154–155
executive sponsor, 89
exit strategies, for alliances, 245–252

facts, vendors' use of, 19–20
financial function, 61–77
  and acquisition process, 35
  cost-benefit analysis, 66–72
  management decisions, 64
  support of other roles, 114–115
financing, and outsourcing, 210
flexibility
  and outsourcing, 211
  and risk, 75–76

gray market sale, 201

IBM Corporation, 20
indemnification, for vendor personnel,
      168–170
independent contractor, vs. employee,
      188–189
indirect damages, 133
industry standards, and contracts, 130
information, and mission fulfillment, 8
information systems, competing for control,
      13
information technology
  acquisition, 12, 119
  acquisition quiz, 31–33
  alternatives, 62
  maintaining control, 12
  personal relationships in sales, 19
  purpose, 119
  reasons for mistakes, 23
  role of department, 51–52
installation of equipment, 196
insurance, for vendor personnel, 168–170
integration, and decentralization, 55
"Integration" contract clause, 135
intellectual property
  indemnities in contract, 133–134
  and outsourcing, 226–227
  in strategic alliances, 236–237, 248, 250–251
Internal Revenue Service, on independent
      contractors, 188–189
invoicing, for outsourcing, 219–220

joint ventures, 240, 248–250
"jurisdiction" contract clause, 136

layoffs, outsourcing and, 220–221
leasing equipment, 205–207
  fair market value buyout rights, 206–207
  and outsourcing, 225
  and tax indemnification, 207
legal advice, for negotiation team, 90
"lemon clause," 201–202
leverage in negotiations, 83, 84
  commission plan as, 89
liability, in outsourcing, 228–229

maintenance
  for software, 173–174
  term of agreement, 204

management, 118
    and negotiating team, 91–92
manufacturer's warranty, 201
market access, in strategic alliances, 238
market prices, and outsourcing fees, 217–218
market research, 47
marketing by consultants, 183
mediation, 228
metering, 215
milestones for vendors, 106
monitoring vendor performance, 106

needs
    defining, 44–45
    negotiator awareness of, 86–88
negligence, 229
negotiating function, 79–97
    and acquisition process, 35
    and communications, 91–93
    controlling process, 83–86
    in Deal Wheel, 39–40
    knowledge about vendor in, 88–89
    seven deadly sins, 80–83
    for strategic alliances, 252
    support of other roles, 115–116
net present value, 67
nonentity strategic alliances, exit procedures
    in, 250–251

object code, 153
objectives, of company, 86–88
one-time project costs, 67–69
operating system software, standardizing,
    100
ordering equipment, 193–194
outsourcing, 209–232
    analyzing, 209–211
    announcement timing, 222–223
    communication, 227–228
    exclusivity of, 214
    information technology assets in, 224–225
    and intellectual property, 226–227
    invoicing for, 219–220
    liability in, 228–229
    pricing in, 215–220
    services description in, 212–214
    and software assignment, 165
    termination, 229–231
overconfidence in negotiators, 82–83
ownership of work from consultant, 184–187

partnering
    by customer, 96–97
    see also strategic alliances
partnerships, real between vendor and cus-
    tomer, 27
payment clause, in software license, 161–163
payroll processing, 10
performance of vendor
    documentation of, 108–109
    monitoring, 40
    outsourcing and, 210

standards, 118, 127
    stopping problems, 105–109
personnel costs, 68
planning, sequential, 65
prepurchase testing, 57
preventive maintenance, scheduling, 203
pricing, in outsourcing, 215–220
productivity improvement, 71–72
products
    determining needs, 55–56
    updates vs. new, 131
profit, technophile impact on, 9
profit sharing, 242–243
project costs, 73–77
purchasing standards, 101

real estate, and outsourcing, 225
reasonable, contract use of, 131
rebidding, provision in outsourcing contract,
    218
refund rights, in contracts, 132
remedies for warranty, 201
requests for proposal, 45, 84, 139–145
    construction, 140–142
    identifying vendors for, 142–144
    information types in, 141–142
    reasons for, 139–140
    reviewing responses, 144–145
    scope, 139
requirements document, 45
resellers, warranties from, 200–201
resources, overextending, 100
response time, 203
retained employees, outsourcing and, 222
rewards, 27, 71–72
risks, 73, 74
    and flexibility, 75–76
    sharing in partnerships, 27
royalties, in strategic alliances, 243–244

sale and leaseback, 206
sales, to individuals vs. company, 22
sales reps
    aid in decision making, 17
    commission plan, 89
    statement and meaning, 124
savings, vs. discounts, 63
scarce resources, and vendor urgency, 24
scope of use, in contracts, 126–127
sequential planning, 65
signing of deal, 48
    in Deal Wheel, 39–40
software, bundling, 76
software companies, suit by, 16
software licenses, 16, 147–175
    acceptance, 157–158
    assignment; binding effect, 164–165
    compliance, 104
    confidentiality, 158–160
    definitions, 156–157
    entire agreement provision, 165–166
    granting, 151–155

software licenses (*continued*)
    infringement indemnification, 168
    introduction, 156
    maintenance and service, 173–174
    most favored nation clause, 163–164
    and outsourcing, 224–225
    payment clause, 161–163
    pitfalls, 149–150
    quiet enjoyment, 167
    recitals or ''whereas'' clauses, 150–151
    rules and protocols, 155–167
    sharing risk, 167–171
    and source code, 153–155
    structure of agreements, 150
    termination, 160–161
    use of name provision, 166
    value pricing trend, 147–148
    warranties, 171–173
software licensing, 126–127
Software Publishers Association, 104
source code, license provisions, 153–155
standards, 99–100
status quo, and change, 12, 13
strategic alliances, 233–253
    contributions, 236
    control, 238–242
    exit strategies, 245–252
    key issues, 235–236
    negotiating technique, 252
    sharing of risks and rewards, 242–245
stress testing, 56
subcontract rights, 136–137
success, defining by user, 44
suites of software, 76
sunk cost fallacy, 82
systems integration, 53
    and contract changes, 58
    difficulty of, 59

taxes, and outsourcing, 211
team
    building, 89–93
    management responsibility for, 118–119
technical function, 51–60
    and acquisition process, 34
    support of other roles, 113–114
technology
    assessment process, 53–58
    glitches in, 8
    implementation costs, 18
    in strategic alliances, 236–237
technophiles, priorities of, 7–11
technophilia, 2, 7–16
    hidden costs, 13–16
    vendor-induced, 11–13

termination
    of consulting agreement, 184
    of contract, 135
    of outsourcing, 229–231
testing, 56–57, 197–198
time, cost of, 15
time-limited task, consultant for, 177
trade secrets, of vendors, 125–126
transaction costs, 73–77
transfer fee, 149
transfer pricing, in strategic alliances, 244–245
transferred employees, after outsourcing,
    221–222
''turnkey'' solutions, 55

update, vs. new products, 131
urgency in negotiations, 96, 124
users
    and acquisition process, 34, 43–49
    risk assessment by, 45–46
    satisfaction measures, 106
    support of other roles, 112–113

value pricing trend for software, 147–148
variable fees, for outsourcing, 215
vendor friend, 92–93
vendor selling ploys
    bait and switch, 25–26
    beating, 94
    divide and conquer, 21–22
    partnering, 26–28
    sense of urgency, 23–25
    smoke and mirrors, 17–20
vendors
    big vs. small, 20–21
    contract form from, 123–124
    focus of, 54
    identifying for RFP, 142–144
    knowledge about, 88–89
    limitation of liability, 170–171
    monitoring performance, 49
    negotiator attitudes about, 80–81
    objectives, 3
    and outsourcing, 212
    personnel in outsourcing, 223–224
    selecting short list, 84
    software license termination by, 160
    stopping performance problems, 105–109
    and technophilia, 11–13
    use of company name, 135–136, 166
    viruses, 14

waiver and estoppel, 107–108
warranties
    for equipment, 198–201
    for software, 171–173
willful misconduct, 229
work-made-for-hire, 185–186